Tranquil Power:
The Art and Life of Perle Fine

Perle Fine in her East Hampton studio in the late 1950s

Tranquil Power: The Art and Life of Perle Fine

By Kathleen L. Housley

MIDMARCH ARTS PRESS
New York City

Publication of this book is made possible with support from the Renate, Hans and Maria Hofmann Trust.

Library of Congress Control Number: 2004115449
ISBN 1-877675-54-7

Printed in the United States of America

Published in 2005 by
Midmarch Arts Press
New York, NY 10025

CONTENTS

Perle Fine at work in her studio in The Springs, Long Island. The painting *The Wave* in the background. *Toward the Sea* painting owned by Dr. Alvin Goff, New York City. c.1957. Photo: Maurice Berezov

PROLOGUE

It is fascinating to read about troubled artists who pick fights, make outrageous statements, have numerous affairs, or abuse family and friends, all the while struggling in the isolation of their studios to create masterpieces. Often the narrative line of their lives is filled with inward torment and outward action; just when things begin to get dull, they decamp to a lonesome place, lop off an ear, find a new mistress, or get dead drunk and wrap their automobile around a tree.

What about an artist who doesn't conform to that worn out, yet compelling, script? One who is reserved, doesn't wear outrageous clothes, has never thrown a bar stool, has strong convictions but is not angrily argumentative, and is monogamous? Where is the drama in such a life? Shouldn't the quality of the art alone be sufficient to command attention?

These questions are not rhetorical. In the United States, where personality and star-quality have always been important, they pertain to which artists get recognized and written about during their lifetimes and beyond. They pertain to Perle Fine in particular because she reached artistic maturity during the period of Abstract Expressionism, a style that the artist Robert Motherwell said had "to do with a certain violence native to the American character."[1] Fine was aware of that undercurrent of violence and refuted it in her art and life. "I couldn't be aggressive. I'd have to do aggressive work to be aggressive," she said.

Yet during the formative years of Abstract Expressionism, Fine helped shape its direction, beginning with her inclusion in Peggy Guggenheim's ground-breaking exhibition "Salon for Young Artists" at her avant-garde gallery Art of This Century. Between 1945 and 1953, Fine had six solo exhibitions in New York City at the Willard Gallery, the Nierendorf Gallery, and the Betty Parsons Gallery, and one at the M. H. De Young Memorial Museum in San Francisco. Over the course of her life, in which her style evolved from Abstract Expressionism into an evocative, color-saturated form of Minimalism, she had 25 solo exhibitions, and took part in more than 125 group shows at the

Metropolitan Museum of Art, the Museum of Modern Art, the Solomon R. Guggenheim Museum, The Whitney Museum of American Art, and numerous other museums, galleries, and universities.

"Really great works," wrote Flaubert, "have a serene look. Through small openings one perceives precipices; down at the bottom there is darkness, vertigo; but above the whole soars something singularly sweet. That is the ideal of light, the smiling of the sun; and how calm it is, calm and strong!...The highest and hardest thing in art seems to me to be to create a state of reverie."[2] Flaubert could have been writing about Fine's art, for the words he used recur in over 40 years of art reviews, along with the words quiet, mystery, power, gentleness, beauty. A critic in the 1940s cited a "mysterious" quality in Fine's paintings that kept even the most turbulent ones from chaos, offering "new and delightful passage into another world." After visiting Fine's first exhibition at the Betty Parsons Gallery in 1949, Robert Coates, art critic for *The New Yorker*, felt compelled to write her a personal letter of congratulations: "I must say I thought the pictures looked, well, stunning, they were so strong, assured, and powerful." Twenty-five years later, another critic wrote: "these are gentle paintings of near unspeakable beauty."[3]

Identical synonyms recur in the remembrances of family and friends: "She had a unique style. There was a soft mystery to it. I liked her but she was quiet and remote, off in her own cloud," said a friend. A family member described her as "a beautiful person not only in her art but in herself. She was not confrontational. She wouldn't raise her voice, but if she really believed in something, she wouldn't back off either."[4]

If there was conflict in Fine's life, it was not against the cultural strictures that kept her work in the eddies at a time when it should have flowed influentially into the mainstream; the protracted conflict was painting itself. And she would have had it no other way. Late in her life, when asked whether it would have been easier had her career started after the advent of the feminist movement instead of in the 1930s, Fine replied, "I don't think it's any easier, not because of women's lib, or anything, because in the final analysis it's always the painting." For her, painting was both a visceral and intellectual effort that was never easy, nor did she want it to be. "I'm very suspicious of it when it's easy. Whether it is easy or looks easy, there might be something lacking," she said, "and, on the other hand, when I'm fighting it out with a canvas, substance is added to the appearance of the work, which makes it all the more convincing. I put it aside, and then when I look at it, that canvas has a lot more to it. Some unseen force or something that gets into it."[5]

Art historian Ann Eden Gibson confirms that by the early 1950s, Fine was "squarely in the center of Abstract Expressionism. Her combination of fluid and brushy rendering was an ideal mesh of personal agency and truth to materials for that style, and her use of biomorphic forms encased and intertwined with a softened and irregular geometric lattice places her in league with Gottlieb and Baziotes. Yet she is seldom included in discussions of Abstract Expressionism. What went wrong?" For Gibson, the question is rhetorical because her thesis is that the very image of the Abstract Expressionist painter was a white male, and that this movement, which perceived of itself as a glyph of individual freedom, constricted the entry of everyone else, regardless of the nature and quality of their work.[6]

No doubt Fine would have agreed with Gibson, although it would have been some of the gallery owners and museum curators, functioning as blatantly chauvinistic gatekeepers, who would have received her greatest opprobrium. It would not have been most of the male artists, for although it was true that many of them were inculcated with stereotypical attitudes toward women artists, they had their own formidable psychological and cultural barriers to overcome. A high level of alcoholism and depression among them was mute testimony to this struggle. Recalling one dealer's pronouncement that there would be no women artists in his gallery — a gallery which helped define and designate the mainstream — Fine was offended. "I know I was as good as anybody else in there," she said.[7] Yet in the fullness of Fine's own life there was little room for bitterness or anger, although she did admit to feeling their sting occasionally. On the contrary, she considered herself to be "very lucky to be able to grow and paint what I want. I didn't expect anybody ever to buy it or like it or anything. I didn't think of that at all because I think that can stand in your way."[8] Had she been given the chance, Fine probably would have reconfigured Gibson's question into a positive: "What went right?" Part of her answer would have highlighted her freedom to pursue arcane aesthetic questions that could be solved only through the process of painting, her willingness to destroy work that did not meet her exacting standards, and her determination to eliminate anything in her painting that was referential to reality or "pleasant." The "Accordment Series," begun in the 1970s, gives a strong indication of Fine's being at peace with her achievement, for the title implies harmony and fulfillment. About the series, she wrote: "Compelling, mysterious, they are yet very tranquil; they are evocations of being in tune with nature and the Universe."[9]

At a certain point, a painting separates itself from its creator and begins life on its own. The artist's personality and the facts of her or his life don't matter any more. Instead, spectators view the painting in the context of their own vastly different lives. If a painting resonates for them, it is because it has been imbued by the artist with the capacity to live beyond the time and place in which it was created. As Fine's biographer, my goal is to present her art and the facts of her life in a way that enables readers to seek on their own what Fine described as "the spell-binding quality, the one that beckons and holds, the unpremeditated, the nameless, touched off perhaps by some transcendental experience, but guided surely by a poetic and creative hand — these are the things hidden beneath the surface."[10]

CHAPTER 1

ART FROM THE DAY SHE WAS BORN

At the height of the Abstract Expressionist period, it became a truism that many of the artists had gone through anguished childhoods, fraught with Oedipal-like entanglements between parent and child, and complicated by sibling rivalry. It was as if the artist played a part in a Greek tragedy as analyzed by Freud. Another interpretation was to cast the artist in the role of an Existentialist hero who created meaning out of the meaningless, having struggled to manhood in a universe that cared nothing for art or its creator.

None of that was so for Fine. In her own straightforward words, she "had a marvelous childhood." As with many gifted children, her abilities manifested themselves very early. Being dairy farmers, her family did not have the economic means to provide her with private art lessons, but they encouraged her nonetheless. In fact, up until the day the family home was sold in the 1940s, approximately forty years after Perle's birth, there were crayon marks in bright colors covering the walls and even the ceiling of her childhood bedroom. "Her parents were so proud of her, they never took them off," recalled Charlotte Fine, the wife of Perle's younger brother Leo. "They were all over, everywhere she could reach, even over the bed. And she started drawing them — flowers, everything — well before she was old enough to go to school. Art was her life from the day she was born."[1]

Fine was born in Boston on April 30, 1905, shortly after her father, mother and older sister Amy emigrated from Russia, sailing from the port of Danzig, Germany. In fact, she was almost born at sea. Her parents were named Sarah and Sholom Hyamovitch. However, their cousins, who had immigrated a few years earlier to New York City, were concerned that the name would be too hard to spell in English. So the cousins counseled them to take on Sarah's maiden name, which was Finegold. Then to make the name simpler for the Russian and Yiddish-speaking family to write in English, one of the cousins broke matchsticks in half and positioned them in straight lines on the

Rose, Amy and Perle Fine on the dairy farm in Malden, Mass., around 1912.

kitchen table, forming block letters. The result was "Fine," without the "gold," although in some early records, including Perle's birth certificate, the name was spelled Feine. First names also underwent radical transformations: Sholom became Samuel; Poule became Perle, which her family steadfastly pronounced as if it had two syllables, Per-le, instead of the Americanized Pearl.[2]

The family settled in Malden, Massachusetts, approximately five miles to the northeast of Boston, where Samuel ran a small dairy farm on Alden Street, delivering milk to the community. Before long, everyone knew him simply as "Fine the Milkman." The farm, with a large barn right next to the house, was one of the last remaining in the area, for Malden was a New England industrial town with sprawling brick factories built in the nineteenth century. Many of its streets were lined with modest wood-frame houses for the factory workers, while its avenues were dotted with lavish multi-colored mansions (appropriately called "painted ladies") for the factory owners. In line with the wealth of its leading citizens, Malden also had its share of monumental civic buildings. For example, the town library (an imposing structure of dark stone, recessed windows and rounded arches) was designed by the renowned architect Henry Hobson Richardson who had also designed Trinity Church in Boston, the city hall in Albany, New York, and numerous other notable civic buildings across the country. To magnify its grand effect, it was sited on a piece of land selected by Frederick Law Olmsted, the famous nineteenth century landscape designer best known for Central Park in Manhattan.[3]

Eventually there were six children in the close-knit family of Fine the Milkman: Amy, Perle, Rose, Leo, Melvin and Robert. The family was poor "but we never knew it," recalled Fine. "We always had lots to eat, lots of fresh good milk, cream, cheese, butter, everything." The only evidence that there was little money was that she had to work hard, washing milk bottles and "doing whatever there was to be done in the house and barn." Fine was not coddled in any way because she was a girl. "I worked like a man, like a boy, every day before and after school just as long as I had to."[4] She never resented the work, seeing it as a necessary part of farm life, even if such a life was an anomaly to the other citizens of Malden who governed their days by the blast of factory whistles and not the lowing of cows needing to be milked. The other anomaly was that the cows were just as likely to be spoken to in Hebrew, Russian, or Yiddish as in English, depending on who was doing the milking.

Both Perle and her older sister Amy took piano lessons on an old upright piano their father had managed to acquire, but while Amy eventually became very skilled, Perle "begged off to do what I wanted to do," which was drawing. "My sister died quite early in life but she inspired me to paint and draw at a very early age."[5] According to Charlotte Fine, Perle's parents were also supportive:

> Sarah and Samuel never discouraged the children in anything they wanted to do. And they were all artistic in some way. That artistic vein was in every one of them. Rose and Leo played the violin, Amy the piano. They could play anything you wanted just by ear, they didn't need sheet music. Sarah and Samuel were two parents like you don't find anymore. Their children were everything to them. They never cared what Perle did — as long as she did. To them whatever she painted was beautiful. Later on, when she began to paint abstract, it was still beautiful.[6]

Fine shared with her family a love of music, although her instrument was paint. In later life, she often described her art in musical terms learned in childhood (vibration, vivace, and harmony) choosing titles such as "In Staccato," "Polyphonic," and "Study for Downbeat." "I can only relate [the painting] to a sound in space: a cry or a chirp or something like that. It's a measured cadence in the painting and it's a very definite weight of tone and sound. I don't seem to be able to convey in words what I mean by this awareness."[7]

Fine found support for her artistic gift outside the family as well. "Starting almost immediately in grammar school at the time of the First World War, I did posters and started winning little prizes and getting encouragement that way." Poster contests were very popular at the time, with sponsors often being local companies. At Malden High School, Fine competed in the "Clean-Up Week Contest" and the "Kindness-to-Animals Contest." In an article in the *Blue and Gold,* the student newspaper of Malden High School, the writer congratulated the winners (of whom Fine was one) of a poster contest sponsored by the International Milk Dealers' Association, making a parallel between them and three famous illustrators of the period:

> That the girls of Malden High are following in the footsteps of the football team in gaining highest honors is seen by the fact that they have just won their fourth consecutive poster contest....Priscilla White received first prize and Perle Fine second. But lo, and behold! At last a boy has managed to get in on the awards. Seymour Goff is the lucky one. Seymour believes that when the boys are heard from they'll be heard around the world. Is it possible that there are more Neysa McMeins than Norman Rockwells or Maxfield Parrishes in Malden High?[8]

Fine grew up in the golden age of illustration. The movie industry was still in its infancy, so the only way that a story could be visualized was through art, and Americans fell in love with it. Due to technological advances in printing methods, illustrated magazines and books gained enormous popularity. It is estimated that by 1925 one in four homes owned a print by Maxfield Parrish, whose bucolic illustrations were filled with nymphs and dyads in languid poses, with skies suffused with a glimmering blue so emblematic it became known as "Parrish blue." It was illustration, not paintings in museums, that shaped how Americans conceived of art. Many artists who grew up during this period remember being captivated by illustration. To open a copy of Nathaniel Hawthorn's *Moby Dick* and see a powerful picture by Rockwell Kent of the great white whale upending the boat with his tail, or to pick up a copy of *Treasure Island* with N. C. Wyeth's dynamic portrayal of the one-legged pirate Long John Silver was to sense the enticing power of art to make a story come alive. The artist James Brooks, a friend of Fine's in adulthood, remembers being "raised on magazine illustration mostly. My family weren't educated in art so I just picked up from comic strips and magazines." Even after he started studying drawing, he did not differentiate between illustration and fine arts. "They all seemed the same. I liked Rembrandt and Pruett Carter and Raleigh — all illustrators," he said.[9]

There was a panache to being an illustrator. Plus the field sported some highly successful women, such as Neysa McMein and Rose O'Neill, the creator of the Kupie Doll, so it was natural for Fine to gravitate toward that profession. One of McMein's best known designs was the original Betty Crocker character, but she was also a respected portrait artist and an occasional member of the prestigious Algonquin Round Table in New York City. This was a group of writers, poets, critics and others, among them the writers Dorothy Parker and Edna Ferber, who met daily at the Algonquin Hotel, to share over lunch their insightful, often acerbic, comments on life, literature, and everything and everybody in between. It was a glamorous, urbane gathering in which women were prominent. What they had to say, particularly Parker's witty repartee, was often reported in the general press.

Possessing a strong sense of self and an equally strong sense of direction, Fine left high school without graduating because she was determined to pursue a career in art. She was not burdened by cultural and religious perceptions of what were appropriate careers for women, nor did she trail into adulthood psychological problems rooted in a troubled childhood. Yet her decision to leave school early and to be an artist was tinged with awareness of what that decision truly meant. "I just knew that what was right for [just] about everybody else wasn't right for me, and it always made me sad because one feels drawn to society as well as to be withdrawn from it."[10]

Fine enrolled in the School of Practical Art in Boston to study illustration and graphic design. In return for her tuition, she was given a job in the bursar's office, "There was no one in the family who was an artist....So it was up to me to find some way to get to an art school and learn to draw and paint." Working in return for tuition was the answer, but at first she had no idea what a bursar did and what her job entailed. "I immediately sent receipts out to everyone who should have gotten a bill. But the people receiving them were brighter than I was. They all came in and paid their receipts."[11]

Increasingly, she found herself attracted to fine art in addition to commercial art and illustration. "At that school I learned how to do

As a young woman interested in new developments in art, Fine moved from Boston, which she found too traditional, to New York City to study first at the Grand Central School of Art then at the Art Students League.

little newspaper ads and learned all the requirements for that, and I made my way as well as learned to draw from the model and paint whenever I could. But that couldn't last very long. I knew that there was an end and that there was no place in Boston at the time where I wanted to study."[12] Then in her early twenties, Fine decided to move to New York City where there was not only a wider selection of schools but also a nucleus, albeit very small, of newly opened museums and galleries dedicated to modern art, although what the words modern, abstraction and non-objectivity actually meant was open to furious debate. There was also debate about whether modern art was morally decadent, a sign of the rapid degradation of society, as were speakeasies, women smoking, and the Charleston. For example, in December 1927, 70 drawings by Pablo Picasso were exhibited at the Wildenstein Galleries. In his review, Henry McBride, art critic for *The Sun,* alluded to the opprobrium that his art generated among many segments of society, stating that Picasso's power was undeniable and should "be recognized even by those who fear that he is a pernicious influence upon the young."[13]

In 1905, the year of Fine's birth, Alfred Stieglitz opened his first gallery at 291 Fifth Ave., referred to simply as "291," eventually showing not only his own photography, which he considered an art form, but the art of avant-garde Europeans unknown in the United States, among them Francis Picabia and Gino Severini, the first a Dadaist and the second a Futurist. Equally important, he showed several contemporary Americans including Arthur Dove, Charles Demuth, Stanton Macdonald-Wright, and Georgia O'Keeffe (whom Stieglitz eventually married).

Then there was the famous "International Exhibition of Modern Art" at the 69th Regiment Armory in 1913, which reporters and critics described with long strings of negative adjectives, including pathological, hideous, vulgar, profane, and poisonous. Whereas approximately 100,000 people had attended the show in New York City (mostly to gawk and snicker at Marcel Duchamp's "Nude Descending a Staircase"), the Boston public was indifferent when the International Exhibition traveled to the Museum of Fine Arts for its final showing.

Attendance was poor. What mattered most in Boston was tradition: still-lifes of flowers in pastel shades, society portraits, and landscapes, particularly of the New England countryside and the seacoast.

At the time of Fine's arrival in New York City, probably in 1927 or 1928, connoisseurs of modern art were few. However, some of them were so dedicated that they made up in zeal for what they lacked in numbers. Among them was Katherine Sophie Dreier who in 1920 established the Société Anonyme with her friends and advisors, the artists Marcel Duchamp and Man Ray. An artist herself who had a painting in the Armory Show, Dreier was also a social reformer; in the Société Anonyme, she was able to combine her two passions. Outwardly dowdy but inwardly avant-garde, Dreier gave lectures, organized exhibitions, and collected the art of Paul Klee, Franz Marc, Wassily Kandinsky, and many others.

There was also the Gallery of Living Art at New York University which opened on December 12, 1927. It displayed works by European artists including the sculptor Constantin Brancusi, whose bronze sculpture "Bird in Space" was considered so radical when it was imported in 1926 by the photographer Edward Steichen that American customs authorities classified it as industrial metal that was subject to duty payment, a classification that was subsequently overturned in court. There were paintings by Georges Braque, who early in the century had been one of the founders, along with Picasso, of Cubism. Paul Cézanne, Paul Klee, Henri Matisse, Joan Miró, and Piet Mondrian were also represented alongside the art of several contemporary Americans, among them Louis Bouché, Charles Demuth, Preston Dickinson, John Marin, Marsden Hartley, and Charles Sheeler. Unusual among museums and galleries, all this art was the collection of one man, A. E. Gallatin, a wealthy connoisseur. Born in 1882, his passion for art was rooted in his childhood, but his interest in abstraction did not peak until the early 1920s when he visited the European studios of Braque, Fernand Léger and others, where he studied their work, talked to them at length, and took numerous photographs. By the time he opened the Gallery of Living Art, he had become so dedicated to promoting modern art that he provided access to the collection to everyone free of charge. It was open six days a week (closed on Sunday), with its doors unlocked until 10:00 o'clock on week nights. He titled it the Gallery of Living Art because he believed that art was indeed alive; a painting should not be a visual representation of something, such as a vase filled with zinnias; instead it should possess its own vitality. He was not interested in presenting exhibitions that attempted to summarize historical periods or styles. Instead he wanted a dynamic gallery in which art shaped artists. To keep costs at a minimum (despite his substantial wealth, he was parsimonious), Gallatin handled all curatorial and administrative tasks himself, from designing announcements of upcoming exhibitions to affixing postage stamps, to which he added one pleasure: he also painted.

For someone interested in art, there was really only one place to live in Manhattan, and that was Greenwich Village. The oldest part of the city with narrow alleyways, crooked streets, stables in the mews, and Washington Square, Greenwich Village had about it a sense of neighborhood. Bounded by 14th Street, Houston Street, Fifth Avenue, and the Hudson River, the Village, as its name implied, felt like a small town within a large city. A literary and artistic center since the 1880s, its reputation for being "Bohemian" was well-established. Theater thrived there, one of the more famous groups being The Provincetown Players on Macdougal Street, which introduced to audiences the plays of Eugene O'Neill.

For artists, the Village was especially magnetic. By the 1930s, it was estimated that over half the artists in the United States lived in New York and of that number most lived in the Village.[14] It was not so much the place itself but the critical mass of artists that attracted newcomers, particularly students and those in the early stages of their careers, who felt the need to see, discuss, and immerse themselves in art on a daily basis. Essentially, it enabled them to be alone together: painting in the privacy of their studios, then going out with other artists to mull over or argue about what was happening. Moving to 215 West 13th Street, Fine joined their ranks. Nearby was The Downtown Gallery, at 113 West 13th St, which showed the art of Yasuo Kuniyoshi, Marin, O'Keeffe and Sheeler. The American Contemporary Art Gallery was at

52 West Eighth Street. The Clay Club (a place for sculptors) was at 4 West Eighth Street. The Whitney Studio Gallery and the Whitney Studio Club were also on Eighth Street. Predecessors to The Whitney Museum which would open in 1931 in four renovated brownstones, they were a hub of activity for an estimated four hundred artists. Gallatin's Gallery of Living Art was on Washington Square.

In November 1929, Fine went to see the spectacular opening exhibition of the newly established Museum of Modern Art (MoMA), which was at that time renting space in the Heckscher Building on Fifth Ave. The exhibition of works by Cézanne, Paul Gauguin, Georges Seurat, and Vincent Van Gogh opened only fifteen days after the stock market crash, hardly a propitious time for the start of a new museum. But despite concerns, the show was a huge success, and eventually so was the museum. On the first day several thousand people lined up on the sidewalk out front, waiting to crowd into the small elevators for the ride up to the four galleries on the twelfth floor. An estimated 35,000 people saw the show in three weeks. Displayed on walls covered in monk's cloth were: thirty-five works by Cézanne including seven watercolors, twenty-six by Gauguin, seventeen by Seurat, and twenty-seven by Van Gogh. The show, the largest of its kind in the United States, had a very strong effect on Fine, converting her into "a life-long Francophile." Those "four great painters really set me off," she declared. "I loved everything French from then on." Of the four, she was fascinated by Cézanne but non-plused by Gauguin. It was just such exhibitions and the intense discussions they generated among artists that Fine had longed for while living in Boston.[15]

That same fall, Fine enrolled at the Grand Central School of Art with the intention of becoming both an illustrator and a painter. As its name indicated, the school was located on the seventh floor of the imposing Grand Central Terminal Building, the city's bustling train station. The school had an enrollment of about 700 students, many of whom commuted to class from the suburbs, taking the elevators up from the train tracks directly to the studios, never having to step outside. Opened only a few years earlier, the school advertised that it developed "individual talent under the instruction of successful artists." Courses

While attending the Grand Central School of Art, Maurice Berezov lost an art competition to a fellow student named Perle Fine to whom he subsequently proposed. They were married in 1930.

were offered in painting and drawing, commercial and applied arts, and interior design. Fine began taking classes with Pruett Carter, a well-known illustrator for *Ladies' Home Journal, Women's Home Companion,* and *McCall's,* who stressed composition, pattern and design in his classes. But it didn't take Fine long to realize that she was headed in a different direction:

> What I found out very quickly was you can only be a painter and nothing else if you're going to be a painter...so there was that necessity to separate painting from just about everything else. And that went right along with the feeling I had about the artist in isolation from society anyway...it had to do with just about everything that was expected of one as a person, as a woman, certainly as an artist, because one had to feel absolutely free to go whatever direction, at whatever time, one needed to do it. There could be no strings attached at all. I knew that painting didn't mean a matter of painting from 9 till 11 in the morning, and doing something else, because you might not want to paint at 9 o'clock. And, as it worked out, very often it took me, I'm ashamed to say, the whole day to get to the point where I knew what it was I wanted to paint. It would be maybe 3 or 4 o'clock and I might only work for a couple of hours on it. But I had to have that free time to think and to walk and to do anything that I had to, to sort of become part of what it was I wanted to do.[16]

Driven by the sense that there was something more to art, something that would challenge a viewer either emotionally or intellectually, Fine switched to the Art Students League. Located at 215 West 57th Street in a building styled after the French Renaissance, the League was one of the largest, most venerable art schools in the country. Famous artists who had studied or taught there since its founding in 1875 included William Merritt Chase, Thomas Eakins, and George Bellows.

James Brooks, Fine's friend who also had been studying with Carter at Grand Central School of Art, reached a similar conclusion about the necessity of changing schools. Working from a model in what he dubbed a kind of Post-Impressionist way, Brooks found that it had become dull and "too easy":

In some respects the relationship between Berezov and Fine was more like an unending love affair than a marriage. Their mutual devotion gave them an emotional resilience many artists lacked. (Photograph dated 1936.)

> We produced pretty effective figure painting but I was getting around just a little. The class next door, which was just separated by a partition, the drawing class, was run by Arshile Gorky, who had just come to this country. I didn't know him then. He used to come in and sit around in the class before it started, and I was generally there early, and he would talk about the difference between colors and color, and odds and ends; not anything definite enough for me to get hold of but which made me wonder a good deal. And I was already dissatisfied. So I quit Pruett Carter's class and went to draw...with Nicolaides at the League.[17]

A deep restlessness with illustration was also Fine's motivation. However, her time at the Grand Central School of Art was not wasted. In 1930, at the annual exhibition of the students' work, she received the first place award for illustration. The second place award went to a fellow student named Maurice Berezov. The article in the paper did not note whether the winners received cash prizes or medals; what is certain is that they won each other. Small and neat in appearance, with dark receding hair, he was a man of genuine warmth with a wry sense of humor. Fine had a look both serious and kind. She had high cheek bones in a heart-shaped face, accentuated by dark brown hair which she wore pulled back. Physically she had a presence that could make itself felt in a crowded room even though she was not tall. A friend described her as "intense looking with glowing dark eyes." Berezov was smitten by her, a feeling he never lost. Berezov proposed to Fine that summer while the two were vacationing in Provincetown at the tip of Cape Cod. As Fine liked to tell it, her acceptance was not immediate:

> We went out for a walk on the breakwater, and when we got way out, the tide was swirling around. It was very hard to get from one rock to another, and Maurice said, "will you marry me?" I said "no." He had an unfair advantage. When we went back to New York, the weather had changed and it was cool and fall was setting in and I said, "I think I would like to marry you. I've changed my mind from this summer." He had a very nice studio and I didn't have a studio. So I could use a studio, and he knew it![18]

Their very small wedding (neither had any money) took place at Temple Emanuel on September 1, 1930, a clear, mild day when the city streets, quiet since June, were crowded with people returning from summer vacation. In fact, the headline in *The New York Times* trumpeted "Vacationing Army 2,500,000 Strong Pours Back into City."[19] Married for 57 years until Fine's death in 1988, they had a very warm, mutually supportive relationship that enabled Fine to withstand the prejudice against women artists that was so deeply embedded in the culture that its perpetrators saw nothing wrong with it. "I could never have been an artist without Maurice's encouragement and love of painting, as well as the fact that he was a painter himself, so he understood what I was going through," she explained. Unlike other artist couples in which the career of the woman was subsumed into the career of the man, or in which competition eventually undercut the relationship to the point of divorce, from the start Fine and Berezov established their own individual spheres. He became, in his own right, a successful illustrator and painter who worked for many years in advertising. As a hobby, he pursued photography, producing sensitive pictures of artists in their studios surrounded by their creations. But he never considered his talent to be as great as Fine's. "All his life, he was crazy about her," one relative remembered. "He affectionately called her Perley, and was happy to 'schlep her canvases around' as he used to say, and help hang her exhibitions." Together they upheld — and honored — the other's separateness. At a time when a woman routinely took her husband's surname, Fine kept hers, never becoming known as Mrs. Maurice Berezov. This was a radical decision on her part. While it was not rare for a woman artist whose reputation was firmly established to keep her maiden name upon marriage (for example, Georgia O'Keeffe never changed her name to Georgia Stieglitz), it was rare for an art student to do so. Equally radical was Fine's decision not to have children because in dedicating her life to art she believed that she "could never have taken [them] on."[20]

Berezov's family had left Russia early in the century, as had Fine's, to escape the pogroms against Jews, moving first to Paris, where he was born in 1902, and then to the United States. As a young man, he had learned how to engrave silver while working for a jeweler, which piqued his interest in becoming an artist. He studied at the Cooper Union, and then the National Academy of Fine Arts in New York before attending Grand Central where he met Fine. Along with her, he switched to the Art Students League where he studied etching as well as drawing and painting.

The League was set up in such a way that students could choose the art teachers with whom they wanted to study. There were no required courses. No one kept attendance, and enrollment was on a month-by-month basis, which allowed students the freedom they needed to come and go, to pick and choose, fitting courses in and around work schedules and the availability of money for tuition. The artist John Sloan, who became president of the League in 1931, likened the non-structured approach to a hungry individual being allowed to choose his food from a varied menu at an automat. Students also had a vote in its operations, which led occasionally to fierce internecine battles, the first occurring not long after Fine's arrival on the proposed hiring of foreign teachers, in particular George Grosz. A German painter known for his gritty, often satirical portrayals of war and societal ills, Grosz was too extreme for the League board of directors, who refused to invite him because he would be, as one board member declared, an unhealthy influence on American youth. As a result, Sloan resigned as president, charging the board with "sentimental and financial timidity," and the students held a mass meeting and drafted resolutions in his support. Nothing much came of it; Grosz came to the United States anyway, despite not being offered a full-time position, teaching instead a summer course at the League.[21] What the incident underscores is that at the League, the nature of art (what was a rehash and what was innovative, who was on the cutting edge and who was frozen in time) was debated continually, not only among the students but among the teachers and staff. Even those students who condemned the League as the epitome of stale academism were proud to say they attended.

While many of Fine's generation would choose to study under Thomas Hart Benton, including Jackson Pollock who began to take classes in September 1930, Fine pointedly avoided him, selecting Kimon Nicolaides instead, as did Brooks. "I thought that one should have a thorough grounding in academic painting which is what I thought I would be getting at the Art Students League," she said. "And since Kimon

Nicolaides was the best painter and teacher there, I thought I would get it from him."[22]

There was another reason for her choice of Nicolaides over Benton: Benton did not believe women should be artists. He was known to ignore women who had the effrontery to attend his classes. Afraid that there was something sissified about art and therefore about artists, Benton prized virility, power, and huge scale. Artists were to be male, their subjects masculine in their energy, and their main connection to females was to be as womanizers. Women were acceptable only as sex objects and subjects. Stylistically, Benton was a proselytizer for American scene painting who, ironically, was simultaneously attracted to and revolted by everything American. He portrayed in his murals and paintings: cotton fields, revival meetings, lumbering work horses, iron forges, lively hoe downs, poker-playing cowboys, and dark movie houses. Occasionally, his style bordered on caricature. One critic commented that his paintings had about them "the tang of Mark Twain's *Roughing It*." Another critic charged that "there is no order whatever in Mr. Benton's America. It is all discord, temporary excitement, roughness and vulgarity."[23] Benton hated what he called modernism and despised the artists in the Stieglitz group, among them O'Keeffe, for being "intellectually diseased," an opinion he also held of European artists.

Nicolaides was much more egalitarian than Benton. In a milieu crowded with larger-than-life egos, he had the reputation of being not only an excellent teacher but a compassionate man. He would help any student, male or female, who was willing to work hard. "I do not care who you are, what you can do, or where you have studied, if you have studied at all. I am concerned only with showing you some things which I believe will help you to draw," he said.[24] Unfortunately, in terms of valuing women artists, Benton was more the norm than Nicolaides, as made clear by several articles printed in *Art Digest* at that time with titles such as "Women and Men," and "The Women Question," in which art by women was judged to be decorative, inconsequential, entertaining, and forgettable. In July 1928, *Art Digest* reprinted an interview (originally carried by the Associated Press) with the artist Wayman

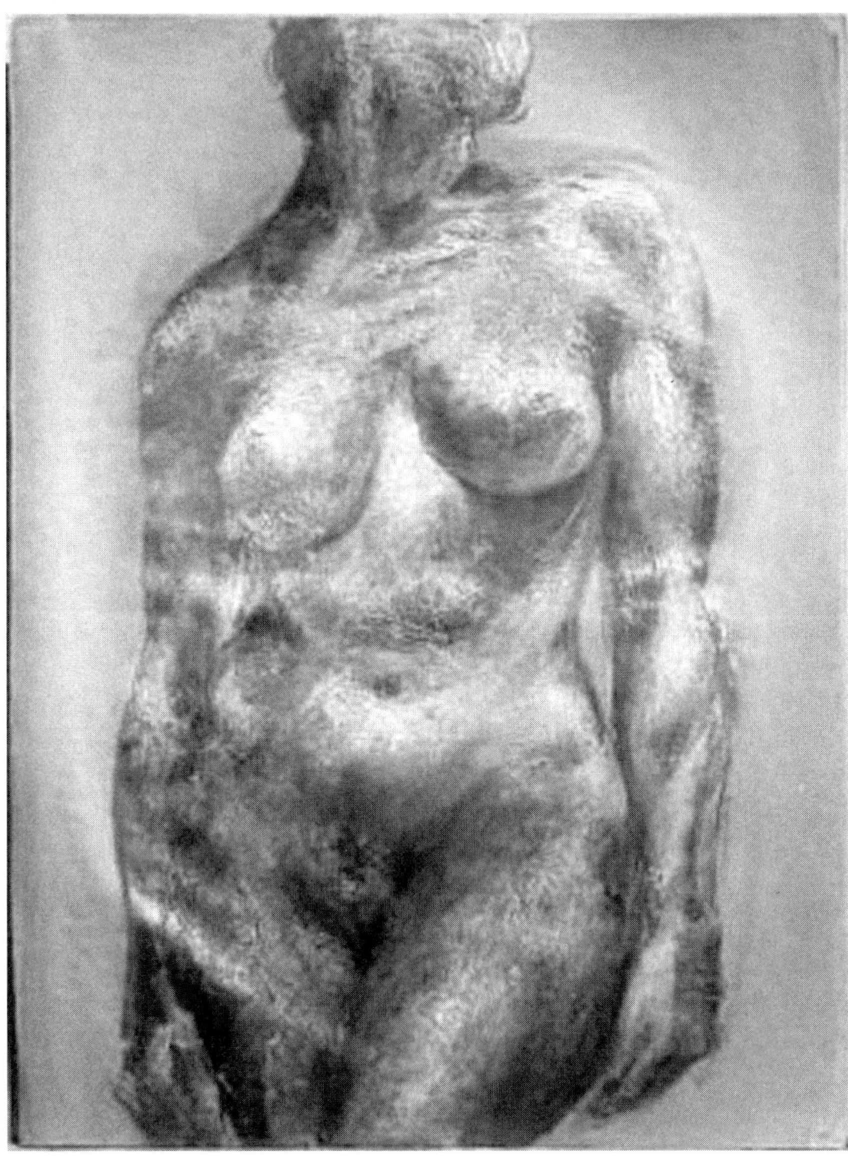

In her sketches and paintings done in Nicolaides' class at the Art Students League, Fine mastered three-dimensionality before studying with Hofmann who stressed two-dimensionality.

Adams, who was a faculty member at the Grand Central School of Art, in which he stated: "There has been a small handful of women painters in the world's history, but in all the history of painting, whenever you find really distinctive work done by a woman it is so rare that it merely proves the case that all really great paintings in the world have been done by men." *Art Digest* attempted to balance Adams's comments by including the opinion of Compton Mackensie, a writer for *Vanity Fair,* who stated that while he did not expect to see a great woman artist in his lifetime, he saw no reason why they should not develop in the coming centuries — hardly a strong vote of confidence in the artistic abilities of women.[25]

Another probable reason for Fine's choice of Nicolaides over Benton was that for her there were uneasy parallels between illustration (from which she was trying to move away) and the story-telling quality of regionalism and American scene painting, touted heavily by Benton. While both Benton and Nicolaides had studied in Paris, Nicolaides had been influenced by Rodin and Matisse, and he was able to pass on his knowledge to his students in a way that allowed them to chart their own direction.

In the fall of 1930, the editors of *ARTnews* noted that the major New York galleries were filled with exhibitions of School of Paris painters among them Matisse, Picasso, Derain, Rouault, Soutine, and Bonnard. Such a concentration was "the most beneficial thing that ever happened to American art," and "the younger and more radical of our painters are sweeping into new strength and courage year by year as a result." This was not occurring due to "bondage" to European styles but to the "glowing challenge" they presented.[26] Adding credence to the idea that American art was finally beginning to make progress, albeit slowly, was a statement made by Matisse while on a tour of U.S. cities. Fascinated by American architecture, particularly the boldness of the skyscrapers equipped with elevators (so unlike older European buildings, the height of which was related to how many stairs a human could easily climb), he believed that American painting had yet to pass through a similar formative stage: "One, perhaps two generations must pass before a solid foundation will have been achieved. France has decades of tradition in back of her art and so can produce masters. The United States is now engaged in building up a tradition."[27]

From the first class she attended, Fine felt an artistic kinship with Nicolaides. One of the most important skills she learned from him was how to do quick sketches, what she called "almost scribbles" that captured "the spirit of the action rather than the outlining of the figure, which was static and lacking in action."[28] Nicolaides became well-known for developing a pedagogy that made full use of spontaneous gestural drawings. He incorporated these principals in his book *The Natural Way to Draw,* which was published posthumously in 1941, three years after his untimely death in 1938. He was more concerned with the ability to see than the ability to copy what was seen. "The job of a teacher," he wrote, "as I see it, is to teach students not how to draw, but how to learn to draw."[29]

Brooks also appreciated Nicolaides's personal manner of teaching and his stress on the intuitive, but eventually he found it a little smothering. "I felt that it was a kind of implication that you might be a genius, you know, and it was a pretty subjective approach to teaching." He decided to switch to Boardman Robinson, another teacher at the League, whom Brooks considered to be more objective in his teaching approach.[30] However, Fine stayed with Nicolaides, absorbing everything he had to offer, including an awareness of three-dimensionality in painting in which the sense of sight was linked with the sense of touch. "Until actually trying to do it in his method, which was using brown wrapping paper and painting with black and white oil on that to the point where the figure almost looked like sculpture coming out of the wall, I never really knew what three-dimensional painting was," Fine explained. "Of course, I had to overcome it later."[31] By this she meant that while the bas-relief quality gave the illusion of three-dimensionality, it was inferior to working within the two-dimensional picture-plane. This emphasis on two-dimensionality, or flatness of the picture-plane, came close to being a mantra of the era. It began in Europe in the latter half of the nineteenth century and gained in influence from thereon, spurred in part by the ubiquity of photography, which was far more efficient at recording reality, thereby lifting from artists any burden they might have felt to paint how the world actually looked. The traditional academically trained painter tried to imitate nature by the use of perspective and other techniques, which was what Nicolaides was teaching, although he was well aware of the newer developments. However, Fine was beginning to believe that the academic approach was artificial, offering nothing more than optical tricks. The superior approach was for a painter to recognize (before touching the canvas with a single bristle) the boundaries and limitations of her art: the flatness of the canvas, the nature of various colors to come forward or recede, the way oil paint flows off the tip of the brush. Starting from that point, the painter could create something real, in and of itself, not an approximation of reality.

As had generations of artists before her, Fine considered the time she spent copying masterpieces in museums to be as formative as attending class, a practice that Nicolaides encouraged. Of the European Masters, Rembrandt was her favorite:

> I remember as a young student that I saved everything I could find on a number of artists that I loved. Of course Rembrandt was one of my great gods and I would cut out and save in a portfolio everything that he did. But I never thought to cut out the whole thing. I would cut out the figure and I never could understand what made it so great. And it had very much to do with what I had cut away...then I realized that where he put what he put was so very, very important.[32]

She received permission from the Metropolitan Museum of Art to copy two of Rembrandt's works in their collection. "The exciting thing was in the copying," she remembered. "I would see, for instance, how in 'Man with the Glove,' his hand was on his knee and there was the slightest suggestion that it was pulled back just a little bit into space, so that it would remain on a two-dimensional plane."[33] To her, it was as if modern theories had been anticipated far earlier by Rembrandt. On completing the copies after several weeks of work, she began to leave with the paintings under her arms when the museum officials stopped her. So perfect were they in execution that they could only be taken from the museum if they were stamped "copy" on the back, which was standard museum policy. But never were her copies done just "for the sake of copying," but instead to seek out "the spirit" that made the paintings great. "It wasn't some hidebound thing I was after but some marvelous inner feeling that existed in those things."

Matisse and Cézanne were also pivotal to Fine's dawning awareness of abstraction. "I looked at Matisse and loved him but I didn't understand him," Fine said. "But I did seem to understand Cézanne, and I loved Cézanne." Matisse's art could be both serene and vibrant with an inner harmony analogous to what Piet Mondrian called "equilibriums." As for Cézanne, Matisse himself had titled him "the master of us all."[34]

Using "The Bather," ca. 1885, as an example, art historian Roger Lipsey clarifies why Cézanne was so important to generations of artists of every stylistic persuasion, including Fine: "Throughout the painting we sense the brooding presence of the artist as mind, eye, questioner. The art of painting has become a visible dialogue between the artist and his sensation of reality, rather than a finished report from which the artist absents himself. Cézanne taught the primacy of questioning and seeking over polished results."[35] Lipsey's explanation sheds light on Fine's use of the word "understand," for she was implying that an intellectual as well as emotional awareness was required. Once when asked by an interviewer about the nature of classicism, Fine brought up "The Bather": "In the statues that you see in the museums, which are very much a part of the education of a student, do you feel or wonder what makes this Greek youth have the same kind of quality that can be seen in the Cézanne painting of a bather? That's one of the most exciting paintings there is for study of what we are talking about."[36]

Fine laboriously translated for herself, using her high-school-level French, an interview with Cézanne in which he used the word "motif" in a different connotation than in English: "Some reporter had found him on the scene at Mont St. Victoire painting, and had finally gotten him to talk, and he would only reiterate the word 'motif' over and over again. Now 'motif' means something completely different in French than it does in English....I interpreted it to mean a kind of order that he was making out of nature which is chaotic and panoramic."[37] That order could only exist "if you have control over that canvas, and that can't exist unless you recognize that the first plane of the picture to be the plane bounded by the north, south, east, and west."[38] What was most significant to her was that Cézanne was "so completely sensitive to whatever was going on and sensitive to what was happening on his canvas and so dedicated to reveal something of what he felt that…he went beyond his own theories," for example, his exploration of perspective, which he was subsequently to "destroy" in his paintings.[39]

As to Matisse, Fine found "his most simple-seeming images impossible to forget," especially his assiduous avoidance of the illusion of depth. "He would have a woman lounging, and then the foot or the hand, or something, would be moved. Why should he have pushed that foot forward or backward?" Her answer was that by so doing, Matisse was keeping it on the two-dimensional plane as had Cézanne.[40] Also important was his strong stress on the value of work: "Matisse may have, as he insists, worked without a theory, but one clear belief he did have: that one must work," Fine said. "He labored to produce a single line and advised, 'Don't wait for inspiration. It comes while one is working.'" The lesson was clear: to paint a great picture, no halfway measures would do. It was all or nothing. "If you don't want to go the limit, you only get approximations," Fine concluded from her study of Matisse.[41]

Equally critical to her was Matisse's receptivity to his own emotions and feelings. "You can ask of painting a deeper feeling which touches the mind as well as the senses," she continued. "On the other hand, purely intellectual painting is nonexistent." Matisse remained important to Fine throughout her life, in particular his use of glowing colors that had the power to affect emotions. He wrote: "Simple colors can act upon the inner feelings with more force, the simpler they are. A blue, for example, accompanied by the brilliance of its complementaries, acts upon the feelings like an energetic blow on a gong. The same with red and yellow, and the artist must be able to sound them when he needs to."[42] Twenty years later in a statement she sent *The New York Times* in conjunction with the opening of her solo exhibition at the Betty Parsons Gallery, Fine echoed Matisse's words: "For me Color is enough — Color has its own palpable reality — Color has its own validity. Through Color I create something which, through its own innate beauty, moves one to feel something."[43]

After completing a sketch in the museum, Fine would return to her studio and paint a work that was analytically derivative, experimenting with light or color, breaking up the image in an impressionistic way. "Mixing color was a very joyous occupation for me because there was so much excitement at what would happen when one color was placed next to another." Non-objectivity and an impulse toward "nothing but the painting itself" beckoned to her with every canvas. She and Berezov occasionally hired models, but she realized one day that the shapes she was painting, in a Cubist style, were "bound to a single object which was the figure." Instead she wanted them to go far beyond the limitations of the object, "to express a mood, a color, almost anything [except] anything recognizable."[44] Other than an impressionistic portrait she completed of her sister Rose not long after her wedding in 1933 (wearing a dress Fine painted in a diagonal sweep of delicate yellow and peach hues, and sitting in a chair of Prussian blue), she rarely drew from a model after the mid-1930s. "Perle came to Malden and had Rose pose for that portrait," remembered Charlotte Fine. "She placed her in a beautiful black mahogany rocking chair with a curved back that we owned. Unfortunately, the chair was lost when we moved to a new home, but the portrait has remained one of our prized possessions. It is a wonderful painting."[45]

Fine attended many classes throughout the 1930s, nevertheless, she considered herself to be largely self-taught due to her habit of setting for herself aesthetic problems and then working out the solutions in the solitude of her studio instead of in the crowded rooms of an art school. "One has to work in one's own studio and be very severe with oneself as to the degree of art that is beginning to happen and try to find out what it is that makes a work of art and why what you've done may not have become a work of art. That is the kind of self-discipline that I gave myself." However, she also acknowledged a great debt to all the teachers with whom she studied, a debt she would repay years later in the style and quality of her own teaching, being both "a severe task-master" as she put it, and also a patient adviser, with the result that her students "usually made terrific progress."[46]

It was fortunate that Fine had the motivation to study on her own because as the Depression worsened, getting the money for tuition was often impossible. Staunchly, the art publications had been maintaining a forced optimism throughout 1930 into 1931, seeing the stock market crash of 1929 as a blip sure to be followed by an economic upswing that would buoy up all artists. Indeed, when 1931 began, the galleries seemed to be humming with an exciting mix of exhibitions: Picasso was at the Valentine Gallery; Jules Pascin was at the Downtown Gallery; Matisse was at the Brummer Galley; Georges Rouault was at the Demotte Gallery; Hilla Rebay (who would become a major influence on Fine in the 1940s during Rebay's tenure as head of the Museum of Non-Objective Painting) had an exhibition at the Wildenstein Galleries. Meanwhile, Georgia O'Keeffe had yet another exhibition at An American Place, Alfred Stieglitz's new gallery on Madison Ave. and 53rd St. But sales were dismal for everyone. Finally in an editorial in the October 3, 1931 issue, the editors of *ARTnews* dropped their mask of optimism and admitted the worst. Because the "artistic Renaissance which has sprung up in recent years in America" was imperiled, they pleaded with museums and collectors to remember that "the finest works of art still appreciate in value" and, therefore, it was an opportune time to buy art. The European art scene was also in terrible shape. *ARTnews* German correspondent Flora Turkel-Deri, who had until then maintained a positive outlook in her column "Berlin Letter" admitted to "a rather strong spirit of pessimism."[47] And everything just kept getting bleaker.

As the Depression dragged on, taking on the adjective Great, no one knew where art was headed except downhill. American Social Realism vied with German De Stijl and Russian Constructivism, each style carrying with it an ideology, and each claiming the others were artistic dead ends. There was a physical hunger and a mental uneasiness that showed up in the classrooms of the Art Students League. It predominated in the endless conversations in the League's cafeteria, and mingled with the smell of coffee at Stewart's, a downtown eatery. This uneasiness was exacerbated by the fact that most art students were receiving information about the European art scene second-hand, often through periodicals. Through the 1920s, it had been standard for

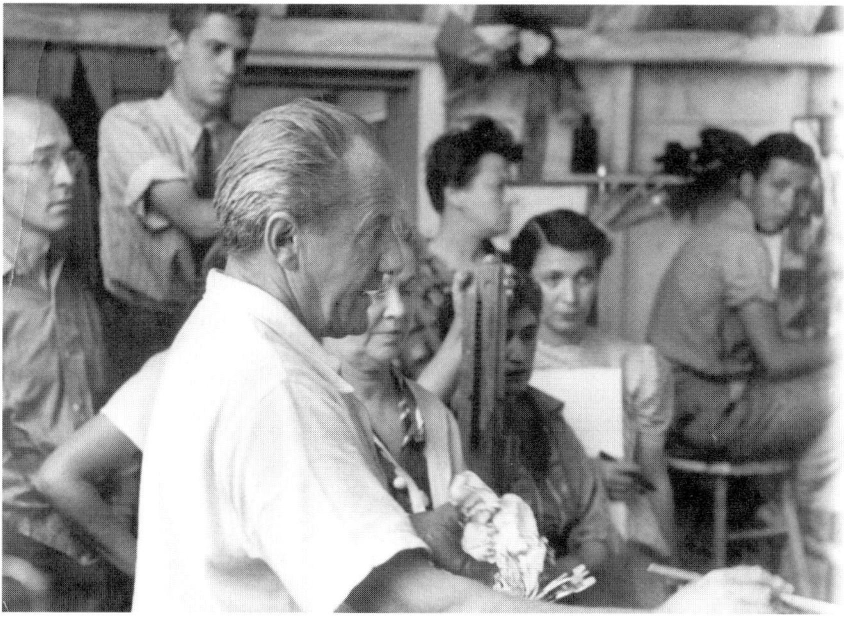

In his school, Hans Hofmann provided an atmosphere similar to a Parisian atelier where American students could learn European art theories. Fine (second from right) considered him to be catalytic for a generation of artists.

art students, even the poorest, to go to Europe at some point in their education, at least for a short while. But the Depression had slammed that door, forcing students to rely instead on *Cahiers d' Art* and other publications, printed in black and white and written in French. The isolation was increased by the fact that several major art texts on Constructivism, De Stijl and Neo-Plasticism had not yet been translated into English.

Young American artists struggled to keep up with what was happening in Europe, but wealthy American collectors, oblivious to the Depression, traveled there whenever they chose to visit the galleries and studios. The result was a major disjunction between artists and collectors, who were well aware of what was taking place in the studios of the Left Bank. Not until World War II would American collectors, suddenly forced to stay state-side, begin to give more than a passing glance at what was being created here.

Unable to go to Europe, American artists turned repeatedly to the art of Picasso that was often on display in New York, scrutinizing it for signs of a new direction. Five months after the exhibition at the Museum of Modern Art of Cézanne, Gauguin, Seurat, and Van Gogh (the exhibition that had turned Fine into a self-proclaimed Francophile) Duncan Phillips wrote in an essay for *ARTnews* that the artist who he felt was far and away the most important for setting the direction of art was not among the four: "Picasso is a colossus who bestrides both camps, inspiring imitators either to look up at his pose as a formalist of quite formidable power or to guess at his meaning as a supernaturalist most strangely disturbing. He is making history-breaking precedents every day. There is no doubt at all of his genius. The only doubt is in regard to the results of his influence."[48]

An undated note in Fine's personal papers gives an indication of her own close study of Picasso: "Great Picasso show. Went again and again. More students followed."[49] What astonished her, as it did so many others, was Picasso's ability to continue to change, not holding on tenaciously to what he had done before but not repudiating it either. Nothing was static. In the mid-1940s, Fine compared Picasso to Mondrian in an unpublished essay: "When Picasso was doing what appeared to be non-representational work, it was certainly extremely beautiful, and when he was painting Analytical Cubism it too was very moving, very beautiful. Every phase of his work, without any symbolical connotation, has extremely beautiful examples in it."[50]

So extensive was his influence that many artists were accused by critics of aping the great European. For example, a reviewer for *ARTnews* wrote: "A man who is destined to make trouble for the experts is Archele Gorki [sic], who paints Picassos and Braques with great skill."[51] A year older than Fine, Arshile Gorky had followed a similar trajectory, having studied at the New School of Design in Boston before moving to New York City in 1922, taking a studio on Sullivan Street near Washington Square, and subsequently teaching a course at Grand Central School of Art while Fine was there. In fact, she recalled hearing his heavily accented voice sounding through the classroom wall, adding a touch of the exotic. However, unlike Fine and other artists in the same age group, Gorky had as a boy been a witness to genocide. Born in Armenia in 1904, he was aware of the massive slaughter of his people by the Turks and had watched his mother die of starvation. He had come to the United States in 1920 at the age of sixteen with his sister Vartoosh to stay with his father. They lived at various times in Boston and Watertown, Massachusetts, as well as Providence, Rhode Island. Emotionally scarred in a way that other artists could sense but could not completely understand, Gorky embodied in his own life the darkness that would be the twentieth century well before the rise of Hitler and Stalin, becoming the tormented survivor who barely survived. For other artists, including Fine, Gorky was the breaker of artistic molds who was himself broken. Even the name "Gorky," which he adopted in place of his birth name, meant "bitterness." Struggling to gain a foothold in America, he struggled equally hard to gain a foothold in the world of art, and during the late 1920s and early 1930s, it was Matisse, Cézanne, and Picasso (the same artists that Fine found pivotal) whom he emulated. The art dealer Julian Levy wrote that in the winter of 1932, he considered giving Gorky a solo exhibition, but after carefully looking at Gorky's portfolio, he told him, "Your work is so very much like Picasso's." Gorky replied, "I was with Cézanne for a long time and now naturally I am with Picasso." Levy promised to give him an exhibition "someday, when you are with Gorky."[52] Similarly, the poet Edwin Denby, who lived in Greenwich Village at the time and who was friendly with many artists, remembered the predominance of Picasso in their talk:

> I began this train of thought wondering at the cliché about downtown painting in the depression — the accepted idea that everybody had doubts and imitated Picasso and talked politics. None of these features seemed to me remarkable at the time, and they don't now. Downtown everybody loved Picasso then, and why not. But what they painted made no sense as an imitation of him. For myself, something in his steady wide light reminded me then of the light in the streets and lofts we lived in.[53]

In the same restless frame of mind that had spurred their decision to leave the Grand Central School of Art and enroll at the Art Students League, Fine and Berezov heard through Vaclav Vytlacil, a painter and teacher at the League, of a new art school opened by the artist Hans Hofmann. Vytlacil had traveled to Munich, Germany, to study with Hofmann from 1922 to 1926, returning to New York to teach at the League beginning in 1928. Heavily influenced both by Hofmann's pedagogical philosophy and the art of Cézanne, he had attempted to incorporate some of these ideas into his own teaching. However, he had been taken to task for "misleading the students" by fellow artists and teachers Reginald Marsh and Kenneth Hayes Miller, a man whom one student derisively dubbed the "the foremost representative of the tradition inherited from the high renaissance."[54] Vytlacil continued to teach at the League, but his censure as well as his willingness to spread the word on behalf of Hofmann based on his own experience as a student is an indication that even among the teachers there was the feeling that the League was no longer on the cutting edge.

Hofmann opened his school in New York City in 1933 after emigrating from Germany. Because his reputation as a superior art teacher had preceded him, he found a ready group of admirers who were chafing at academic constraints. They were eager to learn about what was occurring in Europe not just via reading but in the studio under the guidance of a master teacher who cared enough to take their work apart and help them put it back together again in ways that were exhilarating and novel. Berezov recalled:

> I first heard about the school as far back as 1924 or 1925. A friend of mine came back from a European trip. He had traveled on a National Academy Scholarship and was floating around Paris when he heard about Hofmann in Munich. It seems that Hofmann was all the rage, and all young painters were flocking there, so he went to Munich and stayed there as long as his money held out. When he came back, of course, he raved about it. I couldn't go to Europe, so I put it out of my mind, but when I heard that he had opened a school here in New York, Perle and I immediately joined up.[55]

With regret, Fine told Nicolaides that she and Berezov were leaving the League to study with Hofmann. But there was no changing their minds. "Both Maurice and I felt it was very important to understand what Hofmann was talking about…it was a very exciting time because things that we felt very vaguely were suddenly brought forth face to face."[56] At their last meeting, Nicolaides acknowledged that he could not teach Fine anymore, saying to her without reproach or cynicism, "When you learn something, come back and tell me what it is." Feeling sorry about leaving him, and beholden to him for what she had learned, she replied that she would.[57] However, Fine never got the chance because Nicolaides died at the age of 47 in July 1938 after a brief illness. In a tribute to Nicolaides, Dan Kern, a former student, wrote that "he was a second father to many of us, and the guide and champion of minds that found the struggle sometimes too great to be borne without help.…He died when classes were over for the summer, but in the last mercy of delirium, he was whispering instructions to some imaginary student — some student who was the symbol of all that to which he had given his life."[58]

Berezov and Fine were extremely fortunate when it came to teachers, for Hofmann was as kind and concerned about his students as Nicolaides had been. The artist Nell Blaine, who studied with him in the 1940s, described him as "a kind of jovial, intellectual Santa Claus."[59]

To Fine, "no teacher that I have ever known engendered as much love and loyalty from his students":

> They would hang on his every word, even if they didn't completely understand him and they followed him around the class as he criticized the students' work. They clustered six deep and stood on the stools and window-sills to watch him demonstrate on some student's work-in-progress. He never gave lectures during the class sessions; he only demonstrated, and lectured at other times. When the class session was over, the drawing he had worked on was pinned on the wall for all to study. It helped to clarify many of the principles that were brought out in his lectures.[60]

Hofmann provided for his devoted students the closest thing to a Parisian atelier this side of the Atlantic, rich with an atmosphere of creation and passionate debate. He infused the students with a thorough sense of art history and a solid knowledge of the traditional standards governing the definition of a good painting. Yet he also encouraged them to exceed not only those standards but his own work as well. He brought Europe to America and made it comprehensible, even though his command of English was shaky and his theories were a pastiche of long accepted ideas on the continent. "It was extremely difficult to follow him because of his accent," said Fine, but he hammered through the importance of two-dimensionality nonetheless:

> When he was a young artist, painting in Paris, that was one of the major points of the new discovery — that is, Cubism. One can hardly imagine the discussion that waxed furiously in studios and cafes. Hofmann developed a good understanding of the picture-plane and a workable method of achieving a feeling of three-dimensional volumes with it, which is the basis of modern art. One artist made this quality of two-dimensionality his chief preoccupation and developed it to a degree of prime importance. That was Piet Mondrian who, coming to Paris, had seized upon what he called the "plastic" quality of Picasso's Cubism, and made it his lifework. Hofmann knew and understood Mondrian's theories. On two separate occasions, when I was in his class, he gave a demonstration, using the model, on an arrangement of planes, simplifying the space division, suggesting the feeling of the volumes, and keeping the picture-plane quite flat, until he had a typical Mondrian grid of lines. It was a very impres-

> sive performance. The great value of Hofmann's teachings is that he combined the flat two-dimensional with a strong feeling for the three-dimensional in volume, with movement and a great deal of expression.[61]

Art historian Eleanor Munro attributed Hofmann's influence and his teaching approach to his engineering background. "What he projected was a Germanic feeling for nature imploded into the rational structure of Cubism. An engineer and inventor in his youth, he may have kept a tough, pragmatic feeling for balance of stresses: a work of art, drawing or painting, was to have its own internal life as a system of pushes and pulls acting across the whole surface. Then these interrelated thrusts would generate an all-over field of energy. Physical nature — a still life, a figure, a landscape — was always the model, not to be copied but to be referred to. It was there that these charged relationships between shapes were to be studied."[62]

Despite her respect for Hofmann, Fine did not attend his classes regularly because she never cared for working in a group, a dislike exacerbated by the fact that eventually his classes became so popular they were often overcrowded, with easels crunched together and students vying for the best angle. Instead, Fine attended intermittently over a four to five-year period during the mid-1930s and extending into the early 1940s, both in New York and in Provincetown, Massachusetts, to which Hofmann and his students migrated during the summer to get away from the unbearable heat and humidity of the city, which maximized the smell of oil paints, turpentine, and sweat in the crowded studios. Part of Fine's hesitancy in committing to study full-time with Hofmann was her increasing fascination with non-objective art, to which he was not personally committed, at least not yet. While at his school, Fine realized that abstraction had to be total; there was no middle ground. As she put it: "there was no such thing as semi-abstract painting; one couldn't be semi-abstract — it's like saying 'I feel a little bit strongly about something.' " She characterized Hofmann as "an opening wedge" into what she really wanted to do. Many young artists were involved with regionalism, American scene painting, and social protest painting, conveyed in either bleak or sarcastic realism. But right from the start, Fine was pulled toward the non-objective and the purely abstract:

> I've felt all along that there's something that's drawing me away from the figure and toward the other....I think it has to do with the unexplored. There's so much that's still unexplored in the realm of the non-objective and the abstract. And I feel that I sort of owe it to myself because I know quite a bit about it and I think because I do, I want to know a little bit more. I want to know what I don't know. And so I feel drawn to that exploration more and more. I don't know whether I'll find anything or not, but it's so much fun to look for it. It's strange.[63]

Fine's ability to drop in on Hofmann's classes was facilitated by the location of her studio, a five-story walk-up on West Eighth Street across the street from his school, which was over a movie theater. In the mid-1930s, she and Berezov rented "two cold water flats, very, very inexpensive...and one of them was kept completely free and I worked in there. It was just fine. I was in the rear of the building so that it was very quiet. And we lived in the other. Everyone said to break through, but the whole idea was to have complete separation." Fine worked alone in her studio until she was "absolutely frustrated with not knowing where I stood or what I had to do," at which point she returned to Hofmann's class to reorient herself. Feeling inhibited, she never took any of her non-objective work into his class or invited him to her studio to see it. "Hofmann might have enjoyed it, but I couldn't do it in class. I couldn't show it to him."[64]

In the privacy of her studio, she was determined to understand theoretically what was happening in her painting as she moved steadily away from figuration and toward complete abstraction. This meant retracing the steps first of the Impressionists, then of the Analytic Cubists, and finally of the Synthetic Cubists. To her, these last two groups were involved with breaking down and then building up while rigorously maintaining the picture plane:

> On trying to do whatever I was doing a little better, it would lead me directly into working with planes. I'd set up a still life in my studio, just the way Hofmann did in his classroom. There were always people fighting for places. I didn't have to contend with that in my studio. At first I couldn't use color at all. This paralleled what the early Cubists did. They

During her years as a student, Fine experimented with several styles including Cubism. *Sketch for Cubist Still-life* (1938), charcoal on paper, 6 x13 15/16". Gift of Dr. Thomas B. Brumbaugh Art History Collection, Augustana College Art Collection, 2002.18.14.

> couldn't use color. They used black and white, a little gray, a little brown. Then the big step was when they put in a little green or a little blue, where it didn't intrude, very subdued in color, still keeping the picture plane, not losing that.[65]

The women who attended Hofmann's school during the late 1930s and early 1940s included Lenore Krasner (who eventually changed her name to the more androgynous Lee) with whom Fine became a lifelong friend, Lillian Kiesler, Ray Kaiser [Eames], and Mercedes Carles [Matter]. Among the men were Nicolas Carone, Robert De Niro and Larry Rivers. Hofmann could be very critical; once he ripped up a drawing by Krasner, summarily rearranged the pieces and exclaimed, "This is tension." But he was also encouraging and stimulating. As with the Krasner incident, Fine remembered him tearing up drawings in class and using the pieces for collage, in so doing opening up new creative possibilities and in the process "making movements do things other than what they were doing before."[66] Carone recalled appreciatively that the atmosphere in Hofmann's class was such that "you'd dare go beyond yourself and not be kept back by a climate of acceptance."[67]

Generally the students got along well in the studio which was large, light-filled, and uncluttered. Fine wrote:

> The model stand was placed flat against the wall, that is, free of windows, and screens were placed on the model stand against the wall, and drapery was hung from them in such a manner as to give movements and counter-movements to the pose of the model. The students and their easels were placed in a semi-circle around the room. Other schools pose their models in the center of the room with the students all around them. This is very bad, especially for beginners, because in order to study the model as a form in movement within a given space, the relationship between the model and what surrounds the model must remain constant."[68]

The extent to which unchanging totality and interconnectedness of the model and the environment were considered important in Hofmann's studio is indicated in a humorous incident involving Krasner. The class had been doing a series of sketches of the same model for two or three weeks. One Monday morning, the students had set to work once again when Krasner rushed in a little late. According to Fine, all at once she started to yell, "It's all wrong. It's all wrong! It's all changed!" Seeing nothing different, Fine and the other students looked quizzically at the model, at their drawings, and at Krasner's drawing, trying to find out what had thoroughly upset her. "She's cut her hair," Krasner screamed. Fine also laughed about De Niro's comical contrariness revealed by his occasionally crumpling up a sheet of paper and tossing it in front of the model, forcing someone else to pick it up to return the scene to its original purity.[69]

As did the other women in his classes, Fine found Hofmann to be partial to male artists; nonetheless, he pushed everyone — men and women — to excel. Hofmann told Krasner that one of her works was "so good you would not believe it was done by a woman."[70] Fine also remembered the day early in World War II when the ratio of men to women in Hofmann's classes began to shift radically because the men were entering military service. Complaining bitterly out of frustration, he stood up and pointed at each women, one after another, shouting, "You'll amount to nothing. You'll amount to nothing. You'll never get anywhere. You'll never get anywhere."[71] Yet he could also be magnanimous in his support. One day he looked at the painting on which Fine was working and exclaimed, "Ah, lyrical!" then went on to explain that he meant the term in a positive way because "you can't shout all the time."[72] However, there finally came the point when Hofmann told Fine what she had already been told by Nicolaides: there was nothing more he could teach her.

In a way that Hofmann could not have foreseen, his stress on the totality of a canvas, including the edges, to create tension or balance, was inculcated into the students who would become Abstract Expressionists, many of whom considered themselves to be edge-conscious. Certainly Fine not only learned it and used it, but eventually she preached it to her own students: "I first make a student very conscious of the frame of the picture, which is usually the last thing we do. Everything must be related to that. Expression cannot come about without it."[73]

There is no doubt that Hofmann was galvanic for generations of artists and art teachers, even those who eventually felt compelled to distance themselves from him. Everyone who studied with Hofmann, whether they became Abstract Expressionists or realists, learned the same principles and imbibed the same aesthetics. "To stand behind that man, as the whole class did while he was working," Fine wrote, "seeing suddenly through his eyes the beauty he created, the problems he made and solved, and changed and solved again, the tremendous creative power he infused [into] this lump of clay on the model stand is an experience I have not forgotten."[74]

Although Fine was too reticent to show Hofmann the pure abstractions she was painting outside of class, nonetheless she believed that she played a part in bringing him to see the worth of non-objectivity, to the point that his own painting began to evolve in that direction. That Hofmann was open to the influence of his students, making changes in what he taught and how he painted, was corroborated by Carone:

> Hofmann developed from his students. And a lot of talented people went to him and, if they involved themselves, he was aware of their research and experiences in areas that were opened up in class. I think that the most advanced — and you can quote me now, boy — the most advanced art was done in Hofmann's class. When I first saw…de Kooning, I didn't think he was so advanced. In fact, de Kooning later on began to do what we were doing in the Hofmann school.… Hofmann used to say "You people don't realize what you're doing." He said, "You're doing something more advanced than anything outside."[75]

In the final analysis, Fine considered Hofmann to be catalytic, not seminal. "Hofmann made something come about faster than it would have otherwise," she said. What was taking place in art in America would have occurred with or without him but not as rapidly. "A lot of people agree that this would have happened to me and to all the artists in this country who studied with him anyway, even if he hadn't been on the scene."[76]

Whereas the spirit inside Hofmann's school was exhilarating, the spirit in the world outside was disheartening. Until the stock market crash, artists had often worked odd jobs, making just enough to survive in vaguely bohemian style that had about it a certain living-on-the-financial-edge thrill, at least for artists who were at the beginning of their careers. But by 1933, even those jobs were gone and instead of lines outside museums and galleries, there were breadlines. People sold apples on the streets to get by. The excitement of being an artist in Greenwich Village had faded to a bitter survival mentality. "I remember visiting Perle and Maurice around 1934," said Charlotte Fine. "They lived on the fifth floor, which was at the top of the building, so it was lit by skylights. It may have been wonderful for painting but it meant we had to walk all the way up the stairs. Things were very, very rough for them. When we visited, we often gave them a little money, a dollar or two, because they didn't have the money for the electricity or anything. Or we would slip a few dollars into a letter. There were times when they didn't have a penny."[77]

"It was a very rough time," Fine said. "Maurice had a job. He lost it. I had a job. I didn't lose it, but I left it. We were trying to make just enough to get along, without a penny over that."[78] For a while, Fine worked as a monitor in Hofmann's classes in exchange for tuition. It was the only way she could attend. "Hofmann was very charitable to poor students. His rates were rather steep compared to other art schools, but he gave a large number of scholarships to deserving people. He also gave many lectures, and they were free, or were benefits for some liberal cause of the day."[79]

More often than not, it was the ever pessimistic but acerbically funny Gorky who captured the tenor of the times. Recalling a party at Willem de Kooning's studio with Gorky in attendance, Denby wrote:

> I knew they talked together about painting more than anyone else. But when other people were at Bill's Gorky said so little that he was often forgotten. At one party the talk turned to the condition of the painter in America, the bitterness, the unfairness of his poverty and disregard. People had a great deal to say on the subject, and they said it, but the talk ended in a gloomy silence. In the pause, Gorky's deep voice came from under a table. "Nineteen miserable years have I lived in America." Everybody burst out laugh-

> ing. There was no whine left. Gorky had not spoken of justice, but of fate, and everybody laughed open-hearted.[80]

Many artists received financial support from the Federal Art Project of the Works Progress Administration (W.P.A), but that did not begin until 1935 by which point the Depression was in its sixth year.[81] In the W.P.A's first year, it helped support over 1,000 artists in New York City, but Berezov and Fine were not among them. Fine applied but was turned down. She believed she was rejected for two reasons: she was married, and she owned a phone. It was presumed that married women were financially supported by their husbands, so they were not entitled to help from the government. As for the phone, Fine had acquired it on applying for the W.P.A to make it easier for the officials to reach her, but they saw it as further proof that she did not need assistance. Fine also suspected that she was not friendly with the right people: "I didn't know the social protest artists. Probably if I did know any, I might have gotten in there."[82] This was a reference to her belief that several W.P.A painters and administrators were also members of the American Artists' Congress, a Marxist group, that thought art should be used as a method of protest and persuasion to bring about a collectivist movement for economic revolution. Fine never took part in any organization, art or otherwise, that had a political agenda. Without the support of the W.P.A, Fine and Berezov took turns working as illustrators so that both could attend classes. Fine put her commercial training to good use doing drawings of shoes for the department stores Bonwit Teller and Bergdorf Goodman. If one's economic standard was "barely enough to subsist," then "at that time one could live on what one could make on one or two drawings," she said.[83]

Besides the lack of financial support, not being a part of the W.P.A hurt Fine by distancing her from a tight artistic community. However, there was a small, albeit short-lived, benefit which the W.P.A bestowed on women artists in general: its anti-discriminatory rules opened doors and helped promote an artistic culture that if not totally nurturing of women's talents at least did not stifle them. The artist Helen Lundeberg, who bossed a W.P.A mural crew of six people, said, "Most of us look back on those as the good days."[84] The artist Alice Neel also considered her years with the W.P.A as a positive experience: "You had a world of your own."[85] But those doors soon closed. In later years, many women artists looked back on the 1930s wistfully, because a long period of regression set in afterwards during which the men distanced themselves from the women, insisting that it took "balls" to produce art, as Louise Nevelson was told, or that "only the men have wings," as Hofmann stated.[86] According to art historian Charlotte Streifer Rubinstein, the very openness to women that existed during the 1930s, due in large measure to the W.P.A, led women artists to a false sense of having achieved equality, which created problems for them in the 1940s and '50s. They did not see the need for an active feminist movement: "Therefore, there was no organizational structure or even awareness with which to resist the chauvinism of the period."[87]

Perhaps as a result of being on the periphery, Fine was also not among the group of artists who formed the American Abstract Artists (AAA) in 1936. Yet in terms of her style and her frustration with the lack of interest in abstraction among museums and gallery owners, she could easily have been one of the founding core. She and Berezov joined in the early 1940s at which point the AAA provided them with an important link to many European artists who had sought asylum in the United States, among them Mondrian. From there on, Fine and Berezov took part in the AAA's yearly exhibitions and occasionally headed up committees, remaining active for close to forty years.

The AAA was established at a time when galleries and museums were very conservative in their offerings and exhibitions. Many art critics of the era believed that art should reaffirm the American way of life. It should not present ambiguous or challenging images or ideas. Some suspected abstraction of being un-American because it was derivative of European avant-garde art. Others considered it to be a dead-end. Even the Museum of Modern Art, which in 1936 had presented the vast exhibition "Cubism and Abstract Act," displaying almost four hundred works of art on four floors, came in for its share of criticism from non-objective artists who thought Alfred Barr — its urbane, Harvard-educated director who had rapidly become a major force in updating the American perception of art — was playing it entirely too safe and too European. He was not paying enough attention to new developments in the United States. The AAA encouraged its members to speak out against misguided criticism and ambivalence, to push for the inclusion of non-objective art in museum exhibitions and permanent collections, and to explore and explain the theoretical underpinnings of the style.

Given the fact that artists in general are not drawn to participate in structured organizations, often do not work well together, and are concerned about the risk of being defined or labeled, with a resultant loss of freedom, it is no surprise that the establishment of the AAA was turbulent. Frustrated at not having access to gallery space, four artists, Rosalind Bengelsdorf, Byron Browne, Albert Swinden, and Ibram Lassaw, met in Bengelsdorf's studio in 1935 to discuss the possibility of exhibiting together. Nothing came of the meeting until the following year when a larger group was convened, this time in Lassaw's studio, where the original four were joined by Burgoyne Diller, Balcomb Greene, Harry Holtzman, and George McNeil. All were involved in the W.P.A, in fact, Diller was director and Holtzman assistant director of the Mural Division. Because of heated disagreements about what the mission of the group should be, it did not really began to coalesce until 1937 after the artists rejected the model of a school/atelier put forth by Holtzman (with himself as head) in favor of group exhibitions and the provision of an unstructured forum for the sharing of ideas.[88]

As its members had hoped, the exhibitions provided much-needed exposure. They were reviewed routinely in the New York newspapers as well as the art magazines, although for about five years, the criticism was uniformly negative. Edward Alden Jewell, senior art critic for *The New York Times,* was highly critical of abstraction, preferring figurative art. Despite his dislike, he dutifully attended the AAA exhibitions, writing dismissively about the first in 1937:

> Into the wide open spaces in the thirty-third floor of the Squibb Building, thirty-nine American "abstract artists" have ventured, each of them bringing examples of his own special ingenuity, each arguing in some degree his endorsement as a raconteur of tales from over yonder on the Rive Gauche that have begun to assume, by this time, a sly patina of age. What they have put on display at the Squibb makes a colorful, an often resounding mass demonstration of decorative design.[89]

The charge of being decorative was one many abstract artists found belittling, for Jewell was implying that the art was not to be taken seriously because it lacked a clear subject. In his review of the exhibition two year later in 1939, he added insult to injury by writing "they make their little decorative dingbats turn the very neatest of handsprings."[90] Yet from the standpoint of the artists, negative criticism was better than no criticism because at least people began to take a look at what all the fuss was about, and some of the things they found pleasantly surprised them. Certainly it was more difficult to determine good art from bad, but that did not mean abstraction was an exercise in chaos by the untalented and the untrained. For example, despite the oft-repeated charge that it took no training to create an abstract painting and that "even a child could do it," it turned out that of the 43 artists in the 1939 AAA exhibition at the Riverside Museum, almost all were academically trained, having studied at Hofmann's school, the Art Students League, the National Academy, or in Europe.[91]

The presence of the AAA and their single-minded insistence on pure non-objectivity may also have influenced painters working in other styles; but it is more likely that many artists were on a parallel trajectory not affected by the AAA. For example, in 1939, the painter Ralston Crawford — one year younger than Fine but already well-known for his "precisionist" paintings of factories, railroads, bridges, and other aspects of industry and commerce — was called by one critic an "essentialist" because he had simplified his material forms to the point where the representational elements verged on pure abstraction. The critic added that fortunately his paintings escaped the style's "calculated coldness." Other "essentialists" whose art was almost entirely divorced from subject matter, according to the critic, were John Ferren, John Graham, Stuart Davis, and John Xceron.[92]

Abstract Expressionism was still several years off, but many of the artists who would be identified with it were working towards it already. A description of de Kooning's art written by his friend Edwin Denby provides evidence of Abstract Expressionism's beginnings. The first time they met was when a black kitten, lost in the rain, was crying on the fire escape by Denby's apartment. It turned out that it belonged to de Kooning, which led to a visit to his studio:

> He was painting on a dark eight-foot high picture that had sweeps of black across it and a big look. That was early in '36. Soon Rudy Burckhardt and I kept meeting Bill at midnight at the local Stewart's, and having a coffee together. . . . Seeing the pictures more or less every day, they slowly became beautiful, and then they stayed beautiful. I didn't think of them as paintings of the New York School, I thought of them as Bill's pictures....At the time from the point of view of the School of Paris, they were impenetrable. The resemblances to Picasso and Miró were misleading, because where they led one to expect seduction and climax, one saw instead a vibration. To start from Mondrian might have helped. One could not get into the picture by way of any detail, one had to get into it all at once, so to speak.[93]

While there were no champions coming to the fore, some critics were beginning to change their minds and to appreciate what was happening among the pure abstractionists. Paul Bird, writing in *Art Digest* about a 1938 exhibition of non-objective paintings by Josef Albers (a painter associated with the Bauhaus in Germany who had immigrated to the United States in 1933), found his precise craftsmanship and color values in abstract geometric patterns to be "compelling." So also, the same year at an exhibition of paintings by Jean Helion, Henry McBride, the much-read critic for *The Sun,* was first taken aback by their total abstraction, but then he regained his footing by asking who wants to understand art anyway. "To be understood is to be dead," he wrote, adding that Helion's colors were "delightful," that he "dramatizes his space relations and his darks and lights with such security that each picture seems a very complete thing."[94] Yet most of the critics of the late 1930s still shared the opinion of Jerome Klein, the *New York Post* art reviewer, who wrote about the 1939 AAA exhibition: "Very well, poke among the droppings of modern art, pick yourself a dry bone and suck on it. See what you get."[95]

For Fine, pure abstraction was not a dry bone and would never be a dry bone. Using a different metaphor, she saw it as the "unexplored" realm, which, as Denby said about de Kooning's paintings, had to be entered "all at once." As a student, she had systematically worked through Impressionism, Cubism, and Neo-Plasticism, but Fine discovered that she "actually had to, at a certain point, forget about painting abstract, and forget about everything, and do holistic painting, which is the sum of its parts and nothing could be taken away. The whole idea was there before you." Now in her mid-thirties, Fine's career was ready to begin with that realization.[96]

It seemed in 1938, a quarter century after the Armory Show had shaken up the American art world, that a new movement finally was gaining momentum and was on the verge of breaking through American conservatism. In March of that year *Art Digest* had announced that abstractionists had taken over the town. Not only were the halls of the National Academy filled with the AAA exhibition, but at the Passedoit Gallery, A. E. Gallatin was having his first solo show after many years of being one of the style's chief apologists by virtue of his museum. Fernand Léger's art was at the Pierre Matisse Gallery and while it was not purely abstract, it had "the stuff out of which a new formal vocabulary will grow." Jean Helion's paintings were on view at the Valentine Galleries and were what the *Digest* called "probably the most completely abstract pictures yet shown." While over at the East River Gallery, a young sculptor named David Smith was stirring up excitement with his creations made in his foundry "where he twists and bends and braises it into abstract creations which exploit the tensile implications of poised power that resides in steel."[97] Then on September 1, 1939, Germany invaded Poland. Suddenly the artistic breakthrough was put on hold. The artists who were ready for their first "one-man" exhibitions, Fine among them, would have to continue to wait. When the breakthrough finally did occur following the war, several other factors, including the arrival from Europe of the Surrealists, would bend it in a new direction.

CHAPTER TWO

THE WAR YEARS

Several years prior to the outbreak of war, German artists and art dealers, in particular those involved with modernism and abstraction, began to immigrate to the United States. They were the first wave of what would become a flood from all over Europe, turning New York City into the art capital of the world — a title that was supposed to be temporary but which New York City refused to relinquish after World War II ended. In that flood of people were two who would become pivotal in Fine's life: the German art dealer Karl Nierendorf and the Dutch painter Piet Mondrian; the first helped launch her career and the second helped crystallize her aesthetic perception.

The upheavals of the entire period were so enormous it is not possible to pinpoint one event as being the linchpin in the development of Abstract Expressionism. Yet it is undeniable that the suppression of modern art in Germany beginning in the 1930s, and the subsequent awareness that totalitarianism was anathema to artistic freedom, made a deep impression on all artists including Fine, affecting the way they painted following World War II and how their work was politically interpreted during the Cold War.

George Grosz, whose proposed appointment as an instructor at the Art Students League had caused a brouhaha in 1933 when Fine was a student, was in the first wave. He had acted on a strong "hunch," as he called it, that under Hitler there would be no future for art in Germany, other than that which portrayed in an academic style an idealized and sanitized version of the German people as blond, blue-eyed, and strong. His hunch proved to be correct, for in less than a year Paul Joseph Goebbels, minister of propaganda for the Nazis, announced that thenceforth the government would supervise all artists and that anyone who was judged to be "unfit" would be replaced by "qualified creative artists and art craftsmen." As a German soldier during World War I, Grosz had served for four years in the trenches. The experience so scarred him that he lashed out, via his art, at the savagery of war and the stupidity of humankind.[1] By Nazi standards, Grosz' military service could not counterbalance the unfitness of his angry art, so he took the only route open to him: he immigrated to the United States.

While it was clear why the Nazis would ban Grosz' politically charged works, it was unclear why they would ban the art of Franz Marc, who had given his life for the motherland in 1916, and who was neither Jewish nor Communist — two categories that led to instant repression regardless of style and subject matter. When Hitler was asked why Marc should be labeled as a degenerate and all his work placed on the taboo list, he said flatly "there are no blue horses," referring to one of Marc's most famous paintings, "The Blue Horses."[2]

Art dealer Karl Nierendorf, who would become Fine's supporter and mentor in the 1940s, encouraging her to seek her own style, came to the United States in 1936. Until then, he had run the Berlin gallery established by J. B. Neumann (who had left Germany several years earlier), which featured contemporary expressionist art, the type the Nazi Party had labeled decadent. Nierendorf brought with him a wealth of knowledge about modern art, particularly about de Stijl of which Mondrian had been a member, and the Blue Rider group of German Expressionist painters, which included Marc and Paul Klee. According to an interview published in *Art Digest,* Nierendorf arrived in "New York with little more to show for his 15 years of dealing in art in Berlin than a collection of the works of Paul Klee. He swept out his little shop in the West 50s himself, paid $5 a month on the purchase of a typewriter, showed and re-showed Klee with a devotion that endures today."[3] Klee himself had been forced to leave Germany in 1937 after being labeled a "degenerate" by the Nazis. He moved to Switzerland where he died three years later, leaving behind an enormous body of work that defied labels, being a creative and highly personal, even intimate, synthesis of Cubism and Expressionism. As Klee's dealer, Nierendorf constantly tried to promote his art to American collectors. "Nierendorf was very inspiring to me because he was a close friend of Paul Klee, one of the few friends Klee had," recalled Fine. But Nierendorf's enormous devotion and effort got him nowhere; people were not interested. "Nierendorf went through all kinds of ways to sell Klee's work. He couldn't sell one of his paintings for one hundred dollars — or fifty dollars," said Fine.[4] But his failure didn't make any difference to him. When Nierendorf believed in an artist, whether or not he himself could make money as his dealer was unimportant.

Surprisingly, Nierendorf was not Eurocentric. He was intrigued by developments in the United States, loved New York City far more than Berlin, and was willing to take the risk of giving exhibitions to unknown artists working in new ways. He often told people that "there is only one art though the centuries" and backed that statement up by juxtaposing in his gallery Chinese, Greek, Peruvian, and Mexican ancient art with modern art to the accompaniment of Chinese lute, Peruvian reed flute, or other appropriate music. His exhibitions often bore titles such as "Unity in Diversity" or "One Art in a Thousand Forms."[5] His private collection was eclectic and vast, including art by the German expressionist Käthe Kollwitz, a woman with strong anti-war sentiments who had lost her teaching position in 1933 when the Nazis came to power. All of which helps to explain why he came to be a supporter of Fine as well as of the painter and sculptor Louise Nevelson. Of Nevelson's 1943 solo exhibition at Nierendorf's gallery, a reviewer raved that her "oils display a lack of timidity rare in America." It was just such lack of timidity that marked Nierendorf's own approach to art.[6]

The artists Josef and Anni Albers left Germany in 1933 after the Dessau City Council had padlocked the doors of the Bauhaus because it was, according to them, "a germ-cell of bolshevism." The school, which had been founded in 1919, was well-known for its theoretical approach to form and function, combining arts and crafts in a way that had international impact. Germany's loss was America's gain as several prominent artists and architects connected with the Bauhaus followed the Albers's lead, including Walter Gropius, Mies van der Rohe, and László Moholy-Nagy. Of this group, Fine would get to know Albers and Moholy-Nagy personally through the American Abstract Artists in which they took an active part, exhibiting in the yearly group shows. Fine also knew Moholy-Nagy through the Museum of Non-Objective Painting (eventually renamed the Solomon R. Guggenheim Museum) where they both exhibited during the war. However, the arrival of the

Bauhaus group did not have as immediate an effect on the Americans as did the arrival of the French Surrealists (who began to come in 1939) partially because the Bauhaus artists came individually over a period of years and immediately spread out. There was never a critical mass in one location as there would be of the Surrealists in New York City. Furthermore, their skills and styles were diverse, from the innovative weaving of Anni Albers to the spare architectural designs of Mies van der Rohe.

Receiving less attention than the influx of Europeans was the return of many American artists who had been living abroad. One of the first to arrive was Lyonel Feininger who had lived in Germany for 48 years and who was immediately championed in New York by Nierendorf. Another was the sculptor Mary Callery who had worked in the studio of Jacques Loutchansky and who knew Picasso well. Man Ray also returned, staying in the United States from 1940 to 1950. Alexander Calder, who had maintained a home in Roxbury, Conn., while living in Paris, settled down for the duration in Roxbury.

With the fall of Paris to the Nazis in 1940, the trickle of immigrants became a deluge, among them being Fernand Léger, Jacques Lipchitz, and Marc Chagall. As a writer for *Art Digest* put it, "The bombs accelerated this influx of European culture by blasting a steady stream of artists loose from their Continental moorings and sending them personally to this country. Most of them follow large numbers of their canvases and sculptures, and large numbers of their students. So their coming does not introduce an entirely new element into the American cultural body, but rather intensifies an element already existing."[7]

The Surrealists arrived in force, carrying with them "psychic automatism in its pure state" (as André Breton had described it in his "Manifestos of Surrealism," published in 1924) and a proclivity for being surreal not only on their canvases but in their personal lives. Among them were Breton himself, Marcel Duchamp, Max Ernst, André Masson, and Roberto Matta. And there was the incomparable Salvador Dalí who attracted the most press by his Dadaist antics. Peyton Boswell, Jr., the editor of *Art Digest,* called him "20,000 volts of uninhibited imagery.

His is a diseased, sadistic, nihilistic art expression, but undeniably it has the hypnotic gift of exciting even those who are surfeited with the acres and acres of canvases done with the sole idea of mutilating virginal linen."[8] Only two weeks after his arrival, Dalí was hired by Bonwit Teller to design a Surrealist window display for the Manhattan department store. Among the items he placed in the window was a befeathered mannequin stepping into a fur-lined bathtub filled with water in which three hands floated, each holding a mirror.[9] The management of Bonwit was not amused and within hours replaced the mannequin with one more appropriately attired, whereas Dalí charged into the store and dismantled the entire display, in the process falling through the window onto the sidewalk along with the bathtub. But such absurdity was just a surface aspect, for Dada and its changeling child Surrealism arose from a profound nihilism about everything, not just art, that gripped Europe during and following World War I. Nihilism did not really take hold in the United States, which (despite the Great Depression) was intrinsically more hopeful and forward-looking than Europe largely because it had been spared the absurdly high loss of life and destruction of culture that was caused by the "War to End All Wars." Furthermore, Surrealism was closely connected to the European literary intelligentsia, which was far more cynical than that in the United States, having had its ranks decimated by the war. Surrealism affected American artists in so far as it offered another approach to subject matter by tapping into the subconscious. It also promoted more spontaneity with paint, but the underlying impetus was different than that of the Europeans.

Fine never came to know the Surrealists personally as she did Mondrian and some of the other Europeans. While she admitted that they brought something important to art, she never felt close to them theoretically or temperamentally, not being theatrical or flamboyant herself. She was also monogamous, which put her at odds with many of the Surrealists who considered marriage to be a passing phase passed through several times. Stylistically, Fine placed them in the same category as illustrators except that their story lines were their own irrational dreams and the primordial unconscious. In fact, Dalí called his images dream photographs, a phrase similar to Freudian dream-painting. "I'm not drawn to the Surrealists very much and yet I recognize their importance," Fine explained. "I recognize that 'surreal' is super-real and therefore very expressive. Because it's very expressive, it has a very definite, very important place in art.... The going against the grain, the going against everything accepted, I think is a very attractive thing to me."[10]

Despite her disavowal of being influenced by the Surrealists, when Fine first began to exhibit in the early 1940s, some critics compared her art favorably to that of the Spaniard Joan Miró, twelve years older than Fine, who was one of the few Surrealists to work abstractly. Along with Jean Arp, he painted in a way called "automatism" (so named by Breton) in which Freudian slips, free associations, and dreams gave access to the unconscious unmediated by reason. Miró's curvilinear forms and fluid line tended to evoke in the spectator a connection to natural organisms, hence the use of the term "biomorphism," and his mottled backgrounds gave off an atmospheric quality. Forced to leave Paris at the outbreak of the war, Miró chose not to come to the United States; instead, he returned to his native Barcelona from which he had been in exile since the Spanish Civil War. Even though his first visit to the United States would not occur until after the war, his work was well known here. A retrospective at the Museum of Modern Art in 1941 had a major impact on many artists, particularly Gorky, because it helped to clarify how Miró had made the transition from Cubism to Surrealism, a transition many artists were finding difficult if not impossible to make. But Fine was adamant that the comparison of her art to Miró's was based solely on their working with forms in space; there were no other similarities. Fine was already reaching for a non-referential universality that was not predicated on the unconscious or painterly allusions to objects, whereas Miró's art retained objective elements sometimes painted ironically. What critics may have been responding to in making the comparison was that their paintings conveyed a feeling of non-aggression. To be non-aggressive did not mean to be passive. It meant that their art did not assault spectators; instead it tended to pull them in, requiring meditative involvement. Fine would often use the words intuitive and mysterious to describe this quality in her paintings. What she called "the forthright, the incorruptible mysterious," was the most challenging aspect of art. On a slip of paper, she copied the following quote from "The World As I See It" by Albert Einstein: "The fairest thing we can experience is the mysterious. It is the fundamental emotion which stands at the cradle of true art and science. He who knows it not, can no longer wonder, no longer feel amazement, is as good as dead, a snuffed-out candle." To this quote, Fine appended, "Add to the artist, the degree and intensity of the emotion; it is at once the catalyst and the whole reason for being." [11]

Fine considered Neo-Plasticism a far more important art movement than Surrealism because it conveyed in the parlance of the times not the unnatural or man-made but something that unified space and form yet was simultaneously dynamic and stable — something with plasticity. In 1940, Mondrian, one of its principal expositors, arrived in the United States at the invitation and insistence of Harry Holtzman, his friend and fellow artist. Holtzman was a member of the American Abstract Artists, which as an organization played an important role finding housing for the Europeans, introducing them to American culture, and inviting them to take part in their exhibitions. It was through the AAA that Fine met Mondrian who would become the most influential artist in her life. She visited his studio several times, watched him work, and studied his philosophy. It was his aesthetics and not his belief in theosophy (an amalgam of Eastern and Western metaphysics) that she found compelling, although unraveling one from the other was a difficult undertaking. "As I knew him, he was very sweet," Fine remembered. "I thought he was really great in his essays and in what he had to say beyond what he did in his own work. His work only reflected what he said in his essays. He really made us so aware of the importance of the vertical and horizontal. And I think in everything I've ever done you see a trace of that, in some more strongly than others."[12] Although many people saw nothing in his paintings but cold geometric exercises, Mondrian himself was as tenderly reverential toward his brushes, oil paints, and canvas as he was toward the actual process of creation, which he approached with an intense level of concentration. "It is amazing, really, to see to what extent what appears to be a paucity of means in the hands of a master becomes such a richness of means," Fine wrote a few years after his death from pneumonia in

1944. “In the sense that Renoir caressed his canvasses, Piet Mondrian caressed the color, the ever-changing hues.” Yet the final result was that “great energy was released through his work.”[13] It was exactly that energy that Fine wanted to release in her own paintings. She had seen it as well in the paintings of Matisse, Cézanne, and Picasso. But only in his last painting did Fine sense that Mondrian succeeded in releasing it “far beyond his time.”

Mondrian held a unique position among the European artists in exile. Unlike many of the Surrealists, he was a quiet and polite gentleman respected by everyone including those who could not understand why he painted the way he did. With his horn-rim glasses that made him look scholarly, his dapper double-breasted suits, and his preference for painting in an all-white studio, he was a gracious anomaly who paradoxically loved the clamor and vitality of New York City, especially the verticality of its skyscrapers and the roar of the traffic up and down the straight avenues, so different from those in Europe. He loved jazz, had a great sense of rhythm, liked to dance, and once swung Lee Krasner around on the dance floor at a party given in his honor.[14] He did not remain aloof from the young American artists who sought out his advice, camaraderie, and encouragement, instead he gave unstintingly. Even artists whose work was fundamentally different from Mondrian’s found his approval to be of enormous importance. For example, as a judge for the Spring Salon for Young Artists, presented by Peggy Guggenheim in 1943 at her recently opened gallery Art of This Century, he told her that she should “watch” Pollock because his painting was very exciting. Surprised, Guggenheim retorted, “You can’t be serious. You can’t compare this and the way you paint.” “So, don’t compare this,” he answered quietly. “The way I paint and the way I think are two different things.”[15] Over the years both Guggenheim and Pollock took pleasure in repeating this story as if Mondrian, the master of exquisite control, had given his imprimatur to a wild, young artist whose canvases seemed to be out of control. Fine would have explained it as Mondrian’s recognition of Pollock’s intuitive sense of space, a quality he himself possessed. “Intuition was not lacking in Mondrian, but it was intuition coupled with reason and extraordinary sensitivity,” Fine wrote in an essay a few years following his death. It galled her that many people, including Guggenheim, made the mistake of thinking that Mondrian's aesthetics precluded painting anything but geometric abstraction. "He himself was often heard to urge artists to work out their experiences in their own way," Fine stated emphatically. "Clearly, it is more a violation of the laws of painting, which from the start prohibit the copying of nature, to imitate someone else's manner of experiencing nature."[16]

Robert Motherwell, who was in his late 20s when he first met Mondrian, was thrown off-balance by his perceptiveness as well as his openness to radical styles and opposing viewpoints. Through him, Motherwell became aware of the crucial difference between the "pure" and the "clean" in art:

> I knew him when he was here during the war. He went to an exhibition by the Surrealist Tanguy, and was asked what he thought, and he said he would like Tanguy's pictures better if they were dirtier, that for him they were too "clean." And it seemed like a paradox....I don't think it was. I think he meant that when they were too clean they were essentially lifeless, statuesque, unrevised. As for me, I must say, Mondrian's painting is intensely rhythmic, warm, passionate — restricted as the means ostensibly seem to be.[17]

The presence of the Europeans served as a kind of validation for American artists working non-objectively. Some of the European artists virtually camped out in New York, not producing much but talking a great deal, waiting for the war to end so they could return to Europe and resume their lives. Others found the new world stimulating and responded by making changes in their art. Mondrian, for example, who had numbered his canvases throughout the 1930s, returned to naming them in the 1940s with the "Broadway Boogie-Woogie" and the "Victory Boogie-Woogie." As the titles indicate, he was intrigued by syncopation and the driving bass beat, attempting to achieve a visual parallel wherein the limitations of the black line would be overcome. There was also an exultant quality to the two paintings that ran counter to the tenor of the times. Painted well before the end of the war, both paintings conveyed a dancing-in-the-streets jubilance, but "Victory Boogie-Woogie" went one step further by enveloping it with the serenity of restored peace, conveyed on the canvas by a soft gray at the top.

The war forced New York City to take the place of Paris as the leading art center of the world, not that anyone had the time to notice or care. The truth was that it looked like more hard times. The Great Depression may have come to an end when the factories began turning out guns, tanks, planes and all the necessities of war. However, an improving economy did not mean that there was an increase in the number of art buyers. In 1940, a city-wide endeavor called National Art Week, in which 1,500 exhibits were mounted in all five boroughs, yielded only $5,845 in sales. Edward Alden Jewell called it a fiasco that failed abysmally to reach or even approach the goal envisioned.[18] Just getting oil paints became difficult because in 1941 the government confiscated 14 pigments needed for the war effort, among them titanium white, the cadmiums, cobalt blue, cerulean blue, and the chromium oxides. Looking back on the war years, Adolph Gottlieb recalled, "During the 1940s, a few painters were painting with a feeling of absolute desperation. The situation was so bad that I know I felt free to try anything no matter how absurd it seemed."[19] Some artists spoke out for the continuing importance of art. Others attempted to put their skills to use for the war effort. Gorky spent time developing a course on the nature of camouflage, maintaining that an artist was the best person to teach how color can conceal or reveal. Hofmann pontificated early in 1942 that the standards of culture had to be maintained as far as possible because "a post-war world in which the cultural forces have died would be unworthy of any great effort. It is through the constructive forces of creative art and human development that a better world will evolve."[20] However, his words reached few people and convinced even less, including himself. It was during this period that he lashed out in frustration at the women in his classes (many of the men having gone to war) charging that they would "amount to nothing."

The war resulted in the decline of two styles that had been actively pursued by many artists during the Depression, although not by Fine. Social Realism had been aligned with the left politically with many of its practitioners being avowed Marxists or at least sympathetic to the cause. World War I and the economic upheavals of the following two decades had caused so much suffering around the globe that the Social Realists felt compelled to use art as a means to rail against all kinds

For Fine's parents Sarah and Samuel Fine, the war years were a tense time with two sons serving in the U.S. Army in Europe and the death of their youngest daughter Rose from nephritis.

of injustice. Then to the dismay of American Marxists, Russia became an ally of Germany and invaded Finland, and the entire geopolitical climate changed. The result was that Social Realism came to be seen as at best irrelevant and at worst misguided, even dangerous. Its polar opposite, at least in terms of political focus, was American Regionalism as practiced and proselytized by Benton and others. This style had an America-first, anti-European bias which was acceptable until December 7, 1941, when it was suddenly at odds with the reality of a nation fighting alongside its European allies against the Axis. Of the three styles that had most attracted young American painters during the Depression, only abstraction was left unscathed, partially because of its apolitical, art-for-art's sake focus. But only in retrospect would it be considered seminal. Sidney Geist, art critic and sculptor, wrote in 1956:

> The truth is that in the late thirties and early forties, critics and both museum authorities and W.P.A officials were looking the other way. The latter, intent on their roles as tastemakers, returned from European tours with the observation, "Abstract art is dead." If Americans persisted in working in abstraction, that was because they were not really au courant. Only one American abstractionist, Alexander Calder, was able to achieve not only national but European attention in this period. Nevertheless, the abstractionists were the only group of the late thirties with a dynamic sufficient to perpetuate it beyond the war years.[21]

One thing that did not change during the war was the bitter argument about what was the real American art and who were the real American artists, except that the language used in the argument often took on patriotic fervor. For example, Barnett Newman bombastically elided modernist art with patriotism, charging that artists who painted in a realistic style were false and noncreative and were keeping America from becoming the art center of the world. In 1943, he sent a letter to the director of the Metropolitan Museum of Art protesting an exhibition of contemporary art that did not include modernist painters. Because the exhibition was presented by Artists for Victory, a consortium of artists' groups in support of the war effort, Newman felt compelled to stud his letter with patriotic keywords: "Such an exhibition cannot fulfill its high purpose of stimulating the cultural life of an America at war if it excludes the modern viewpoint. In these crucial times, when all our cultural values are at stake, no cultural enterprise can stand that excludes the vital, creative forces of modern artists and builds on the feeble support of noncreative elements."[22]

There was also an undertone in the letters and manifestos of the era that the real artists (those who were painting abstractly) were courageous to the point of being tragic, which meant they were willing to take great risks, whereas the unreal artists (who, ironically, were the ones painting realistically) were cowardly and not free, being subservient in their painting to outmoded styles. In response to a negative review by Jewell of the exhibition of the American Federation of Modern Painters and Sculptors in June 1943 (in which Jewell had written that he was "befuddled" by the modernist art, some of which had heavy references to myth and archaic images), Adolph Gottlieb and Mark Rothko, aided by Newman, sent him a tirade in which one of their main points was that "art is an adventure into an unknown world, which can be explored only by those willing to take risks." While the subject in art was crucial, "only that subject matter is valid which is tragic and timeless." But there was about all this a sense of the apologists over-pleading their case, as if deep down they were uncertain. The last paragraph of the letter to Jewell was mean-spirited and carping: "Consequently, if our work embodies those beliefs, it must insult anyone who is spiritually attuned to interior decoration; pictures for the home; pictures over the mantle; pictures of the American scene; social pictures; purity in art; prize-winning potboilers; the National Academy; the Whitney Academy; the Corn Belt Academy; buckeyes, trite tripe; etc."[23]

For Fine and Berezov, even summers spent in Provincetown, Mass., at the tip of Cape Cod, to get away from the oppressive heat of the city, barely lifted the contentious gloom. Berezov recalled that the exodus of artists each summer was so great that finding sufficient studio space in Provincetown was difficult. "First, fishing shacks were converted. Then some of the garages were pressed into service. Prosaic looking cottages, even a lumber-yard, have gradually become studios, and none of this seems the least bit incongruous."[24] Years later, Robert Motherwell recalled that due to the required black-outs at night to keep the German U-boats from targeting the town, "the claustrophobic silent dark of the World War II nights here remains with me like a black stone. So does the Depression poverty of the town then — peeling paint, askew shutters, holes in roofs, primitive stoves, and occasional kerosene lamps — as well as my own poor means."[25]

To the shared concerns and frustrations of the war years, including falling behind in her rent with regularity and not having enough money for art supplies, Fine had personal worries. Two of her brothers, Melvin and Robert, were in the U.S. Army in Europe. Melvin, who held the rank of captain, saw action in Italy. Robert was wounded while serving in France and received the Purple Heart. At a greater remove was the fact that Fine's family had immigrated from the section of Russia that after World War I had been reshaped into Poland. While her mother's side of the family had all settled in the United States, there were still distant relatives on her father's side in Poland, and what might be happening to them — what was rumored — was deeply disturbing. No Jew whose family had immigrated to the United States in the twentieth century was immune from an all-pervading sense of dread.[26]

Yet for all the darkness and uncertainty, the rationing of food and gas, and shades pulled tight over windows both in Provincetown and New York City, Fine's career started auspiciously with her inclusion in the Spring Salon for Young Artists, May 18 to June 26, 1943, at Art of This Century, Peggy Guggenheim's new gallery. Opened in October 1942, the gallery featured Cubism, abstraction and Surrealism in exhibits that *Art Digest* pronounced would "make an academician scream," but in which the cognoscenti would find not only their old favorites but "a few new idols." Guggenheim herself had swept in from Europe like a cork floating on top of a Surrealist wave. Married shortly after arrival to the Surrealist painter Max Ernst, she was exuberant, flamboyant, irrepressible, and wealthy, being the daughter of Benjamin Guggenheim (who had gone down with the Titanic) and the niece of Solomon R. Guggenheim. She hired Frederick Kiesler to design her gallery (located at 30 West Fifty-seventh Street) knowing full well that what he came up with would be eye-popping wild, which would help to attract the press and increase attendance regardless of the quality of the art. Prior to his immigration to the United States in 1926, Kiesler had been an avant-garde architect and stage designer in Europe. He constructed the walls of the gallery's Surrealist section of curved gum wood and illuminated the paintings with blinking spotlights, making the environment itself feel surreal. In the Cubist section, the walls were covered with a blue canvas curtain drawn taut by ropes to the ceiling and floor. Kiesler himself described his design as "a demonstration of a changing world, in which the artist's work stands forth as a vital entity in a spatial whole, and art stands forth as a vital link in the structure of a new myth." *ARTnews* saw in the Spring Salon a symbiotic relationship between the artists and the gallery's design, offering proof that the fantastic and the abstract were not worn-out, dead-end styles and that "work of this type can gain new courage from being displayed in such dashing surroundings."[27]

The Spring Salon was the first of several exhibitions presented by Guggenheim featuring the work of artists who were supposed to be no older than 35, although Fine was 38. It may have been at this point in her life that Fine began to list her date of birth as 1908 instead of 1905, lopping off three years, which put her at Guggenheim's upper age limit. But apparently she was not the only one who was older than 35. In fact, when it came time for the 1944 salon (in which Fine was one of only 20 artists chosen from approximately 200 who submitted art for judging), the editor of *Art Digest* charged, "We are reliably informed that in order to admit certain favored 'youngsters' the age limit for 'young' was upped several years to include those who will never see 40 again. Which perhaps proves either of two things: artists are forever young, or we are embarrassingly indefinite with our definitions."[28] While Guggenheim herself admitted that she had extended the age category, she insisted that only one artist was over 35 and only by a year. For Fine, the significance of this nonsensical controversy was that she was already considered older, although the 1943 Salon was her first important group exhibition.

Artists were invited to submit work that was then selected by a panel of jurors who voted not by a simple yes or no but by placing a number from zero to ten on each work of art indicative of the degree to which they approved. To be accepted for inclusion, a work had to receive a vote of thirty.[29] For the first salon, the panel was comprised of Guggenheim and her able assistant and eminence gris Howard Putzel, who was the salon's organizing force, the artists Marcel Duchamp, Piet Mondrian, and Max Ernst, along with art patrons and museum administrators James Thrall Soby and James Johnson Sweeney, whom Guggenheim listed in the press release as "critics." In a selfless gesture that was out of character, in that same press release Guggenheim listed herself and Putzel as "amateurs." Competition for inclusion in the exhibition was apparently fierce with artists lined up outside the gallery carrying their canvases under their arms. The list of the artists who made the cut at thirty points included among the women Hedda Sterne, Sonya Sekula, Esphyr Slobodkina, Virginia Admiral, Xenia Cage, Fannie Hillsmith, Alice Trumbull Mason, and Irene Rice Pereira, and among the men William Baziotes, Ilya Bolotowsky, Jimmie Ernst, Ibram Lassaw, Robert Motherwell, Jackson Pollock, and Ad Reinhardt. Fine had two paintings in the show, "Gabun" and "Tensions Dynamique." In a review for *The Nation*, Jean Connolly wrote: "Perle Fine, a name to conjure with Robert Motherwell, Fannie Hillsmith, and Ralph Rosenberg, each show small paintings which it would be a pleasure to own. Baziotes who had a picture in the last exhibition, has two tenebrous ones in this, and there is a large painting by Jackson Pollack [sic], which, I am told, made the jury starry-eyed." The painting that Connolly considered to be unequivocally the best in the show was not Pollock's "Stenographic Figure" but "Composition No. 30" by Irene Rice Pereira, in which one abstraction was painted in glass over another on canvas, "precisely complementing it," an unusual technique which Pereira would use to great effect over the next decade.[30]

Just after the Spring Salon closed, Fine was included in her second important group exhibition, this time at the Museum of Non-Objective Painting, the place which would become her most important locus of artistic exposure during the mid-1940s. One of the personal quirks of the museum's director was to lean paintings against the cloth-covered walls instead of hanging them, forcing viewers either to look down or get on their knees. Fortunately, the floors were covered in thick gray carpet, and the music of Bach, Beethoven, or Chopin was piped in to provide a kind of cosmic atmosphere, so kneeing was not entirely out of the question. Attendance at summer exhibitions was invariably poor; nevertheless, Fine's paintings were mentioned favorably in the reviews, with *ARTnews* recommending to viewers that they "should be sure to note the incredible plastic modulations of Moholy-Nagy, the precise and delicate work of Perle Fine, and the constructions of Fernando Martinez."[31] Only three months later in November, she was included in yet another exhibition at the museum. About her painting, Maude Riley, the art critic for *Art Digest,* wrote that Fine "has declared her subject in "Le Cirque" and expressed the high wires, and acrobatic equipment in an all-gold arrangement."[32] From thereon, Fine's work was mentioned regularly in reviews of shows at the Museum of Non-Objective Painting. These were frequently what were called loan exhibitions, indicating that the paintings were loaned by the artists and were not owned by the museum, although subsequently some were purchased for the permanent collection.

At the same time as Fine's paintings were on view at the museum, Pollock had his first solo exhibition at Guggenheim's gallery about which James Johnson Sweeney declared, "It is lavish, explosive, untidy." Riley in her review surmised that "Pollock is out aquesting and he goes hell-bent at each canvas, mostly big surfaces, not two sizes the same."[33] Fine was equally impressed but concluded that her own style was headed in a different direction:

> I didn't see very much of what he was doing until his first one-man show at Peggy Guggenheim's. Oh, I thought it was very exciting. It didn't have very much effect on me, on my work. But I thought it was exciting work. I was pretty well determined to continue working these forms in space. In some cases my forms were going almost completely across the canvas so that it almost looked as if they were tied to the edges which is the all-over manner of working, but they still were free forms in space.[34]

Trying to capture on canvas "a feeling of air and space and objects moving in it," Fine compared her efforts to what Alexander Calder was trying to achieve via his mobiles, and he, in turn, compared his

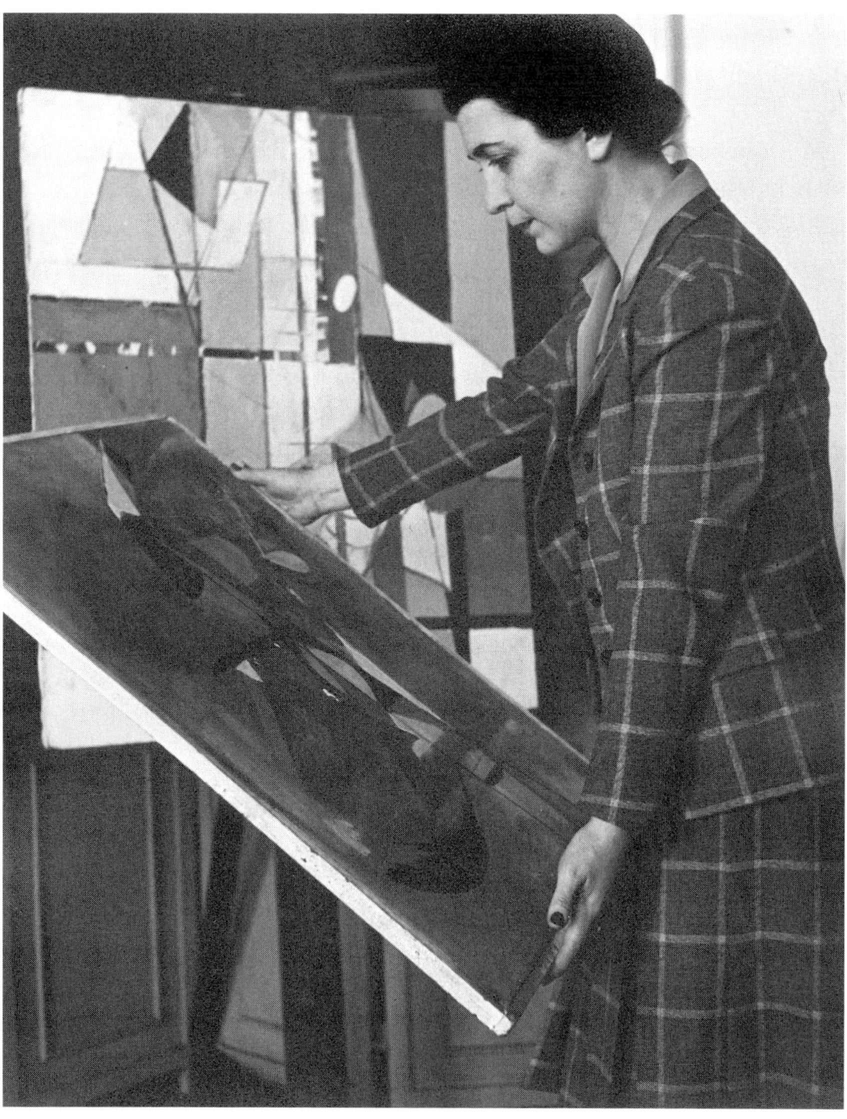

During the 1940s, Fine received grants from the Museum of Non-Objective Painting to purchase art supplies, but the grants came with the stipulation that the paintings created with those supplies had to be non-objective.

efforts to Mondrian's. On a visit to Mondrian's studio, Calder had been deeply affected by the stark white walls divided by black lines and rectangles of color as if the entire studio were a work of art. He had found himself thinking, "how fine it would be if everything MOVED," although he had to admit that Mondrian would not have approved.[35] To achieve movement on canvas similar to Calder's mobiles, Fine started with what she called "a color idea." Then she did complete sketches in color, not charcoal, that "might have had absolutely nothing to do with what I was going to do later. But by the time I was through doing these sketches — which were in themselves quite beautiful little things — then I would know what I wanted to do as a painting, and I'd go directly to it as a painting. I wouldn't even sketch it out."[36] Fine's canvas "Midnight," (see color plate) painted in 1942, provides an excellent example of how she developed "a color idea." It is a dynamic canvas with areas of dark warmth, on which the austere quality of thick and thin lines is held in tension with small circles. It is as if for an instant one of Calder's mobiles suddenly stopped moving. Fine wrote about "Midnight," "I have employed limited color and means in an effort to create the drama of the play of these forces in space, and then suddenly, the tensions of these forms as they seem to be arrested in their play at a single moment — midnight." About her style as exemplified by "Midnight," the art historian Henry-Russell Hitchcock wrote: "It is rather her intention to dramatize fundamental elements that she apprehends in nature: the tension of related spaces, the rigor of straight lines, and the contrasting grace of fluent curves. The geometry of her paintings is never without emotion. Warmth and sensuousness infuse her most schematic pictures; vitality and drama can be sensed in her severest compositions."[37]

Dynamic tension coupled with a sense of rhythm, like visual music, is also apparent in another canvas of this period. "In Staccato" (1941) (see color plate) is as faceted as a stained glass window, but there the resemblance ends. Originally titled "Still Life on Checkerboard," Fine changed the name to indicate the emphatic role of color, used sparingly, against the planes of white, black, and gray, similar to the role of staccato notes within a smooth passage of music.[38] In both "Midnight" and "In Staccato," there is a playful sense of stillness that is not still:

in the next moment a move will be made on the checkerboard, the clock will tick, a note will be played. Something in these paintings is gathering force; something is hovering.

In 1943, Fine was awarded the first of several grants from the Solomon R. Guggenheim Foundation. It was indeed an honor to be a grant recipient, but Fine found the amount awarded to be too small to make a major difference: “It just about paid for paints and that kind of thing.”[39] Furthermore, the scholarship came with a long list of stipulations and requirements. Recipients were expected to turn in monthly reports on their progress and attend sessions where their work was critiqued, often by the artist Rudolph Bauer and the Baroness Hilla Rebay, director of the museum as well as an artist herself. From this group of paintings, a few would be chosen by Rebay to show to Solomon R. Guggenheim, who would usually give his approval for purchase.

Even before she received the grant, Fine had been attending the monthly meetings. “I am one of the artists who attends the criticisms regularly and find myself being helped immeasurably by Mr. Bauer’s guidance,” she wrote to Rebay on March 2, 1943. “But more than that, I find enjoyment of the pictures in the museum so greatly heightened by those stimulating monthly sessions that I do not know how to express my gratitude to you, to Mr. Bauer, and to the Foundation.”[40] Less than a month later, having received the grant, she wrote again remarking that the critiques had: “given me the courage to paint the way I know now that I have always wanted to paint. I used to wonder why, when looking at pictures in galleries, some would make me feel as though there was great breathing space all about me, as though the wind and all the elements of nature were all around me and I could breath deeply, and others made me feel as cramped and small. You have helped me to understand a little better why this is so.”[41]

On September 1, 1943, while the loan exhibition was taking place, Fine was working at fever-pitch under pressure from Rebay. She wrote to Rebay that she had three or four oil paintings to show her as well as three watercolors and that she had “worked every day as long as daylight lasted.” Finding that the scholarship did not provide enough to live on, Fine wrote to Rebay yet again on October 12, 1943, to inquire whether the museum would purchase some of her work:

> I think there are paintings among them that may prove valuable and interesting additions to the Solomon R. Guggenheim Collection, notably the larger canvasses: "Le Cirque," "Héroique," and "Joyeux," and perhaps among the water-colors "Formes Rouges" or "Serein." I am writing again only because I have been hard pressed lately with doctor and dentist bills as well as the need to provide a heater for my studio which is a cold-water flat, so that I sincerely hope I shall be able to see my way clear to go on painting without interruption of any financial sort.[42]

Not long after, she and Alice Mattern, also an abstract artist, were invited for a personal visit to Rebay's home, named Franton Court, in the area of Westport, Conn., known as Greens Farms, about an hour northeast of New York City. Rebay had transformed a Victorian-style house and barn, situated on 14 acres, into an estate and art studio, filling the house with modern furniture and non-objective art, mostly by Bauer. The music room was reserved for art by Kandinsky, Chagall, Delauney, Mondrian, Seurat, and a mobile by Calder. One entire wall in the living room had been replaced by plate glass to maximize the view of the formal gardens, laid out with green precision. Even her books were arranged artistically, not by size but by the color of the bindings, with rows of reds abutting pinks, and violets sharing shelf space with purple.[43] In the barn which she had converted into an art studio, there was room on the ground floor for her concert grand piano, with two guest bedrooms and a little kitchen in the loft. Following the visit, Fine wrote to Rebay: "It was a truly memorable day for me — to see such a jewel of a house in such a setting as that one, rivaling only the house itself — the trees — those magnificent trees, I am sure I shall never forget. Standing under that wonderful dark green fir and looking up was indeed like being in a cathedral and very very close to God."[44] But despite her praise for Franton Court and for Rebay's vision in making it "work with nature," as Fine put it, nothing came of the visit in regard to the sale of paintings, and Fine's financial condition continued to deteriorate. She was forced almost to begging on March 7, 1944:

> I stand at this moment in grave danger of losing my workshop, my studio, for falling three months behind in my rent. There are no leases on these cold-water apartments, and if I should lose it, I fear it would be some time before I could find one as inexpensive as this one again. Do you think that the S. R. Guggenheim Foundation might be interested in taking the pair of pictures — the two little black ones from the previous exhibition, "Black on Black" and "Midnight," or perhaps the oil called "Clockwise" to help me out of this difficulty?[45]

It was not Rebay but the art collector Emily Hall Tremaine who bought "Midnight" (see color plate) for $65, which may have been to Fine's advantage, because money received from Rebay, whether via purchase or a grant, never came free. Rebay wanted to encourage the pursuit of non-objective art in the United States, but in so doing, she could be over-bearing in exerting artistic control. Although she purchased for the Guggenheim collection paintings by Klee, Léger and Helion among others, Rebay was devoted to the art of Wassily Kandinsky, the Russian painter who in 1910 began to paint non-representational art. In fact, the collection had its beginning in 1929 when Rebay traveled with Solomon R. Guggenheim to Dessau, Germany, to meet Kandinsky. The Museum of Non-Objective Painting, which opened ten years later in 1939, served almost as a shrine to Kandinsky. Art historian Dore Ashton described the museum as "the child of the liaison between an infinitely wealthy collector, Mr. Solomon Guggenheim, and an infinitely eccentric devotee of certain expressionist brands of abstract art, the Baroness Hilla Rebay."[46]

Indicative of the level of control that Rebay exerted is the grant application that Fine and other artists had to sign which spelled out in no uncertain terms that the money was not to be used to paint in an objective style: "The undersigned in asking for a grant to buy painting material declares that he is financially not able to conduct his work of non objective painting and study independently and acknowledges that the grant is made with a view of disseminating the ideas and promoting the work of the Solomon R. Guggenheim Foundation and [the artist] does not use the grant to paint objectively and for no other purpose than non-objective study."[47]

Despite the draconian restrictions, the list of grant recipients throughout the 1940s was long and, in retrospect, prestigious, including Isamu Noguchi, Richard Pousette-Dart, and Ad Reinhardt. Rebay even hired Jackson Pollock to work as a handyman and janitor at the museum. However, anyone who did not abide by her rules was summarily cut off, as would happen to Fine. Similarly, when Pollock became a success, Rebay dismissed his work as "meaningless scribbles and scrawls."[48] However, for a five-year period (1943–48), Fine got along well with Rebay. She even had the temerity to make suggestions to her, although she tended to phrase them in soft ways. For example, on June 5, 1946, she wrote about the inclusion of a painting by Moholy-Nagy in an upcoming exhibition at the museum, and mentioned that she was "saddened to think how dangerously ill" he was. "Would it not be a lovely gesture to offer him a sort of retrospective some time in the near future, while he is still with us to enjoy it?" she asked tactfully. Suffering from leukemia, Moholy-Nagy, director of the Chicago Institute of Design and one of the Bauhaus emigres, died five months later, November 24, 1946, at the age of 51. Belatedly, Rebay acted on Fine's suggestion and presented a memorial exhibition the following May. It is also possible that Fine had a hand in encouraging Rebay to give a retrospective for her friend Alice Mattern with whom she had visited Greens Farms in the fall of 1943. Mattern died in 1945 at the age of 37.

The peculiar way in which Rebay displayed art, often overriding the artist's decision as to top and bottom, left and right, was described by Ben Wolf, who went to see the Mattern retrospective in October 1945:

> The pictures nudge the gallery floorboards and give the spectator the curious sensation of being a Gulliver in Lilliput. Once one has surmounted this, there is a fresh problem. Some of the canvases have been hung upside down while others are to be viewed on their sides. Now it is not to be denied that the exhibits so hung do balance, but obviously they were not so intended for showing by the artist, else the signatures would not appear upside down and perpendicularly.[49]

Rebay's decision to hang the paintings without regard for Mattern's intent was typical of her imperious treatment of artists. People both respected and feared her. Artists complained of having to grovel to get her approval. In her letters, Fine herself tended to be overly complimentary of Rebay's own artistic talent, which is not surprising considering that Rebay was not only dictatorial to the point of being despotic, but also vengeful. However, she could also be very generous, even occasionally paying medical bills. Once when the artist Stuart Davis broke his leg, she sent him a check and groceries.[50] Likewise she invited the artist Jeanne Miles and her daughter to stay in her Carnegie Hall studio apartment, which she had stocked with food for them, after they fled from France to the United States.

As important as her dispensation of money was Rebay's unyielding belief in the value of non-objectivity. One critic on seeing an early portrait of Rebay described her as looking like "a Pre-Raphaelite heroine," by which he meant she was classically beautiful in a mythic way. While she might have disagreed with the Pre-Raphaelite comparison, she certainly saw herself as heroic, and as is common with heros and heroines, she also saw herself as fighting alone against the Philistines. She was accused of being manipulative, having tunnel vision, and of being parsimonious when she should have been lavish and lavish when she should have been parsimonious — all true. But it was also true that she had money, power and drive. With the world at war and artists feeling adrift, Rebay's adamant belief in pure abstraction (which she demanded be called non-objective art) counted a great deal. Furthermore, she had no qualms whatsoever in supporting women artists.

At the time that Fine was having serious financial difficulties, one exhibition that probably took her mind off her problems, at least briefly, was the first solo exhibition of her old teacher, Hans Hofmann, who after many years of teaching, had finally returned to painting, and who had been cajoled by Peggy Guggenheim into an exhibition at Art of This Century. Hofmann's status in the New York art community guaranteed a good turn-out as students came from near and far to get the answer to the question that had long hung in the air: could the master teacher, then in his 60s, actually do what he professed in the studio. The exhibition proved that the answer was a definitive yes. *ARTnews* proclaimed that the show should be of interest to painters as well as laymen: "In their directness and robust handling they have this in common: a vivid presence." As the critic Maude Riley wrote in *Art Digest*, "if you think of all teachers of middle age as cautious and wise gentlemen who carp on the subject of drawing, and in general take the joy out of life for young students, you'll be surprised." Riley saw a parallel between Hofmann's style and Pollock's. "There is a likeness in this debut show to one that preceded it in these galleries earlier in the season. Jackson Pollock comes to mind at the first step within the Hofmann show." But whereas Pollock seemed serious, almost obsessed, to Riley, "Hofmann has as much fun as any youngster. The walls fairly sing and dance with a succession of untitled exuberances in brilliant colors."[51]

In 1945, Fine participated in her third group show at Art of This Century, a juried exhibition titled simply "The Women." This was Guggenheim's second gendered show, the first being "31 Women," which was held early in 1943. In both, the artists were Surrealists and abstractionists, although in the first show (in which Fine did not take part) there were a few people whose inclusion could only be attributed to Guggenheim's need to be amused, specifically the striper Gypsy Rose Lee and her surrealistic self-portrait in which she portrayed her body with the head of a dog on a vaudeville runway. Also included was Baroness Elsa von Freytag-Loringhoven, a Dadaist who was eccentric enough to wear ice cream spoons and sardine cans on her head. Others were: Frida Kahlo, Leonora Carrington, Leonor Fini, Buffie Johnson, Suzy Frelinghuysen, Louise Nevelson, Meret Oppenheim, I. Rice Pereira, Kay Sage, and Dorothea Tanning. In helping to select paintings for the first exhibition, Guggenheim's lover and most recent husband, Max Ernst, visited Tanning's studio and was smitten by more than her art. The upshot was his divorce from Guggenheim, his subsequent marriage to Tanning, and Guggenheim's oft told joke that she should have limited the exhibition to 30 women, not 31. Apparently, no such hijinks marked the second exhibition, titled simply "The Women" perhaps to eliminate the risk of numerical and matrimonial betrayal. Nonetheless, it underscored the reality that at that time there were perceived to be four basic roles for women: muse, mistress, model, and wife. By being married to an artist, critic, or gallery owner, a woman artist had a slightly better chance of being seen, but she also ran the risk of being erased. For example, Krasner was already truncating her own creativity to further Pollock's. Jacqueline Lamba had to fight constantly for an identity separate from André Breton's, who often referred to Lamba not by name but by the pronoun "her" used pejoratively. Of the other artists included in Guggenheim's women-only exhibitions, many were part of artistic couples: Virginia Admiral/Robert de Niro, Louise Bourgeois/Robert Goldwater, Xenia Cage/John Cage, Suzy Frelinghuysen/George L. K. Morris, Frida Kahlo/Diego Rivera, Alice Rahon/Wolfgang Paalen, Kay Sage/Yves Tanguy, Hedda Sterne/Saul Steinberg, Muriel Streeter/Julien Levy, Sophie Täuber-Arp/Jean Arp, and Pegeen Vail/Jean Hélion.[52]

Not a single artist in the two exhibitions harbored any hope that Guggenheim herself, who was hostile towards women, would champion her work, although subsequently she did give solos to several women, including Virginia Admiral and Marjorie McKee. Hedda Sterne, who immigrated to the United States in 1941, remarked that Guggenheim was so negative toward women that she hung her kitchen pans on a painting by Sophie Täuber-Arp. "Her generation, or even my generation, were mean towards women; when a woman was exceptional she wanted to be the only exceptional one."[53] Buffie Johnson considered that the "31 Women" show in 1943 marked the point at which she became a feminist. She had called her friend Jimmy Stern, art editor at *Time,* to encourage him to go to the exhibition. His reply to Johnson was brusk: "There has never been a first-rate woman artist, a first-rate woman writer. Women were made to create with their bodies, and I am not going to look at thirty-one women's paintings." According to Johnson, "That was the end of a beautiful friendship." As for the second exhibition, Guggenheim confided cattily to Johnson that she had scheduled it from June 12 to July 7, which she considered "a throwaway date" just before the gallery closed for the summer months.[54]

Even some of the artists who participated thought twice before saying yes, concerned that being in a gendered show would label them as female painters, conjuring up images of pastel flowers in vases and beatific children with pink cheeks. Since her marriage in 1930 when she had decided to keep her maiden name, Fine had never hidden her gender. Unlike other women artists who took on male first names, used only their surnames, or initialed their canvases, Fine always signed her paintings clearly with her full name. For example, it was during this period that Lenore Krasner changed her name to the more androgynous Lee, and initialed her canvases. Rice Pereira used the initial I instead of Irene. Joan Mitchell introduced herself to the art world as George, although by the 1950s she dropped the ruse. Fine did not have the fashion flamboyance of Nevelson or the black swathed drama of O'Keeffe. None of it concerned her. Throughout her life, Fine remained adamant that who she was, her gender, her position in life, her marriage, where she lived — in short, everything — made no difference; only the painting mattered. "The painting goes out there and it represents you, and thank God for that, because I'd hate to go out there and talk about my work. I let the canvas do everything that I say it should," said Fine.[55] It was an idealistic position in a culture where the name on the canvas was often more important in determining value than the quality of the work, but she staunchly held to it anyway. When interviewers pressed her for details of her private life, she was not forthcoming, always turning the questions back solely to art.

Despite Fine's belief that only the painting should matter, many of the reviews of the first exhibition were loaded with derogatory statements about women. Henry McBride wrote in the *New York Sun* that the artists in the "31 Women" exhibition were better than any of the men Surrealists, but his compliment was back-handed:

> This is logical now that one comes to think of it. Surrealism is about 70% hysterics, 20% literature, 5% good painting and 5% saying boo to the innocent public. There are, as we all know, plenty of men among the New York neurotics but we also know that there are still more women among them. Considering the statistics the doctors hand out, and considering the percentages listed above...it is obvious women ought to excel at Surrealism. At all events they do, hysterics insure a show.[56]

However, the reviewer for *ARTnews* was impressed by the exhibition, cautioning that the women should never be laughingly referred to as ladies, because "they present a chinkless armored front, Kay Sage's "At the Appointed Time" having particularly steely dramatics."[57]

By the time of the 1945 exhibition a change was beginning to occur, and some critics were complimentary. Yet their praise was tinctured by genuine surprise that the women were able to produce such strong art, which was in their words "refreshingly unladylike" with an "almost masculine vigor of ideas." Edward A. Jewell wrote that there was "nothing save the catalogue to indicate that these artists are women. The work might as well have been produced by 'the Men.'"[58]

In these comments can be glimpsed a serious problem for women artists. In Freudianism, women were taken to be emotional and irrational, as underscored by McBride's comment about their being hysterical. Men were intellectual and rational, as made clear by Jewell's comment about the "masculine vigor of ideas." The realm of the super ego belonged entirely to males. These beliefs were inculcated throughout the culture. Yet within the art world, paradoxically the male artists who would become dominant in Abstract Expressionism were already beginning to talk about emotion and the need to express their feelings on canvas. In order to do this and not be considered effeminate, they had to go to extremes in touting their masculinity as they arrogated for themselves artistic terrain that had been heretofore female. Sculptor Dorothy Dehner, then married to David Smith, said it succinctly: "There had never been a great American art before: in fact art had always been regarded as somewhat sissified in this country. By God, these men were not going to be sissies."[59] The presence of several articulate male theoretician/artists and theoretician/critics among the nascent Abstract Expressionist movement, including Barnett Newman, Robert Motherwell, Mark Rothko, Clement Greenberg, and Harold Rosenberg, led to the development of a fierce apologetics to justify the reversal, putting a positive gloss on emotion and a negative gloss on purist control in painting. For example, Motherwell stated, "to choose emotion rather than intellection can be an intellectual position."[60] Newman declared that non-objective abstract art (the province of Kandinsky and Mondrian) was really identical to primitive decorative art which was "a separate function carried on by women."[61] By

Lee Krasner became friends with Fine and Berezov while they were students of Hofmann. In this series of photos shot by Berezov in the early 1940s, she was painting geometric abstractions. After her marriage to Jackson Pollock, Krasner worked to advance his career to the detriment of her own.

1951, when the hegemony of the men among the first generation of Abstract Expressionists was virtually complete, Motherwell could proclaim without flinching: "The emergence of abstract art is one sign that there are still men able to assert feeling in the world. Men who know how to respect and follow their inner feelings, no matter how irrational or absurd they may first appear."[62]

Despite Guggenheim's own ambivalence toward women and the negativity of some of the critics, the women artists who were included in the 1943 and 1945 exhibitions were still pleased to be taking part because Guggenheim, for all her craziness, had a personal magnetism that attracted attention to her gallery and the paintings therein. Years later, Lee Krasner summed up Guggenheim's catalytic role: "What one should say about Peggy is simply that she did it, that no matter what her motivations were, she did it."[63]

If Guggenheim's taste could best be described as eclectic, spanning a broad range of styles and artists, the opposite was true of the American Abstract Artists, which Fine and Berezov joined in 1944. During this period, the organization tended to be dictatorial in defining what pure abstraction was and, as a result, occasionally alienated, or worse bored, critics as well as artists working in other styles. The AAA had started out quite literally as a voice crying in the wilderness in the mid-1930s when of necessity it had to be strident in defending abstraction in opposition to realism. But eventually the stridency wore thin. As early as 1939, Paul Bird wrote in his *Art Digest* column "The Fortnight in New York" that the dullest controversy of the year was "the syllogism that batterdored about concerning non-objective painting."[64] Jewell, who complained about the AAA's "all-or-nothing persuasion," could only summon up "a cordial interest" in their exhibition.[65]

Lee Krasner, who had a painting in the AAA's 1941 exhibition, left the organization in 1943 because, "the AAA wouldn't allow a Surreal breath to pass the door," she said. "They were provincial like any groupie. I tried to keep it open. I tried for example to get Calder invited and was told No. Tried to get Hofmann to lecture and was told No. On the other hand, they did invite Léger and Mondrian."[66] While Fine remained a member, she shared some of Krasner's concerns about the group's narrow focus. At one point, she nominated Pollock for membership. "They practically threw me out!" she recalled, because they considered his work to be "impure."[67] Nell Blaine affirmed the dedication of the AAA members to Neo-Plasticism. Noting that in 1943 she was the youngest member at 23 years old, Blaine said, "I was very dogmatic, in those days, about purist abstraction. I thought it was the only way to work. It was very narrow of me. But it was also very much in the air, that we were pioneers of American Neo-Plasticism."[68]

However, the AAA was not as closed-minded as it may have appeared. The active presence of artists such as Ad Reinhardt — brilliant, acerbic and utterly independent — kept the theoretical pot perking. Labels (including, later on, the label of Abstract Expressionist) slid off Reinhardt like water droplets off waxed canvas. Whatever organization or group of which he was formally or informally a member he graced with potent and intentional uncertainty, helping to maintain a healthy (albeit stressful) fluidity of thought. The artist Ilya Bolotowsky described Reinhardt as having an unusual "gift for space. He could be in and out, all at the same time."[69] There was also the occasional presence in the AAA's yearly exhibitions of artists with different sensibilities, among them the sculptor David Smith (1938), the highly regarded abstractionist Stuart Davis (1940), and Gorky (1940). So also the participation during the war years of Europeans with very different aesthetics (including Léger, who participated in the 1941 exhibition at the Riverside Museum) kept the organization from ossifying.

Equally important was the AAA's gender mix. At the time that Fine joined, there were several women members already, including Nell Blaine, Lee Krasner, Alice Trumbull Mason, Irene Rice Pereira, and Charmion von Wiegand. Moreover, there were several couples, including Rosalind Bengelsdorf and Byron Browne (who had been part of the founding group), Gertrude Glass and Balcomb Greene, Suzy Frelinghuysen and George L. K. Morris, and Esphyr Slobodkina and Ilya Bolotowsky. Often taking leadership roles within the organization, the women were not simply note takers and providers of refreshments at meetings; instead, they helped articulate the organization's theoretical position. Over the years, Fine held several positions including chairman of the membership committee and the exhibition committee. This gender equity was highly unusual and remained so for decades to come.

Many women were attracted to pure abstraction because it was a style in which the gender of the painter made little difference. Subject matter was problematic for women painters. If they painted flowers (as did O'Keeffe) or women and children (as did Mary Cassatt), they were categorized as presenters of female things, embodying nature. Loren MacIver, whose gauzy paintings of the commonplace (such as a window shade, a hopscotch board, and a puddle) were first shown in a "one-man" exhibition in 1938 at the East River Gallery, met with far more success than most women during the 1940s. But she still had to contend with the female label even from her dealer Pierre Matisse.[70] O'Keeffe, to whom MacIver was often compared, was heavily criticized for her subject matter. A reviewer of her 1937 exhibition at An American Place said bluntly that she had reached a "saturation point."[71] About O'Keeffe's May 1946 retrospective at the Museum of Modern Art, Clement Greenberg wrote cuttingly in *The Nation* that her art had "very little inherent value." Pure abstraction gave women a freedom they did not have when painting realistically. Fine contended that it offered her more possibilities because it did not have what she called "oppressive particularities."[72]

The artist with whom Fine worked most closely during the war was Stanley William Hayter who had no connection to Art of This Century, the AAA, or the Museum of Non-Objective Painting. In fact, he was a master etcher. Hayter was not so much a teacher of line engraving and soft-ground etching as a provider of equipment and technical guidance to anyone interested in experimenting. Highly respected as an artist himself, he had been forced to move his lithographic studio, Atelier 17, from Paris to New York at the outbreak of World War II. While in Paris, Hayter had revived interest in etching, combining his classical technique with an awareness of modern art, thereby attracting Miró, Picasso, Chagall, and Ernst among others. His arrival in New York City spurred similar interest among American artists, most of whom came to appreciate the expressive quality of line even if many of them

Fine produced a series of etchings at Hayter's lithographic studio Atelier 17, including ***Omnipotent One,*** (1946), 7 15/16" x 5 3/4," a complex composition printed in muted grays and greens. Courtesy of Hirschl & Adler Galleries, New York.

never used the burin (an engraving tool) again. A writer for the *Museum of Modern Art Bulletin* wrote in 1944:

> With Hayter and his associates burin engraving has recovered its dignity as a medium of original expression. For them the copper plate is not merely a plane surface on which to draw, like paper, a lithographic stone, or a canvas. Thanks to the different depths and types of stroke possible to the burin, line engraving exists in a middle realm between relief-sculpture and drawing — perhaps closer to goldsmith work than to either.[73]

Hayter's studio was initially located at the New School for Social Research; then he purchased a house in Greenwich Village that was in a tumble-down condition. With the help of his friends, he remodeled it, placing his studio on the top floor so that the toplight could be placed correctly, and adding florescent lights so that work could continue all night long.[74] Hayter was also a painter known for strong use of color, which one critic called "bold, even cruel, shocking," and definitely surprising: "Timidity of mimicry in its use would be expected since his graphic compositions have relied mainly on movement and a remarkable line of dynamic strength and powerful follow-through."[75]

In Fine's paintings of this period, there is an emphasis on line that is clearly related to her work with line engraving and soft-ground etching. Achieving great skill with the burin, she won the respect of other artists because of her ability to convey depth and complexity by means of virtuoso technique and subtle use of color. Describing the effort the burin required, Rosamond Frost wrote in *ARTnews*: "Infinitely more difficult to handle than the etcher's needle, the burin leaves its own masculine signature in the clean tension of the lines. Almost like the prow of a boat, it travels through the metal, its steel end facet perfectly balanced to the smooth copper surface."[76]

Fine's etchings were in a group exhibition at the Wittenborn & Co. Gallery in 1944, with more than 60 prints from etched or engraved copper and zinc plates, as well as carved plaster reliefs and original plates.[77] The Wittenborn, located at 38 East 57th Street, was actually a bookstore that reserved one long wall for gallery space. It was always a lively place to visit, especially for artists, because its owners, George Wittenborn and Heinz Schultz, were booksellers with an abiding interest in the fine arts. Because of their multiple interests and their egalitarian approach to selecting artists for exhibitions, Wittenborn and Schultz were able to provide one of the few places in the city where the literati and artists mingled easily. Not only did they display art and sell books about it, but they also sponsored publications that were unfailingly interesting and often seminal, albeit financially unsuccessful and short-lived. For example, in 1946 they launched the Documents of Modern Art series, hiring Robert Motherwell as editor. A bit of a dilettante, Motherwell would become the era's most educated art apologist. In the prospectus for the Documents series, Motherwell wrote that the goal was "to show that modern art is the expression of feelings and ideas which are complex, but not arbitrary in origin," a statement with which Fine would have concurred.[78]

As the war finally turned in favor of the Allies, a major change began to occur in art with abstraction moving from the margins to the mainstream. An indication of the enormity of the shift came in the spring of 1944. For the first time, the majority of 57th Street exhibitions were abstract, an event that according to Edward Alden Jewell made "a tingle of excitement" run through the art world. Peyton Boswell, Jr. editor of *Art Digest* was also struck by the phenomenon:

> It's all very exciting, but at the same time confusing. Is this a war-inspired recrudescence of ultra-modernism, which attained its peak with and following the last war? Or is it a deeper current of international thinking, world politics and broken barriers? Is art, once again, casting its prophetic shadow ahead of coming events, or is this merely a reaction against nationalism and will it, in turn, breed its own counter-revolt as creative artists continue to seek artistic independence?[79]

Fine was ready for a solo exhibition. In fact, she had been ready for a long time, slowly garnering attention in group shows at the Puma Gallery, besides those at Art of This Century, the Museum of Non-Objective Painting, and the yearly AAA shows. Critics had mentioned her name favorably in their reviews. All that was needed was to find a dealer willing to take the risk.

CHAPTER THREE

GOING SOLO

A "one-man" exhibition is analogous to breaking out of the pack. Visibility and name recognition do not come from group shows, which are like samplers, but only from solos where the combined impact of several paintings in one space provides critics and spectators with enough substance to ponder and assess. When and where it takes place is important in gauging the strength of the breakout. Fine's first "one-man" exhibition was in February-March, 1945 — a strong time of the year as opposed to May and June when everything is winding down and attendance is low. It was at the Willard Gallery on East 57th Street — a very good location. Whereas Greenwich Village was the place art was created, 57th Street was the place it was sold. The first was slightly seedy, the second up-scale. Art of This Century, the Wittenborn Gallery, and the Puma Gallery were all located there. On visiting 57th Street, Michael Seuphor, a French writer and artist, wrote that it seemed to him to be always "drenched in sunlight, even on a snowy day," due to its "very wide pavements," and tall houses that "are bright outside as well as within. Space and light for all." But then he added a cautionary note: "And yet it seems there is not enough space for everyone. Let those who are not pushers take care. Among the modest, the non-intriguing, who will have a chance? I get the impression that in New York everyone gets his chance. Although there too it passes, perhaps even more quickly than elsewhere."[1] Fine's chance had come.

Like Betty Parsons and Peggy Guggenheim, Marian Willard was from a monied background that insulated her somewhat from having to make her gallery into a financial success. Nor was her gender an issue because running a gallery was seen as similar to maintaining a literary salon, a role traditionally played by socially connected and aesthetically sensitive females who provided the milieu for creators and connoisseurs to meet and mingle. Other prominent women dealers in the era were Antoinette Kraushaar, who inherited her father's gallery, Eleanor Poindexter, Bertha Schaeffer, and Martha Jackson.

In Provincetown, Fine was able to relax yet also paint uninterruptedly in preparation for her solo exhibitions first at the Willard Gallery then at the Nierendorf Galley.

Willard began her career at the East River Gallery on East 57th Street from 1936 to 1938, giving the sculptor David Smith and Loren MacIver their first solo exhibitions. She then worked with J. B. Neumann from 1939 to 1940, during which time she gave Mark Rothko a solo exhibition. In 1940, she opened her own gallery with financial support from her parents. As a dealer, Willard was a good match for Fine because she described her taste as complex and poetic, words which could be used to describe Fine's art as well. Artists in her gallery included Morris Graves, MacIver, Richard Pousette-Dart, and Mark Tobey. Graves, whose solo preceded Fine's in January 1945, had studied Vedanta and Zen Buddhism extensively; his paintings had a quiet, almost mystical quality. The same was true of Tobey, who had studied Zen and Baha'i. Pousette-Dart had the reputation of a spiritual loner who also used the word mystical in talking about his paintings. If any galley line-up was homogenous, it was this one, not due to style or personality but to a capacity for mystery, and Fine fit in well. [2]

Her exhibition received good critical coverage, with reviews in *ARTnews, The New York Times, The Herald Tribune, The Sun and The World Telegram.* Typical is the following by Maude Riley for *Art Digest* in which she compared Fine to Miró:

> It is nothing to her discredit, since so many have demonstrated that it is unavoidable, that her most successful paintings are those which stem by a very short stem from Miró. Most attractive painting done, you might say, on her own, is a sort of white on white arrangement which goes on to include also large grey areas, black and pink movements, and two minute touches of two other colors. This is very charming and so, too, is a small canvas in which solid and transparent paint passages relate pleasurably in color and also texture.[3]

In line with Fine's earlier contention that her paintings paralleled Calder's experiments with space, the reviewer at *ARTnews* wrote that "Polyphonic looks not unlike an immobilized Calder mobile, for the rhythmic use of the forms creates a spatial illusion which, though shorn completely of ordinary pictorial devices, is nonetheless present." Fine's titles were evocative, with "Witches Flight" being a silhouette of black forms against a background of white, yellow, and what the reviewer described as "eerie saffron." "Secret Place" was evocative of "childish treasures hidden in marsh grass."[4]

The year 1945 was in every respect a successful one for Fine. In early spring, she and Berezov took part in the American Abstract Artists' annual exhibition in which over 100 paintings and sculptures were spread out in four galleys at the Riverside Museum. Open every afternoon to the public, the show struck one critic as "good, substantial, and most entertaining." Josef Albers, Fannie Hillsmith, Ad Reinhardt, Ibram Lassaw, and I. Rice Pereira were among the participants, but the Europeans were absent, Léger having returned to France and Mondrian having died the previous year. Fine's painting "Composition" was printed in *ARTnews* accompanying a favorable review of the show.[5] At the end of the year she was in the Whitney Museum of American Art Annual as were Rothko, Motherwell, and Gottlieb. Traditionally, the Whitney annuals were the shows that critics and artists loved to hate. Part of the incentive to cast aspersions on the annuals arose from the Whitney's stated commitment to American art in contrast to the Museum of Modern Art that was still heavily committed to European art. To artists, the Whitney annuals (and eventually biennials) promised more than they could deliver. However, everyone wanted to be in them anyway, and everyone attended so they could carp about them later. The one in 1945 was no exception, the only thing unusual about it being the use for the first time of the label Abstract Expressionism. Hilda Loveman in her review in *Limited Edition,* wrote: "The Eighth Street museum, which has taken a lambasting for years on the charge of emphasizing the conservative side and its own favorite 'regulars' has this year dropped a number of old timers, added fifty new names, and keynoted the abstract-expressionist trends in painting."[6]

It was a critical time for Fine to break through because the galleries were jumping with activity. With the end of the war, there was an effervescent hopefulness in New York that the art business would finally revive and collectors would begin paying attention to American artists, although there was no uniformity of opinion as to who deserved attention. At the same time as Fine's solo, Samuel Kootz, an old-style

Southern gentleman with a penchant for new-style salesmanship more common among used cars dealers than among art dealers, mounted a group exhibition at the Feigl Galleries (not yet having a gallery of his own) in which he began to broadcast the superiority of his favorites: William Baziotes, Fritz Glarner, Carl Holty, and Motherwell. Not long after, he added Gottlieb, Hofmann, and Lassaw to his lineup, juxtaposing their work with that of Europeans, including Léger, Picasso, and Miró, as if to say that the Americans were their equals. Over at the Julien Levy Galleries, the enigmatic art of Arshile Gorky was on display, while at Art of This Century, Jackson Pollock had yet another furious solo. The critics were nonplussed about both exhibitions. Maude Riley wrote that Gorky's paintings were "incoherent accident paintings" as evidenced by "running drips of turpentine," while Pollock's paintings conveyed belligerence:

> Jackson Pollock is surely on easy terms with a paint box. As he whales into the mounds of pigment he must lay out on his palette, he seems to run into no resistance from the medium and no anxiety rears its head between the first flush of purpose and the ultimate achievement of it. But I feel a sort of belligerence in the partnership of paints and Pollock towards all other things — which includes the subject, and you and me. His paintings have to be taken one at a time. Complete readjustment must be made in turning from one to the next. So that the antagonism seems also to exist between paintings.[7]

There was the feeling of expectancy in the New York air, but no one could discern just what it was they were expecting. About the exhibition aptly named "A Problem for Critics," mounted by Howard Putzel at the 67 Gallery, Riley wrote in her review that he "is looking for the front end of an ism to apply to the group of artists he shows," among them being Matta, Gorky, Gottlieb, Hofmann, Pollock, and Rothko. But Riley was aware that, name or no, this group of artists had already begun to receive heightened attention, noting that four of them had been represented in the Museum of Modern Art's Anniversary Exhibition the previous summer. Tongue-in-cheek, Riley concluded her review by inviting her readers to come up with their own names for the new movement. "Readers, don't leave that ism dangling! Here's your chance, if ever there was one, to call modern painting that name you've had in mind for it."[8]

There was as yet no definitive list of who was part of this new ism. However, several of the men had begun to refer to each other over and over again when asked by gallery owners and critics for their opinions. Furthermore, the men frequently wrote the text for each other's exhibitions. Newman wrote the introduction to Gottlieb's exhibition at the Wakefield Gallery in 1944. He also collaborated with Gottlieb and Rothko on many statements and letters to the press. Motherwell, always prolific as well as facile with words, intoned the names Baziotes, Gorky, Gottlieb, Hofmann, de Kooning, Pollock, Reinhardt, Rothko, Tomlin, and, of course, his own, as often as possible. Sweeney had offered his initial list in 1944 in an article in *Harper's Bazaar* extolling the work of five painters: Milton Avery, Morris Graves, Pollock, Gorky, and Matta. "Each of these men in his vitality, individuality of outlook, and present freedom from obvious debts to his predecessors, holds the promise of a new and encouraging phase of American art." About Pollock, he wrote that were he to attempt to achieve harmony in his work, it would lead to its "final emasculation."[9] Over the next few years, the critics Clement Greenberg and Harold Rosenberg developed their own lists. List making and numbering (The Five, The Eight, The Ten) was a kind of game everyone played and because there was overlap, the lists were reinforcing. But there were three groups whose names usually did not appear on the lists: men who had served in the military during the war and, therefore, had not had a chance to establish themselves yet, minorities (although Norman Lewis and Romare Beardon were occasionally included), and women. In regard to women, there were a few exceptions: in Sidney Janis's groundbreaking book *Abstract and Surrealist Art in America,* published in 1944, while men predominated, women were well represented. Janis included paintings by Mercedes Carles (Matter), Fannie Hillsmith, Gina Knee, Lenore Krasner (Lee Krasner), Georgia O'Keeffe, Irene Rice Pereira, Janet Sobel, and Dorothea Tanning. The other exception was the eclectic list put together by Dorothy Miller at the Museum of Modern Art in the fall of 1946 for the exhibition titled "Fourteen Americans," in which Rice Pereira, Loren MacIver, and Honore Sharrer participated. But by and large, women were not included in the lists. Art historian Michael Leja, who in his book *Reframing Abstract Expressionism* analyzes art in relation to film noir and what became known as the Modern Man discourse dominant in the 1940s and early 1950s, put the reasons for the exclusion of women succinctly: "A dame with an Abstract Expressionist brush is no less a misfit than a noir heroine with a rod."[10] Nor did the women mention each other, make their own lists, or gather together in common cause. The desire was to win recognition from the men, to be the exception rather than the rule. It was simply the way the culture worked.

Fine had inner resources many women lacked, the primary one being her determination to work hard, as she phrased it "to be severe" with herself. Another resource was her independent mindset which meant she was not overly affected by what other artists were doing, choosing instead to take a long view. In an interview she gave when she was in her seventies looking back over her career, she said that immediate success had never mattered to her: "I don't paint to sell. I don't paint not to sell. I am very aware of the future, twenty years hence, forty years hence, and I feel that if something will not stand up forty years from now, I'm not much interested in doing that kind of thing."[11] Her other resource was a family who steadfastly believed in her talent. When she became discouraged, they did everything they could to let her know they had faith in her. "I don't think religion had any effect on her. Art was her religion," recalled Charlotte Fine, Perle's sister-in-law. "And that was all right with us. She was a beautiful person not only in her art but in herself. She was not confrontational. She wouldn't raise her voice. But if she really believed in something, she wouldn't back off either." Fine often traveled by train to Malden, Mass., for birthdays, bar mitzvahs and other special family occasions. They, in turn, visited her in New York and during the summer in Provincetown, making certain, however, to bring along food, for neither Fine nor Berezov cooked much, surviving on the most basic of meals. (One relative remembered a dinner of burnt pancakes.) Without money to buy presents, Fine gave them paintings instead. Charlotte Fine recalled a humorous mishap with one of the gifts:

> We had hung one of her abstracts that she had given to us in our living room. It was a lovely leaf-like painting in blues and greens. Then one day she came to visit. She

> stood quietly in front of it for a while, with her head cocked to the side, not saying anything, just looking. "What's the matter, Perle?" I finally asked. "It's upside down." she said softly. Trying to make her feel better, I replied that it looked wonderful either way, but she said she would take it down, mark on the back which side was up, and rehang it, which she did. Not long after, my husband Leo, who was Perle's younger brother, confided to me and his mother that he didn't like the painting very much, liking her realistic paintings more than her abstracts. So Mrs. Fine, feeling sorry for Perle, offered to trade it for the copy of the Rembrandt that Perle had done in the 1930s, the one the Metropolitan had stamped copy on the back, which is how the Rembrandt came to reside in our living room.[12]

When her younger sister Rose was married, Fine's wedding gift had been her impressionistic portrait, its worth increasing exponentially to the family following Rose's death early in 1945 of nephritis. Fine's older sister Amy, who had encouraged her to draw as a child, had died of cancer in 1933, so the death of her only remaining sister affected her deeply. Attractive and talented, as was everyone in the family, Rose had fallen ill in 1943. Fine made many trips to Malden during her last months. In one of the rare times when Fine confided personally in Baroness Hilla Rebay, she wrote of her loss:

> These past few months have been months of great emotional strain for me, for a very near and dear member of my family had become gravely ill and after months of bitter pain and agony passed on. I was very close to God during all that time, and I seem to have experienced a sort of purification and uplift. I seem to be able to judge values more clearly and bravely now than ever. I think I have grown through this experience because I have suffered so much. Forgive me for burdening you with this, but it is all still so fresh in mind.[13]

In the same letter, Fine informed Rebay that she was leaving the Willard Gallery because she had been offered a much better deal by Karl Nierendorf whose gallery was across the street from the Willard Gallery at 53 East 57th Street. Apparently Fine had written to him about joining his gallery prior to making a commitment to the Willard Gallery but had not received a response:

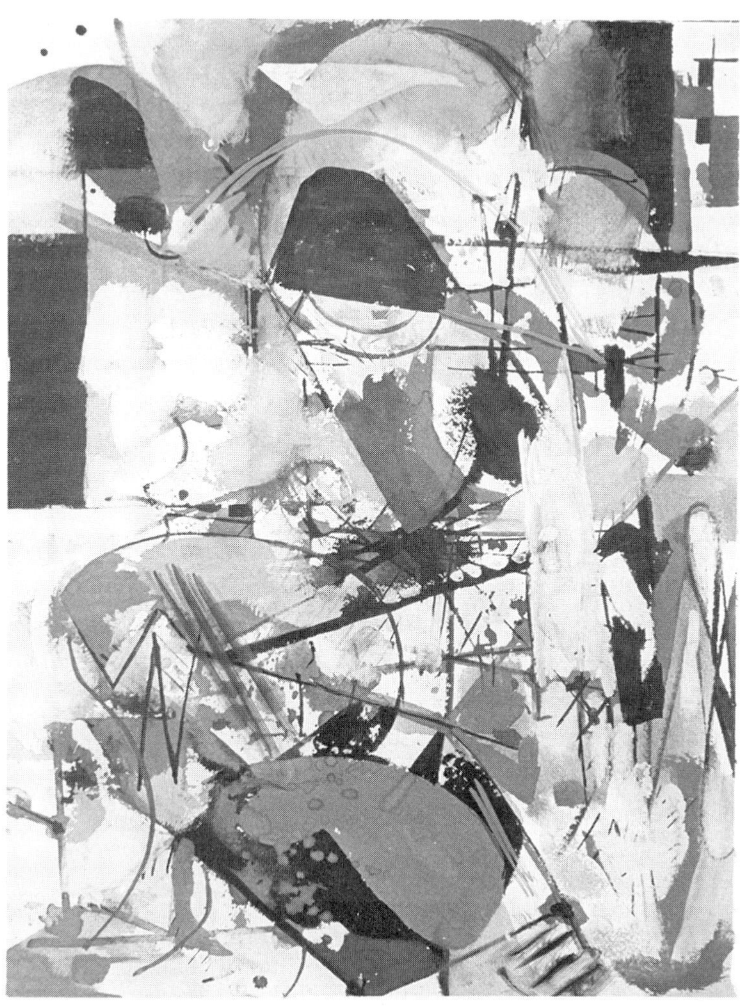

Fine's whimsical *Harlequin*, a 1946 watercolor, was included in her solo exhibition at the Nierendorf Gallery.

> I think you may be interested to know that I have left the Willard Gallery and find my new association with the Nierendorf gallery much more suitable for my work. It was with Mr. Nierendorf that I originally wished to be connected, but unfortunately I did not have the sense to speak with you about it, and by the time he did answer my letter, I had already given my word to the other gallery, which I was honor-bound to keep. They did seem to have a very high regard for the Non-Objective painters there, however, and never spoke an ill-word about them in my presence. Since then, I have been approached by several others whose leanings toward surrealism were so marked that it was obvious it would be bad for my work — and I resisted all offers of all kinds.[14]

For an American artist, it was a privilege to be represented by Nierendorf whose intent was to show, in his own words, "the same progressive movement in art to which my previous efforts were dedicated." Nierendorf offered Fine a subsidy of $150 a month (the same amount Peggy Guggenheim was paying Jackson Pollock) so that she could paint full-time as he had done five years earlier for the painter and sculptor Louise Nevelson whose work he also championed, mounting her first exhibition in October 1941. When Nevelson had initially approached Nierendorf to request that he give her an exhibition, she was so desperate that she was considering cutting her throat if his answer was no. She wrote:

> At that time I had a little place on 21st Street. When the W.P.A closed about six months before, they had taken all the sculpture and broken it up and thrown it in the East River. But the man who was in charge asked me if I wanted my work returned, and I said yes. And so I had it in the cellar. So Nierendorf came the next evening, looked at the pieces, and said, "You can have a show in three weeks."[15]

In regard to subsidies, Nierendorf was continuing a European tradition in which the dealer functioned as a kind of patron, whereas Willard's arrangement with artists was usually sale-on-consignment. He was also willing to buy paintings outright to help an artist who was short of cash as he did for Fine on January 27, 1946, paying $250 for five gouaches.

One of Nierendorf's unique characteristics, besides his perennial sunny nature, was that he offered in his gallery a salon environment in which musicians, architects and actors mingled with artists after hours, either informally for discussion, or formally for recitals and lectures. Rarely did the atmosphere get acrimonious in his gallery. In fact, one of Nierendorf's favorite expressions was "it's love that dominates the world." Internationalism was also important. An interviewer who had been impressed with the "unusual beauty and intelligence" of an "East-West" exhibition that Nierendorf had presented was pleasantly surprised to find on a subsequent visit that on all the window sills, lining the shelves, and filling glass cases were "little reflections in stone, bone, bronze," of ancient Chinese, Greek, Peruvian and Mexican art, indicative of his enduring passion for internationalism.[16] Nierendorf even showed movies as he had done in Berlin where he had been a member of the League for Independent Film. These included color animations made experimentally by Léger and Man Ray. Ahead of his time, he liked to combine media in his gallery often projecting slides in and around photographs and sculptures of ancient civilizations. "I look for unity in the beautiful: for the strong, expressive things in life," he told the interviewer, who noted that Nierendorf "will probably never grow disappointed with life and will never wear a look of gloom on his animated happy face."[17]

Nierendorf's humanism went beyond his encouragement of the artists in his gallery and his jovial hosting of thought-provoking gatherings after-hours. In the years immediately following the war he was actively involved in raising funds to send food parcels to Europe. Twice in 1946 he underwrote art auctions at the New School for Social Research. About the second, titled "Artists and Quakers Join in Helping The Hungry in Europe," he wrote: "Many artists have known privation themselves. Perhaps for that reason they have been especially generous in this undertaking." The art, including a painting by Fine, was exhibited for five days at the school at the end of which an auction took place with Nierendorf's old friend J. B. Neumann as auctioneer.[18]

Because he had personally experienced artistic repression, Nierendorf was willing to take on both the financial and social risk associated with

In a nod to Provincetown, Fine painted *Nautical Composition* (1946) in which identifiable objects, including rope, curve playfully. It was included in her 1947 solo exhibition at the Nierendorf Gallery.

promoting the avant-garde. Fine was well aware of the antipathy his strong stand occasionally generated: "Gottlieb was with the gallery then, as was Louise Nevelson, whose show came hot after mine. Modern art was resented and the guest book had to be cleaned up every few days."[19]

For Nevelson, Nierendorf was not only forthcoming with financial support but he also provided essential psychological support often being the only encouraging voice she heard. He told Nevelson once "you're going to have every desire in creativity fulfilled." When she asked him why, he replied, "I know Picasso and Matisse, I know all the great artists, and I know how they move."[20] Similarly, Fine found that his encouragement helped her establish her own individual style and increased her productivity.

Fine's first solo exhibition was in April, 1946, about which a critic for *ARTnews* wrote, "Her non-objective abstractions have both taste and dignity. Her work ranges from delicacy to strength. Her forms seem at times derived from punctuation marks and musical signs but are more often pure invention. They are placed with a marked sensitivity to intervals of space." Prices were listed from $75 to $500.[21] Ben Wolf, associate editor for *Art Digest,* was equally impressed:

> The artist combines a sense of design with a subtle though strong attitude towards color. There is a struggle sensed here in the direction of underivative expression that Miss Fine seems to be well on her way toward winning. Oddly enough it frequently seems more difficult for an abstractionist to find a clear unfamiliar path for himself than for his more objective cousin. Here and there in this painter's expressionism Miro's impact is sensed. However, along with Perle Fine's development, this is felt less and less until we come to something that is quite her own, such as her swirling "Rhythm of Form and Line," where a highly individualistic stabbing line has been called into play and in "High Point" that employs what might be likened to an aesthetic Morse code.[22]

During this period, Fine continued her association with Hayter and remained an active member of The Society of American Etchers taking part in their annual exhibition in November, 1946, at the always lively Wittenborn Gallery where art, books, and conversation were mixed into a potent brew. About her small engraving, only 5 3/4" by 8", an item appeared in the magazine *The Print Collector*: "Atelier 17's Perle Fine and Alice Trumbull Mason have just issued two interesting abstractions. Fine's "Omnipotent One" is an intricate composition of weaving calligraphy printed in soft greys and greens. Mason has engraved an interplay of amorphous forms in a spiraling composition printed in a harsh red-and-yellow. Both prints show expert use of the burin and soft ground texture." There were fifty in the edition at $15 each.[23] Technically demanding, etching played the odd role of counterweight in the development of Abstract Expressionism, because its difficulty required forethought and skill instead of spontaneity. For Fine, who always claimed that her work had a strong underlying structure, etching sharpened her sense of line. It remained an important influence well after she had returned totally to paint.

New York had no rival in the United States when it came to being the capital of the arts. On the West Coast the only city with any interest in the avant-garde was San Francisco. This was largely due to the efforts of Dr. Grace Morley, director of the San Francisco Museum. In fact, Morley had purchased Pollock's "Guardians of the Secret" from his first solo exhibition at Peggy Guggenheim's Art of This Century. In August 1947, Fine had a solo show at the M. H. de Young Memorial Museum in Golden Gate Park, San Francisco. The curator for Fine's show described her art as "provocative," "alluring" and evocative of the "poetry and magic of color," concluding that Fine's creative vision gave "each work a joyous life of its own." The art critic for the *San Francisco Chronicle* wrote admiringly: "Miss Fine works in oil, water color and gouache, and in each of these mediums produces pictures that are firm in design, attractive in color, and delightful in their use of the fantastic and imaginative."[24]

Her work also began to be shown in Europe where museums were bringing their collections out of storage and repairing damage and to which the exiles were returning. (Even Peggy Guggenheim, never happy and always restless in the United States, was preparing to leave.)

In May 1946, Fine had five etchings ("Calm After Storm," "Carousel," "Omnipotent One," "With Abandon," and "Deep of the Night") in a show Hayter organized for Paris. Having spent so many productive years there, he was not trying to prove via the show that the Americans had surpassed the French, nor did the Parisians see it as an assault on their coveted position as center of the art universe. However, the exhibitions that were to follow had exactly that intent. In the summer of 1947, Fine's paintings were in the Salon des Réalités Nouvelles, which was subtitled "Art Abstrait, Concret, Constructivisim, Non-Figuratif, Orphisme" to make clear its range. The salon had been conceived by the painter Robert Delauney in 1939 to be held at the Galerie Charpentier, with the purpose of tracing annually the development of non-objectivity, sometimes called by the French "Abstract Creative." Then World War II had begun, followed by Delauney's death in 1941. Not until 1946 would his friend Frédo Sidès take on the responsibility of getting it going again, in the process enlarging it into an international salon. He approached Rebay who agreed to send 42 paintings by 14 artists, each represented by three works. When Nierendorf heard about the arrangement while traveling in Europe, he wrote to Rebay immediately: "It is so important that non-objective paintings make a breakthrough here too. It would have repercussions in the U.S.A. as well."[25] In a review published in *Carrefour,* Frank Elgar wrote that Fine was one of the group of artists who "are better than our own at working the same vein," but his use of the phrase "for the time being" in connection with the superiority of the Americans to the French indicated that he thought it would not last:

> For the time being I can only observe that the foreign abstractionists are superior to their French colleagues. This, I think is the first time in a hundred years that a new school of art has arisen outside our influence. A visit to the American section of the salon des réalités nouvelles leaves no doubt as to the scope and vigor of a movement that, one day, perhaps, will emerge here as well, as a movement that has nothing more to learn from Europe and that surpasses similar work being attempted in our aging countries in number, fantasy and simplicity.[26]

In his book *How New York Stole the Idea of Modern Art: Abstract Expressionism, Freedom and the Cold War,* Serge Guilbaut contends that Elgar's comments were self-serving for the French, and were motivated by "the regenerative boons to be expected from the Marshall Plan." However, it is also possible that they were generated by the largesse of Rebay and the Solomon R. Guggenheim Foundation, one of the exhibition's principal underwriters. To Guilbaut, Elgar's comments were marked by an "anxious resignation in the face of the future which might well yield a new style of painting to replace an old and moribund one but which nevertheless left something to be desired." Throughout Elgar's review there was a thread of scepticism as made evident by the last sentence: "If true painting were to reap the benefit, there would be no cause for regret. But will it? That is the question."

Although the reviews of the salon were lukewarm, they were far more positive than those of "Introduction à la Peinture Moderne Américaine" held at the Maeght Gallery the previous spring under the auspices of the U.S. Information Service, featuring artists then in Sam Kootz' gallery: Baziotes, Bearden, Browne, Gottlieb, Holty and Motherwell. *Carrefour's* damning review was typical: "Clumsy compositions, clashing colors, gratuitous aggression, absence of style, and above all a frightening spiritual dryness — must the art of a young and powerful nation pass through such a barren phase before setting foot on the shores of a new world?"[27]

While the art skirmishes between Europe and the United States showed no signs of abating, with Paris refusing to yield to New York City, at least for Fine and the other artists chosen by Rebay, there was a positive ripple effect from the Salon des Réalités Nouvelles. After the show closed, Rebay arranged to have the 42 paintings shown in museums in Switzerland and Germany for the next two years. In December 1949, they were ready to be returned to the United States when Rebay received a telegram, about which she wrote to Fine:

> A cable requested our consent that exhibit be taken over by the American authorities, so that once again it can be shown in all the American Houses of all larger cities of Germany. Since you have given me permission to exhibit your work further on, I consented. I hope this will show you how effective our show has been. And you probably will also

> be pleased that this is a proof that non-objectivity is becoming officially represented by our own government due to the great interest there, and praise we received, over press and radio and again at each different opening.[28]

In the United States, Fine was coming to the attention of the national press, not just the New York-based art publications. She was featured in the May 1947 issue of *Arts & Architecture,* with a painting on the cover and a two-page spread illustrated by black-and-white reproductions of "Mythical Being Mask," oil on canvas, "Interchromatic Penetration," oil on paper, "Tyranny of Space," (see color plate) gouache, and "Transience," gouache. Fine was in eminent company, for the other articles in the issue were on the architect Richard J. Neutra and the sculptor Henry Moore.[29] In the accompanying text, Benjamin Baldwin wrote that there was an intuitive three-dimensional quality in Fine's paintings, yet her fundamental approach was two-dimensional. "To Perle Fine, modern art is a conscious art and a very complicated phenomenon. It demands that the artist have erudition and at the same time ease of execution." While her paintings seemed to begin with a form or color idea, Baldwin concluded that it was "the playing back and forth between form and space which brings about the final expression the picture takes. This struggle to attain greater expansion and perception involves a destruction of the static and a search to establish it again to achieve a sense of tremendous space and enormous form." He surmised that her use of the right-angle provided a sense of stability and kept her canvases from "chaos," the final result being the emergence of a "strange, mysterious" image that offered the viewer "new and delightful passage into another world."

Equally important was the full-length article with the prescient title "Perle Fine and the latter-day mystics" in the Fall 1947 issue of *The New Iconograph,* which also included a feature on Mark Rothko, selections from Mencius, Chinese philosopher, translated by Ezra Pound, "The Swan" by Charles Baudelaire translated by Helena Hersey, and three pages from *The Book of Singular Encounters* by Henri Michaux, a highly individualistic Belgian writer, loosely assorted with literary surrealism. Similar to the equally short-lived but seminal publication *Possibilities,* which appeared the same year and was edited by Harold

Rosenberg and Robert Motherwell, and *Tiger's Eye,* the brainchild of Ruth and John Stephan, *The New Iconograph,* showcased modern art and theory, interlaced with literature. These publications served up an intoxicating mix of philosophy (mostly Existentialism), anthropology (principally "primitive" cultures), linguistics and semiotics, myth (heavily Greek), and psychology (slanted toward Carl Jung). But what they were really about was a longing: first, to find meaning, and, second, to find words. Fine's statement in *The New Iconograph* embodied both the high ideals of the editors, writers and artists who produced or were featured in these publications, as well as the daunting seriousness with which they, and she, undertook the task: "It is as true in art as it is in life that the purest expression of truth is also the purest expression of vitality. Thus, the new reality, constant, palpable, born of truth, free of oppressive particularities, reveals itself clearly in the continuous and reciprocal play of intrinsic forces in a good modern work of art."[30]

The New Iconograph was preceded by four issues of *The Iconograph* in 1946, both taking their titles from that unique property of an icon — its transformation from painting to reality, a process that was paralleled in the transubstantiation of the bread and wine in communion into the real body and blood of Christ. The difference between the two publications was that the latter was more modernist in its overall approach while the former focused on work arising from an appreciation for Indian art, which the editors perceived to be "primitive," a word that the anthropologist Franz Boaz had used in the title of his widely read study *Primitive Art.* Like many literary and artistic people at that time who considered themselves avant-garde, the editors saw Indian art as powerful and symbolic. It was a way for humankind — battered by wars and economic depression, and ripped away from God by the determinism of psychology and the materialism of science — to reconnect to the primordial and thus to themselves. It also was interpreted as an embodiment of the universal and was, therefore, a visual manifestation of the ideas espoused by Jung. At the same time, there was a heavy Existential strain in the magazine as evidenced by a statement made in the first issue by its editor Kenneth Beaudoin about the nature and need for change: "It is the business of a healthy national consciousness to be aware of the art form which will satisfy the existing moment with its eloquence; for in the moment of fresh achievement, then only does the art form enjoy its truest reality."[31]

Of the five paintings that were printed with the article, all but one retained a touch of objectivity. For example, in the photograph at the top of the article, Fine stands in front of "Forms Fugitive" (see color plate) (1946) a large oil on canvas (60" x 46").[32] The apt title referred to the barest hint of a hand, buttons on a shirt, cuff links, even a music clef painted in a thin medium blue line over large curving shapes of light blue, light green, tan, and yellow, with heavy black arrow-like shapes interjecting mass that neither recedes nor comes forward. In the watercolor "Harlequin" (1946), there is again the slight suggestion of a clown, with his multi-colored hat and costume, and a smile, rather like the grin on the Cheshire Cat. "Running Figure," which for Fine was a highly unusual three-dimensional construction completed in 1946, was evocative of both the real and the universal abstraction. About this construction, Jean Franklin, editor of *The New Iconograph* along with Oscar Collier, wrote:

> In the construction "Running Figure," for example, the title is illustrated by a subtle and economic suggestion of a figure in motion, which is however, clearly subordinated to a much more generalized and abstract representation of motion qua motion. The artist has achieved this rather conceptual expression by emphasizing a rhythmic opposition of shapes and textures, harmonious yet constantly moving one against another, as the eye follows the direction of the composition.[33]

In the oval to the right side of the gouache titled simply "Head," painted in 1946, there is the suggestion of a human head. The oil painting "Procession" (1945) conveyed a powerful sense of horizontal movement as if its shapes and lines were in a slow ceremonial parade. Only "Composition" (1940) was totally non-objective, with no hint of an object provided by the title.

Franklin found Fine's work to be hard to classify, which she considered beneficial, most classifications being uninformative: "So the terms abstract and/or non-objective apply to the delicate and sensitive work reproduced on these pages only in a very superficial way." Although Fine was a member of the American Abstract Artists, Franklin considered her art to be different in spirit and intent from that of the artists Ralston Crawford and Robert Motherwell, nor could her art be reconciled to that of the group associated with the Museum of Non-Objective Painting. Instead, Fine had developed a completely personal language, establishing a private reality in her art. Franklin then quoted from Fine: "The stamp of modern art is clarity; clarity of color, clarity of forms and of composition, clarity of determined dynamic rhythm in a determined space. Since figuration often veils, obscures or entirely negates purity of plastic expression, the destruction of the particular (familiar) form for the universal one becomes a prime prerequisite." Aware of the strong connection between Fine's statement and the aesthetic principles put forth by Mondrian, Franklin pointed out what she considered a flaw in Fine's logic — a flaw that Franklin contended ultimately worked to Fine's advantage:

> If Miss Fine were sufficiently aware of all the implications of her statement she would recognize a disturbing contradiction in her approach to painting. Since the "clarity" of which she speaks can only mean an absolute reduction, the only possible artistic products of such a theory are the beautiful and barren designs of Mondrian. The particular aspect of any object is composed of those qualities which serve to individuate it from all other objects in the same category and to place it in a unique temporal-spatial position. Briefly these qualities may be defined as follows: 1.) Those aspects of appearance and structure that vary from the mean; 2.) Any illusion of three dimensional space; 3.) Impure color (only the three primary colors are "pure" in this sense); 4) A source or sources of light. Only by eliminating, as Mondrian has done, all four of these elements from a picture can an artist eliminate the "particular." Miss Fine has merely substituted for familiar objects imagined ones which yet have all the qualities of particularity listed above. The unreality of a form does not automatically establish its "universality." The inconsistency of which Miss Fine is guilty is in my opinion a very fortunate thing. The logical conclusion of her ideas would be an art as restricted as that of Mondrian who succeeded in limiting his genius to such an extent that for most people his work is as meaningless as it is uninteresting. Delicate colors, varying effects of light, subtle complexities of formal and spatial relationships, these are pictorial

> elements that Perle Fine disowns in theory but happily includes in paint for they are the very things that make her pictures so exciting.[34]

By 1947, Fine had paintings in several private collections including those of Frank Lloyd Wright, Francis (Frank) Welch Crowninshield, Alfred Barr, Jr., and Burton and Emily Tremaine. That Wright owned one of her oils ("Composition," 1940) gave Fine distinct pleasure because he was not known to collect abstract art or even to place much value on paintings. To have a painting in the collection of Crowninshield was significant given the fact that his penthouse apartment was already jammed with an important collection of art including paintings by Modigliani, Pascin, Matisse, Derain, Braque, Dufy, Rouault and Bonnard as well as a significant collection of African masks and sculptures.

Until the sale in 1943 of a portion of his collection, Crowninshield's living room was walled on three sides with floor-to-ceiling bookcases in which were approximately 2,000 beautifully bound books, every last one on art, many hundreds of which contained original etchings, lithographs and color engravings.[35] On February 6, 1946, he wrote to Fine: "I was very lucky in being able to buy a charming painting of yours at the Wittenborn Gallery. I have it in my room and it really looks extremely well."[36] Tall, handsome, and dignified, Crowninshield was the influential editor first of *Century Magazine* (1910–13), then of *Vanity Fair* (1913–34). He was a long-standing patron of the avant-garde, having been one of the organizers of the ground-breaking 1913 Armory Show. He frequently reproduced art in the pages of Vanity Fair including paintings by Matisse, Picasso, and Braque. Also, he was one of the few collectors and editors who routinely supported the work of women, having published a poem by Gertrude Stein in 1917, promoted the literary career of Dorothy Parker, and brought the work of Colette to the attention of the American public. In fact, he considered one of the missions of *Vanity Fair* to be feminist: "We dare to believe that they [women] are, in their best moments, creatures of some cerebral activity; we even make bold to believe that it is they who are contributing what is most original, stimulating, and highly magnetized to the literature of our day, and we hereby announce ourselves as determined and bigoted feminists."[37]

For Fine to have a painting in Alfred Barr's collection was also significant because he traveled in some of the same influential circles as Crowninshield. A graduate of Harvard, in 1929 he had been recommended by the eminent art historian Paul Sachs to be the first director of the Museum of Modern Art. Since then he had continuously wielded a great deal of power in shaping the American perception of art.

Emily Hall Tremaine and her husband Burton were newcomers in the New York art collecting scene but were rapidly making up for lost time by putting together a significant collection of modern art. They already owned "The Black Rose" by Braque, "Woman With a Fan" by Picasso, "Le Chat Blanc" by Miró, "Stability Animated" by Kandinsky, and "Victory Boogie-Woogie" by Mondrian and were beginning to purchase the work of younger Americans. Eventually the collection would be considered by many cognoscenti to be among the best in the nation. Consummate art patrons, the Tremaines were known for giving parties either at their New York apartment or their home in Madison, Connecticut, with the intent of showcasing the work of up-and-coming artists. The Tremaines owned at least four works by Fine: "Midnight," "Sunblinded," "Climax," and "Driftwood." Burton, who had not been a collector prior to marrying Emily in 1945, followed her knowledgeable lead in making purchase decisions. President of The Miller Company in Meriden, Connecticut, Burton recalled that the first purchase he ever made on his own was a painting by Fine: "I was at the Non-Objective Museum and I saw one picture and suddenly I thought of our combustion engineer, and I said to myself 'that picture shows just how his mind works.' That particular canvas wasn't for sale, but we went to the artist's studio — and I bought my first Perle Fine."[38]

In 1946, Fine gave the Tremaines a painting as a gift out of gratitude for their support. In her note of thanks, Emily wrote:

> We are both so crazy about the picture you have sent us I can't wait to have it framed and hung near my desk where I can enjoy it. The colors are so exquisite like precious jewels — I can't tell you how sweet you are to remember us and with something that gives us so much joy. I wish you could come sometime and see how wonderful all your pictures look

> — "Climax" is in Burton's office — the lyrical pink one in our bedroom — "Sunspot" or is it "Sunblindness?" is breathtaking in the dining room.[39]

Fine's work had already evolved well beyond plasticism and biomorphism. In fact, critics writing about her second solo exhibition at Nierendorf's Gallery in January 1947 concluded she was a "highly original painter."[40] Jewell wrote for *The New York Times* that Fine's paintings were "full of witty allusions" and that she explored "with aplomb" and "native resourcefulness."[41] The reviewer for *ARTnews* noted that in dealing with plastic problems of creating space while respecting the two dimensions of the canvas surface, Fine "has permitted, even encouraged, a number of metaphorical, literary meanings to enrich her work. Thus human heads, animals, steeples, and boats appear briefly through her interlocking rectangles and lozenges."[42]

That spring, art critic Clement Greenberg singled out Fine's "Bather, Seaside" as one of the best in the Whitney Annual, although his praise for the entire show was equivocal: "The successes are pleasing rather than moving or upsetting," he wrote. A portent of things to come, Greenberg's need for art to upset, to trouble, even to overthrow, was in line with his assiduous promotion of Pollock, which would work to Fine's detriment. There was enigmatic power in Fine's art but not fury. Greenberg wanted fury.[43]

Then came a major blow that set Fine back. On October 13, 1947, Nierendorf dropped dead of a heart attack at 58, just a year and a half after Fine had joined his gallery. In remembrance of him, Peyton Boswell, editor of *Art Digest,* wrote in an editorial that Nierendorf "was a rare combination of a shy scholar and sagacious businessman. So firm were his personal convictions that, once his finely-trained mind was convinced of the rightness of his opinion, nothing could alter his decision."[44] In December, Rebay described his death in a letter to Maria Marc, the widow of the painter Franz Marc: "You knew Nierendorf died suddenly. Two months ago we buried him in the old cemetery here in Greens Farms, where I have my home. He just fell and was dead." Later she told Hilde Prytek, Nierendorf's assistant, about her efforts to get Alexander Calder, who lived nearby in Roxbury, to make him a headstone: "Mr. Calder refuses to make the tombstone for Nierendorf. He just rolled a simple field stone on his grave from my garden and said that if I got a man to sculpt it, he would pay half of the expense."[45]

As was Fine, Nevelson was also shaken by Nierendorf's death to the point that she didn't exhibit for several years. "I always considered Nierendorf my spiritual godfather," Nevelson said. "He was convinced that I could fulfill myself on a totally creative level, and that meant that he gave me that heritage."[46]

Nierendorf had given Fine the confidence to paint in her own way. But one person in particular was not at all pleased with the outcome: Hilla Rebay. Fine had started to digress from Rebay's narrow brand of non-objectivity, and had even began using the term abstraction, to Rebay's utter dismay. On January 12, 1948, Rebay fired off a letter to Fine in which she explained, as to an obtuse child, why only the term non-objectivity would do:

> I am enclosing a statement by Wei Lang which will tell you that the essential of all mysticism and Eastern wisdom, the "Non," was already not only recognized but even in its vast importance worded in the seventh century. Mr. Dwinell Grant recently wrote that through extensive study he — at last — has learned to understand why it must be called non-objective painting and not abstract painting. You again call yourself an abstract painter....Can you abstract also rhythm or space or absolute forms? I cannot. Maybe when you get older you also some day will understand what it meant. And not accept scholarships for non-objectivity and regress to a title as foolish as abstract after the scholarship ended. You will also find that "non" in all eastern ancient traditions of wisdom is called the essential. It is a clear cutoff of all materialistic external and excentric illusion.[47]

As with the case of other very strong personalities, Rebay's obsessive support of non-objectivity eventually had negative repercussions on the artists who remained closely identified with her and the Museum of Non-Objective Painting. Her controlling demeanor was totally at odds with the post-war world of New York City in which most things German were tainted and in which anything that smacked of upper-class Europe was considered not only effete but artistically passé. In the long run because of Rebay's narrow focus, those artists who stayed within her sphere were viewed as lesser than those who broke away.

CHAPTER FOUR

PROVINCETOWN INTERLUDE

In Greenwich Village, Fine looked through her window onto a cityscape of congestion and noise with delivery trucks crowding the avenues. There were no trees or grass, and at night the stars were occluded by the glow of the street lights. But in Provincetown, Massachusetts, she found that her studio window was "a frame for the stars that make up the Big Dipper."[1] In the winter, New York City wore shades of gray, steely and cold, but in the summer, Provincetown wore all the hues on the color wheel depending on the time of day and the weather; instead of black automobiles parked on Eighth Street, there were red and green dories pulled up on sand.

On the extreme tip of Cape Cod, jutting like a bent arm into the Atlantic Ocean, Provincetown satisfied the paradoxical double craving of artists for sociability and solitude. Like seagulls, they could flock together — for leisurely picnics on the dunes, provocative lectures at Gallery 200, and lively summer theater performances — and they could fly solo, spending long unbroken hours in their airy, well-lit studios talking to no one.

From the time that Berezov had proposed to Fine on the breakwater in Provincetown, only to be turned down because of the unfair advantage he had due to the incoming tide, until 1954 when they built a four-season studio home in East Hampton, N.Y., Provincetown was their summer retreat whenever finances allowed. Fine usually spent the entire season while Berezov visited when he could, traveling by train from New York City to Orient Point on the eastern end of Long Island, there to catch the ferry across the Sound, connecting with yet another train or bus to travel through Rhode Island and out to the Cape. With his camera always in hand, he took many black-and-white photographs of the life of the summer community: the artists at Days Lumberyard leaning on the railing of the second-floor balcony in the warm sunshine; Gottlieb sitting at his drawing board with pictographs pinned to the wall behind him; Fritz Bultman backlit by the light

Art studios abounded in Provincetown, allowing an easy interchange of ideas. Berezov's photographic skills were much in demand.

streaming through the angled windows of his studio designed for him by Tony Smith; Perle in a baseball cap riding her bicycle to the beach; parties on the waterfront; sailboat races in the bay. Berezov was as well-known as she, and his skill as a photographer was always appreciated, particularly by artists who needed publicity shots for upcoming exhibition catalogs. On occasion, he even joined Fine in teaching and painting, sharing her space in a lumberyard that had been converted into studios.

They were not alone in deciding to leave New York City each summer. In fact, they were part of a mass exodus instigated by the sweltering heat in the studios with only small fans for relief from the fumes of oil paint and turpentine. Furthermore, the Manhattan art galleries were closed from June to September, so there was no reason to stay. Provincetown had long been one of the preferred destinations (along with East Hampton and Rockport, Mass.), becoming a kind of coastline Greenwich Village. Hordes of students came to study at Hofmann's summer school, to take informal classes with individual artists including Fine, or simply to wander through the studios and seasonal galleries to find out what was germinating on canvas under the beneficent influence of the warm light and sea breezes.

In 1949, Stuart Preston, art critic for *The New York Times,* was enticed into making the long trip to check out the rumor that Provincetown had become once again the "summer capital of American art." He had also been invited to take part in a panel discussion about French versus American art to be presented by Forum 49, a thought-provoking series of panels and exhibitions organized by the artists themselves. Preston described his complete surprise on arrival, after a dull journey out U.S. Rt. 6 during which time his spirits had lowered with the passage of each "weather-beaten" town increasingly distant one from the other, situated on land that looked like an abandoned golf course:

> Suddenly, improbably, an over-life-size granite replica of Siena's great watch-tower punctures the skyline. In a minute the visitor is at its feet, milling through the crowds in Commercial Street, sensing the indefinable atmosphere of a port town. What is at the Playhouse? Where is the forum

Berezov and Fine went to Provincetown each summer from the late 1920s until the early 1950s when they purchased land in The Springs on Long Island. (Photographed in the late 1930s.)

> on American Jazz of the Nineteen Twenties? Isn't that Hans Hofmann talking to Karl Knaths and Adolph Gottlieb? No doubt about it, Provincetown is becoming again what it was thirty-odd years ago, a meeting place of the arts. Here painters, writers and musicians are forced to awareness of the work of each other instead of languishing in the customary state of suspicious, crippling isolation. Paradoxically, an atmosphere of mutual recognition seems to strengthen painters' individualistic tendencies.

Visiting the galleries in Provincetown, Preston noted that there was as yet no "artistic crucible" that had melted into a particular Provincetown style; instead he found an "even balance between conservative and advanced works of art." However, it was Fine's painting that impressed him the most: "Far and away the most striking abstract is Perle Fine's dazzling canvas at Gallery 200, a flat pattern of laminated strips of sensuous color, blues, pinks and yellows, that pulsates from across the room."[2]

Therese Schwartz, one of the art students drawn to the sun and sea and the fabled art life at Provincetown, remembered the summer she became friends with Fine and the powerful impression she made:

> I met Perle Fine who was the first *real* woman painter I had ever known, and was at that time one of the group of abstract expressionist painters — such as Motherwell, Gottlieb, [Jack] Tworkov and Hofmann — then summering in Provincetown. Of all the painters, she was the only one who completely opened her studio to me, letting me hang about while she worked — an invaluable experience for me, for which I have always been grateful. She was an intense looking woman with glowing dark eyes and cropped black hair. Her costume was almost invariably rolled up jeans, a man's shirt, and a bona fide baseball cap, and always with a belt buckled with a military trophy, a souvenir her brother had saved from World War II. She rode a bicycle everywhere. She lived a very sparse existence in a studio complex built in an abandoned lumberyard.[3]

Some artists compared Provincetown's diffused light to that of the Greek Islands surrounded by the sea. Berezov dubbed the town "Montparnesse under the sun," after the section of Paris where many artists lived. To Motherwell, who also summered there during the 1940s, it offered "a distinctly warm southern light compared to Northern Europe, a light as seductive to painters in the modernist tradition as geometry was to the ancient Greek philosophers and musicians, not to mention Mohammedan designers."[4]

Provincetown allowed artists flexibility to do whatever they chose whenever they wanted. "The publicity which has centered on the landscape, the quaint streets, and the very popular art schools crowded with starry-eyed students, has left the professional artist in comfortable obscurity to work or play undisturbed," wrote Berezov. Provincetown had water on three sides: the Atlantic Ocean to the east and north, Cape Cod Bay to the west. One could watch from the same location the sun rise and set over water. To the south were empty beaches, rolling dunes, and scrub oak woods. But Provincetown also had numerous cafés where artists could gather and talk. "[The artist] merges with the crowds on the beaches, goes to picnics or sails a boat, but many an evening is spent in a sort of endless discussion of art and atelier gossip that one hears in the little bistros of Montmartre," wrote Berezov. "It is a comfortable existence except for the struggle and anxiety in creating a work of art."[5]

The principal goal of the professional artists was not only to relax but to find fresh inspiration in a lower-key environment to prepare for fall exhibitions. "In the comparative quiet of the side-streets of this little New England town, much of the avant-garde work of 57th Street is created, and canvasses being painted now will be exhibited in the coming Fall and Winter," wrote Berezov. "Theories and new ideas unfolding themselves on canvas will be tested before the eyes and judgement of the art world."[6]

Another major advantage was that Provincetown was inexpensive. There was ample studio space that didn't need to be heated, and when more space was required, there were fishing shacks, garages, and small cottages that could be pressed into service, and artists could live in their studios if they so chose. New York City had zoning regulations (often flouted by the artists) restricting the use of studio space to work only; artists could not live and paint in the same location (at least not legally), which was an onerous imposition on their ability to work at all hours of the day and night. Provincetown presented no such problems. Also, the town had a fishing fleet comprised of a large contingent of Portuguese fishermen, imbuing it with a working class and an ethnic flavor that was conducive to creating an artistic atmosphere. It also meant that fish were plentiful and cheap.

With the basics of life pleasantly and inexpensively provided, there was nothing to prevent an artist from painting. To Berezov, the atmosphere of Provincetown sparked creativity:

> The artistic bohemian quarter of Paris that lies in a soft haze of romantic nostalgia, on the left bank of the Seine, seems a far cry to a bustling summer colony on Cape Cod. The sleek, shiny cars driving through a fishing village, bright store facades built onto quaint cottages, the hordes of vacationists pouring out of buses and the daily boat from Boston, the whistle of the popcorn vending machine, the children with their picnic baskets, and the surprising number and variety of curvilinear forms on the beach under a bright, bright sun, would tend to discourage or at least soften the resolve of the most dedicated sycophant of the muses. But no, inspiration seems to thrive under these conditions.[7]

Besides the atmosphere itself, Fine had found inspiration at Hofmann's summer school, which she had attended in the late 1930s. But by the mid-1940s she was teaching on her own, although never on the same scale. Hofmann had sixty to eighty students, Fine four or five. Despite the difference in numbers, there seems to have been a little antagonism between them generated by competition. "Hofmann students follow me to beach, to lumber-yard, studio, everywhere, but do not dare to join my class, or risk not being asked to H's [Hofmann's] parties," Fine wrote.[8]

In a notice about her school published in the column "Art School News" in *Art Digest* in the spring of 1949, mention was made of Fine's unique approach to the problems of painting. "Those who saw Miss Fine's recent show in New York know that, as she herself says, she likes to make her paintings speak with color. Her teaching will make students proficient philologists in the language of paint. The basic aim of the instruction will be to bring out each individual student's expression."[9] A notice the following year included more information on the nature of the instruction:

> Still in New England, older schools include Perle Fine's summer painting group at Studio 6, No. 24 Pearl St. in Provincetown. This is a group working very much in modern idioms. Students having some experience in the understanding of modern art, or at least the desire to understand it are preferred. Criticisms and lectures are conducted more or less as group discussions. Rates are $50 per month, with special low rates arranged for school teachers.[10]

What Fine's students lacked in numbers, they made up for in loyalty. Schwartz found her to be "tremendously sensitive — openly responsive to others, easily moved to tears."[11] Fine enjoyed teaching particularly when the group of students was small enabling everyone to enter into discussion. "It's interesting to me that students given a very tired old problem will come up with such marvelous responses partly because they don't know completely what the problem is and partly because they're new people in a new world," she said. "That's one of the exciting things about teaching."[12] However, her willingness to speak her mind about aesthetic principles and her insistence that a certain level of painterly erudition was essential did not always win her friends. "The unspoken animosity of the artists in Provincetown to her superior abilities and authoritarian manner, found voice in underground stories circulated among the art community attributing this to oncoming menopause," wrote Schwartz, who thought that it would have been easier for Fine if she had "staked out an area of painting that the male painters could accept or did not consider a threat, such as Hartigan's Grand Street wedding costume display windows or Mitchell's delicate abstractions — which stemmed from her past as a figure skater."[13]

In the spring of 1950 when Fine turned 45, she considered not returning to Provincetown for the summer. Her reputation as an artist and teacher had developed to such a point that she had received an offer to teach at Black Mountain College in the hills of North Carolina. Es-

Fine's studio was in Days Lumber Yard, a building filled with natural light and an abundance of space. L to R: Fine, Hofmann, Bultman, Kootz in doorway, Peter and Florence Grippe.

tablished in 1933, Black Mountain was not actually a degree-granting college but principally a summer art school unusual not only for its location but for its interdisciplinary focus and its emphasis on experimentation. Established by Josef and Anni Albers, at various times the school was illustriously staffed by the dancer Merce Cunningham, the composer John Cage, the architect and visionary Buckminster Fuller, the writer Arthur Penn, the poet Charles Olsen, and the painter Willem de Kooning. Many of its students were to become equally famous, among them being Robert Rauschenberg. While never large (in its entire twenty-year span, only about 1,200 students attended), its influence was enormous and long-lasting, extending beyond its closing in 1953, particularly in respect to arts education and the importance of cross-disciplinary fertilization. Albert William Levi, head of the school, wrote to Fine on February 27, 1950, about the upcoming summer session: "In addition to teaching in sculpture, drama, writing, dance, music, and photography, we are very anxious in having with us a first rate painter. Do you think that you would be at all interested in coming to the college this summer?" One of the reasons why Levi was seeking a "first-rate" painter was that Albers had taken a position at Yale University in New Haven, Conn., and would not be returning to Black Mountain. Levi offered Fine and Berezov room and board, studio space, $80 a month in cash, and up to $100 of traveling expenses. As tempting as the offer was, Fine turned it down, choosing to return to Provincetown. With a major one-man exhibition scheduled for the following winter, Fine had to concentrate on painting, and for that her studio in the lumberyard was the place to be.[14]

Days Lumberyard housed the studios of many artists including Motherwell's who described what he called the barn as follows:

> The barn was beautiful to behold then, shingled, with arched barn doors on each floor (which I incorporated on the street side of my present studio-house at 631 Commercial Street); windows on all sides, with the radiant summer light of Provincetown that rivals the Greek Islands, because, I have always supposed, like them, Provincetown is on a narrow spit of land surrounded by the sea, which reflects light with a diffused brilliance that is subtly but crucially different from the dry, inland light of Tuscany, the Madrid pla-

> teau, of Arizona or the Sierra Madres in Mexico, where the glittering light is not suffused, but crystal clear, so that each color is wholly local in Hue, as in the landscape backgrounds of quattrocento Italian painting or in the late collages of Henri Matisse....At any rate, the Days barn was filled with lovely light, and with clean, open, large, aged space.[15]

The spaciousness of the lumberyard was to Fine's advantage, for her canvases were getting larger and larger, as were the canvases of all the Abstract Expressionists. With one of the biggest studios in the lumberyard, she had the ability to spread out, working on several paintings at a time, and seeing them in relation to each other. This was helpful in preparing for solo exhibitions because paintings needed to convey uniqueness and unity of vision simultaneously when hung in close proximity in a gallery. The high ceilings, long walls and large windows were a major improvement over the compression of her studio in New York City and encouraged contemplation of the art. "I did a lot of painting in the summertime and I had the paintings around all the time so that one would tell me what was wrong with another. One did have to study them," she said. "But I don't think you can work and study at the same time. It's too inhibiting. I think you work and work and stop. And when you've stopped, you can't just — at least I couldn't — go right back to working. I'd have to stop and study it."[16]

Just as spreading out and spending time was easier in Provincetown, so also the social life was unforced, combining the light-hearted and the serious. Besides sailing parties (Gottlieb had a boat he loved to race) and picnics on the beach, there were formal art exhibitions presented by the Provincetown Art Association and informal ones all over town wherever a studio door was left open. Gallery 200 also served as the setting for the popular Forum 49 lecture series, held every Thursday at 8:30 p.m. Organized by the artists Fritz Bultman,Weldon Kees, and Gottlieb, as well as his cousin the poet Cecil Hemley, admission was only 60 cents including tax. Sitting on folding chairs and surrounded by paintings, the audience listened to a wide-range of provocative speakers and topics, with participants drawn from the full complement of summer visitors: artists, writers, poets, architects, and psychologists. For example, the discussion on August 4, 1949, was on

James Joyce and T.S. Eliot with commentary by Howard Nemerov and Nathan Halper. The following week, August 11, Gottlieb chaired the discussion on "French Art vs. U.S. Art Today," in which Stuart Preston took part. This was always a hot subject for American artists who were still uncertain of their place in the world. On August 18, the topic was "Direction in 20th Century Architecture," with Marcel Breuer and Gyorgy Kepes. For the psychologically inclined, the topic on August 25 was "Finding Yourself Through Psychoanalysis."[17]

Psychology was of major interest to abstract artists because of the supposition that they were painting from their unconscious. Words such as sublimation, neurosis and gestalt spiced the conversation in Provincetown, often in odd, even humorous, ways. Fine, who said she never quite knew what the word gestalt meant, remembered a student, a well-known psychologist, trying to explain it to her:

> He was very enthusiastic about what I was teaching. He said, "But this is it! This is it exactly! This is Gestalt psychology." He was a very poor student I must say. He saw me after the session and he said, "I must bring you my masterpiece and show you because I'm sure you will understand." And he brought me the most horrible picture, surrealist, you know, the world in chaos. Absolutely nothing to do with painting.[18]

In a lighter mood, there was the annual Beachcomber's Costume Ball with the theme of infamous people, the crazier the costume and the more infamous the person the better. This was followed by the Artists' Costume Ball, held at the town hall, with the theme of famous people, for which Fine was one of the judges in August 1948. Appropriately the prizes were original works of art by Hofmann, Ben Wolf, Florence Leif, Gordon Peers, and George Yater, displayed beforehand at Cutler's, the local pharmacy.[19]

Despite the occasional frivolity, Provincetown was not shielded from what was going on in New York City, and in the summer of 1949 an incident occurred that troubled everyone. While artists may have felt acceptance in Greenwich Village and on the Cape, outside their immediate environs they were suspected of being leftists, a suspicion that was intensifying with the start of the Cold War. Artist groups, particularly those established in the 1930s, such as the American Artists Congress, often had a leftist political agenda. But when Russia joined the Axis, many American Marxists had undergone a radical change of heart, becoming staunchly pro-United States. In fact, the Federation of Modern Painters and Sculptors was formed in 1940 by a group of disaffected Trotskyites (including Clement Greenberg, Harold Rosenberg, and Meyer Schapiro) with the goal of making the United States the cultural world leader.[20] But none of this mattered to conservative politicians: as tensions with the Soviet Union increased and fear of total nuclear holocaust pervaded the country, a brief flirtation with Marxism in the 1930s was enough for branding. Art critics were especially vulnerable to the charge of being Communist sympathizers because they were perceived to be members of both the art left and the literary left, which meant the evidence against them was in print. It was much harder for right-wing politicos to determine whether an abstract canvas was essentially leftist than it was to determine that an art column was — at least by their standards of judgment.

One of the politicians who launched a sustained war on modern art was George Dondero, Michigan's representative, reading into the "Congressional Record" in March and again in May 1947 an attack on Communism and modern art, with his fury directed most heavily at critics. He called obliquely for censorship of art, although he did not use the word. From then on, a debate raged as to whether the new styles in art were "totalitarian" or "democratic." For example, in November 1947, a reviewer wrote that the Chicago Art Institute exhibition was "a mess of gibberish," and that it was "not art at all because it lacks meaning and beauty; it is not American because it stands for totalitarian dictatorship in the realm of ideas." Samuel Kootz promptly wrote a rebuttal: "What the modern artist seeks is greater feeling, greater emotional impact, through new inventions and intensified color. Why call him 'Totalitarian' because he refuses to remain academic? Wouldn't that accusation come strange from people who so strongly resent his departure from outworn standards?" Certainly, the word "totalitarian" would have been hard to affix to Fine's painting in the exhibition, about which Daniel Catton Rich, the director of the Institute, had written to her, praising its "color and fantastic power."[21]

In June 1949, Dondero increased his thunder from the right. Pleas for tolerance voiced by many people in the art community went unheard. That same month, Fine had a solo exhibition at the Betty Parsons Gallery, which she had joined following Nierendorf's death. The art critic Howard Devree used his review for *The New York Times* as a chance to goad Dondero: "Perle Fine makes an impressive singlehanded report — her first in several years — at the Betty Parsons Gallery. Doubting Thomas and carping Congressional critics are urged to attend instead of criticizing at long range and attempting to operate by remote control."[22]

The war of words took its first casualty the next month: Emily Genauer was fired by the *New York World-Telegram* after 18 years as art critic for the newspaper. Dondero had accused Genauer of being "very kindly" toward "left-wing so-called artists," and had pressured the newspaper to fire her. They obliged by eliminating the art page, thereby eliminating her job along with it, which made it seem as if it were merely a benign editorial decision. However, it was clear that the paper had capitulated. Dismayed that Genauer had not even been given the chance to answer Dondero's charges, Alfred Frankfurter, editor of *ARTnews* wrote, "The smear technique — of loose suggestion by mentioning casual associations, yet proving nothing — has apparently had its usual results."[23] Peyton Boswell, editor of *Art Digest,* was so troubled that he wrote in the September issue, "Congressman Dondero's near-sighted and totalitarian attempt to link modern art with Communism continues to cause more disruption in the art world than the weight of his childish arguments deserves. And yet there is so much danger to our democratic way of life concealed in Dondero's similarity to Hitler and Stalin that we cannot ignore his attacks on our system of free cultural enterprise."[24]

On receiving the news of the firing, Fine immediately wrote to Genauer from her Provincetown studio to express her outrage and to provide encouragement:

> I want you to know that the many fine articles that you've written have not gone unnoticed by me at least and many of my friends who are artists. They have been discussed privately and openly at art forums, etc. I've followed your work for years and considered you one of the most liberal,

> open-minded and generous writers in your craft. Perhaps we did not always see eye-to-eye but I always respected your opinion and the thoroughness with which you performed a really difficult assignment. I guess I just liked you.[25]

Despite the protests, the *New York World-Telegram* refused to rescind their decision and rehire Genauer. Even the strong stance of New York City's Republican Congressman Jacob K. Javits in support of artistic freedom made no difference. Javits had upbraided Dondero in Congress: "My colleague's personal opinion of modern art is one thing, but my colleague's suggestion that it should all be lumped together and discredited — perhaps suppressed — because he believes it is being used by some — even many — artists to infiltrate Communist ideas, is a very dangerous use of 'Communism.'"[26] Genauer herself was not intimidated by Dondero's bombast and in September thumbed her nose at him in an article provocatively titled "Still Life with Red Herring." Neither was *The New York Herald Tribune* intimidated: they promptly hired Genauer as art critic. Shortly thereafter, Fine wrote to congratulate her, although it was clear that the smoke had not cleared and more attacks from the right could be expected throughout the winter.[27]

The following summer, artists once again took the organizational lead in Provincetown, attempting to push back the boundaries of art, free of the oppressive hand of museum curators, exhibition organizers, and cultural philistines, challenging spectators to develop new definitions that not only transcended styles but also geographic borders. Highly unusual in this respect were interlinked exhibitions on both sides of the Atlantic in which Fine and Berezov participated. The first was the yearly "Réalités Nouvelles" (in which Fine had taken part in 1947) which ran from June 10 to July 15, 1950, at the Palais des Beaux-Arts de la Ville de Paris.[28] This was followed in August by "Post-Abstract Painting 1950: France, America," which was billed as the first international exhibition of advanced contemporary art in the United States since the Armory Show in 1913. Under the leadership of Fritz Bultman and Miz Hofmann, it was presented by the Provincetown Art Association at the Hawthorne Memorial Gallery.

In the "Réalités Nouvelles" exhibition catalog, which printed statements from the participating artists, Berezov wrote: "What is modern art? It is a new WORLD of the senses where the line may be lyrical, the form dramatic, and the color sensuous, gay, or bold; where the sensitivity of the artists creates beauty, the like of which has never existed before." For her part, Fine wrote of the role of fine arts in Ancient Greece where it was considered one of the servile arts, not one of the liberal arts, because it required manual labor. But finally the role of artist as an artisan had changed:

> There is no question but that today the modern artist has assumed his rightful position in the Liberal arts. His transformation has been a slow one. Over the centuries, through a constant process of renunciation and rejection of all that was obvious, pretty or puerile, he has at last come face to face with what is real in art. It has been no easy process of purification, for he has literally performed a miracle — he has made of as tangible an object as a canvas as intangible a spiritual work that it rightfully ranks with Music, Mathematics and Logic of the Ancients.[29]

While the exhibition was ongoing, Fine gave an impromptu lecture at the Provincetown Art Association. Since no subject had been announced for the evening, she asked the indulgence of the audience while she expounded some of her ideas regarding nature and reality. Exploring the need of the artist to "denaturalize Nature to deepen one's experience of it," she attempted to clear up a misconception held by many students and teachers about "imitating" nature. She did so by broadening the perspective into the realm of belief:

> But what are we to *believe* in Nature? What we see? My studio-window is a frame for the stars that make up the Big Dipper. I have *seen* them go away with the approach of dawn; and I have seen them reappear night after night, and take their *same positions* in the *same section* in the frame of the studio window. I have seen black skies and green skies and the ocean pale blue — the color the sky should have been. And even now, as we sit here quite calmly, I see men and women *hanging* on the walls of this room. In the studios of the artists, I have seen broken bottles and rusty wheels and yellowing newspapers and empty doughnut-cartons; and on their easels, inspired from

> these moulding, lowly objects were beautiful paintings, rich, moving and mysterious.[30]

The following month Fine returned to New York City, transporting the canvases on which she had worked over the summer back to her cramped studio on Eighth Street, five stories up with no elevator, in preparation for her upcoming exhibitions. From 1945 to 1953, Fine had seven solos, one at the Willard Gallery, one at the M. H. de Young Memorial Museum in San Francisco, two at the Nierendorf Gallery, and three at the Betty Parsons Gallery — a significant number, made possible in part by summers spent on a narrow spit of land, sheltered from the Atlantic Ocean by sand dunes, a place known affectionately to its summer inhabitants as P'town.

CHAPTER FIVE

MONDRIAN AND THE NATURE OF CLASSICISM

In the late 1940s, a multitude of isms — Existentialism, Freudianism, totalitarianism — vied for dominance, and all of them agitated the art community. If life had no meaning, then what was the role of the artist confronting the tragic void? Was painting a form of sublimated sexuality curable by psychoanalysis? Was abstract art playing into the Communist takeover of the world? Or was it the embodiment of freedom, as intrinsically American as the lone cowboy? And what about the lone cowgirl? The term was a non-sequitur.

Within the art world itself, there was an entire dictionary of yet more *isms*: Cubism, Synthetic Cubism, Surrealism, Automatism, Plasticism, Neo-Plasticism, Expressionism. How did these fit together, if at all? Which one was the opening to the future? What was objective, what subjective? The difficulty in finding answers was twofold: first, none of these questions could be answered separately from the others; second, many of the debates, fueled by alcohol, became heatedly verbal, and on occasion, violently physical.

Virtually all of these issues, *isms,* and personality clashes have a bearing on why many people in the New York art world changed their opinion of the work of Piet Mondrian following his death in 1944. What may appear on first glance to be an off-the-subject, arcane, even sterile, argument among artists and critics turns out to be a window into the era. It also provides insight into why Fine was not recognized along with Motherwell, de Kooning, Kline, Pollock, etc. as one of the major Abstract Expressionists, over and above the fact that she was the equivalent of the lone cowgirl — the non-sequitur.

Fine had a clear understanding of why she painted what she painted and was willing to defend the aesthetic principles she believed underlay pure abstraction. She also had the capacity to live with ambiguity, not becoming dogmatic or doctrinaire in defense of what she believed. She appreciated the mystery that her best paintings conveyed, knowing full well it could not be explained by an encyclopedia of art principles. Still, she believed that such principles did exist and that it was essential for the artist to know them well. While some had been promulgated by Hofmann, particularly two-dimensionality and the importance of the picture plane, for Fine the apotheosis of all of them was Mondrian's last unfinished painting, the incomparable "Victory Boogie-Woogie." Its broken jazz rhythms gave the canvas what she called "a wonderful swelling and receding quality." It was the only work in which Mondrian himself felt he was achieving the universal, as he put it, to move "the picture into our surroundings and give it real existence." He had told James Johnson Sweeney in an interview while he was working on the painting: "Many appreciate in my former work just what I did not want to express, but which was produced by an incapacity to express what I wanted to express — dynamic movement in equilibrium. But a continuous struggle for this statement brought me near. This is what I am attempting in "Victory Boogie-Woogie."[1] Without argument, no other artist in the world knew that final painting as thoroughly as did Fine.

It all came about because of an unusual double request made by Emily Hall Tremaine in 1947: First she asked Fine to make an exact copy of "Victory Boogie-Woogie." Then she asked her to paint what she called an "interpretation" that would reveal the painting as it would have been had Mondrian lived a few weeks longer.

Perceiving in it a transcendent power, Tremaine acquired the great diamond-shaped canvas in 1944 not long after the artist's death from pneumonia:

> I feel that the "Victory" was an intense breakthrough that was the culmination of Mondrian's whole life. The experience of it is wonderful. There is drama caught in it. It is like Beethoven's Ninth Symphony — the full orchestration — the chorus forcing octaves almost beyond human ears. Mondrian felt that nothing is ever finished — always processing from the material to the spiritual, just as high as you are able to go with it. There is no beginning and no end.[2]

Fine worked on the copy of *Victory Boogie Woogie* in an all-white studio with the same type brushes and paints that Piet Mondrian had used.

When Tremaine first saw the painting at the Dudensing Gallery in New York City, she asked her cousin A. Everett "Chick" Austin, director of the Wadsworth Atheneum in Hartford, Conn., to come to New York City immediately. "I've seen a picture where every door that Mondrian closed he has opened again," she exclaimed over the telephone. "There's a whole century of inspiration and art and ideas and vision in this thing." Upon seeing it for himself, Austin concurred: "Yes, isn't it true! He's opened every door."[3]

To give more power to the vertical and horizontal, Mondrian had chosen a diamond-shaped canvas, in essence, as he put it, hanging the painting "diagonally, as I have frequently planned my pictures to be hung," so that "only the borders of the canvas are on 45% angles." He also used small color planes instead of the black lines common in his earlier paintings, his goal being to "destroy those lines also through mutual oppositions." Only weeks before he died, Mondrian had completed the painting. But as was his way, he was not totally satisfied. Scrutinizing the canvas as it hung in his all-white studio, he concluded that it needed more rhythm and beat, in short, more "boogie-woogie," a form of music that he loved because he perceived of it as a "destruction" of melody. "I think the destructive element is too much neglected in art," he said. Just before he became ill, he reconsidered the location of some of the color planes, adding small pieces of tape as a means of experimentation. He died before he had a chance to replace the tape with paint, the result being a masterpiece that was, unfortunately, incomplete and unstable.[4]

Tremaine wanted a copy as a reference for restoration should the tape fall off. "Almost from the day it arrived, this collage began to tremble, and I realized that even losing one element might throw the whole thing off that Mondrian was working on, he was so exact," said Tremaine. She also wanted a fully rendered "interpretation," based on thorough analysis, that would serve as a stand-in for the original on the upcoming national tour of the Tremaine collection (then known as The Miller Company Collection). She was convinced that the original with its precarious pieces of tape could not stand the strain of traveling to 24 museums over a two to three-year period. Fine was a natural choice for the task because she had known Mondrian personally and was conversant with his theories of Neo-Plasticism. However, she was not the first one approached. Tremaine initially asked the artist Harry Holtzman because he had been instrumental in bringing Mondrian to the United States at the start of World War II and had been personally close to the artist. For unknown reasons, he did not follow through on the project at which point Tremaine approached Fine.

In a memo to an executive of The Miller Company (of which she was art director and her husband president), Tremaine wrote about Fine's visit to the Meriden, Conn., plant in October 1947 to determine whether she would take on the commission:

> Miss Fine realized that her position was that of a musician who finds a lost score which has never been played. It is one that requires extremely intelligent and sensitive interpretation. After studying the picture for several hours, Miss Fine has decided that she wants to accept the challenge and I have arranged that the "Boogie Woogie" be shipped to her studio on Monday October 20th, 1947. Miss Fine intends to keep a notebook as she proceeds with the work, noting her reasons for each decision as she proceeds with her canvas. I believe the result will be a most exciting contribution to the art world and particularly art students. Miss Fine has been an ardent student of all of Mondrian's paintings and writing and I feel there is no one in the country better equipped to carry out this very important work — a work that should be important in the history of art.[5]

Tackling the double task of painting an exact copy and an interpretation, Fine wrote to Tremaine shortly thereafter about the difficult transition of the project from Holtzman to her, for he was very possessive of everything that had to do with Mondrian and considered such a project to be his by rights. She had tried and failed to make clear to him "that it would be as conscientious an interpretation of a great work, that I, in all humility and love for that artist's work could make. Furthermore, since it is to be an interpretation upon which my integrity as an artist who has studied and practiced the laws of plastic spatial art as propounded by Mondrian stands, I stand ready to defend it, should it be necessary, to the fullest extent." Fine kept her word about conscientiousness. She painted in a pure white room with the same type of brushes Mondrian had used (all carefully numbered), and the same type of paint. As she told Tremaine, "Mondrian used pre-war unattainable cadmiums, permanent blues, etc., which very fortunately I have stocked up well on." In the process of painting, she discovered that Mondrian had used more than 20 shades of white, a fact which Tremaine had suspected and by which both she and Fine were intrigued. Fine wrote, "The whites are of such a nature that they actually have in them every color which was used in the canvas, red, yellow, blue, etc., in varying degrees. Thus the whites relate themselves to the various complexes; they unify and divide, according to the artist's wishes."[6]

Marian Murray, a journalist, visited Fine's studio while she was working on the interpretation and was impressed by the meticulous care coupled with reverential enthusiasm with which Fine approached the task. The "Victory" was covered by a sheet of transparent plastic for protection, while beside it:

> stood another, of exactly the same size, on an easel. Because Mondrian never held a palette, but mixed his paints on a white-topped porcelain table, there too stood a table, with mounds of red, blue, yellow, and white pigment....While painting, she wore a grey smock. Even that was deliberate. She placed Mondrian's canvas and her own side by side in exactly the same northern light. But when a white building across the court was repainted yellow it increased her difficulties by reflecting a light slightly different from that before. She changed her blue smock to grey, because the blue had cast back a fraction of its color onto the canvas.... Applying the paint requires a special technique, and Perle Fine congratulates herself that she had been able to watch Mondrian at work. "He caressed the paint," she said. "When you look at each area, it seems absolutely flat, but there is much underpainting, and he put down each stroke with infinite loving care. Look at those exciting complexes — here, for example, and here. See how the whole moves toward that largest unbroken area at the top. See how the form goes in and out, in that lovely controlled plastic quality, yet the sense of predetermined surface is never destroyed!"[7]

Yet another aspect of this unusual assignment was Tremaine's insistence that Fine do a complete analysis of the painting. To facilitate

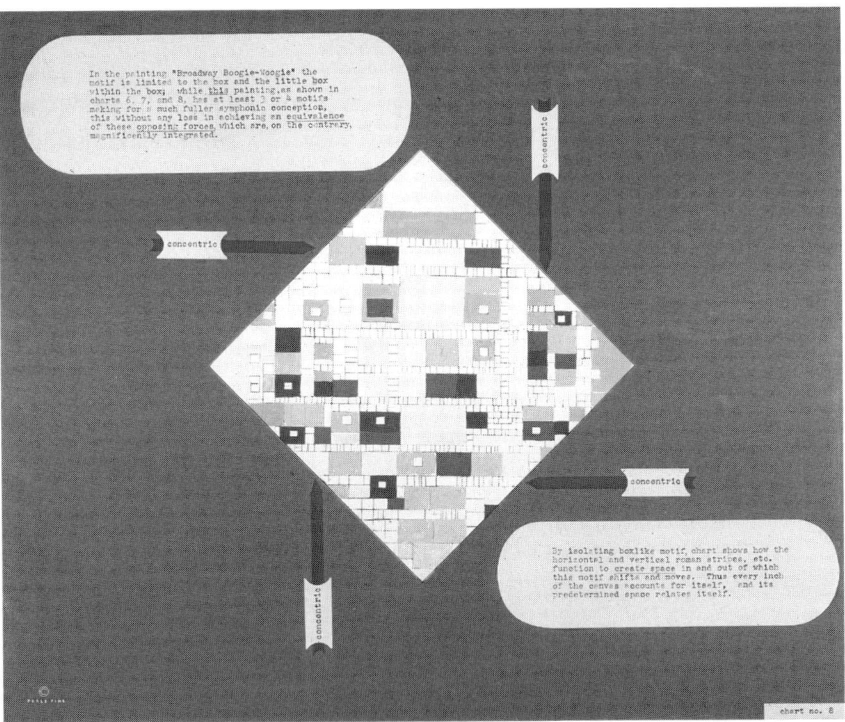

Fine completed a series of analytical charts of *Victory Boogie-Woogie*, which Tremaine intended to collect in a booklet for artists and architects, thereby enhancing Mondrian's influence, but for some reason it was never published.

the process, she sent Fine a dictaphone so that she could record as she was working "all the changes you feel Mondrian would have made in completing the picture." Tremaine also requested a set of annotated charts that she hoped to print with Fine's analysis in a booklet to be distributed to artists and architects thereby increasing Mondrian's influence. Fortunately, Fine shared Tremaine's sense of mission and was enthusiastic about the extra work. She wrote to Tremaine that Holtzman had complained to her about the enormity of the undertaking, "the canvas being so large, bending over, the great skill needed to match the colors perfectly, the fumes of the turpentine, etc. Of course, I know it's going to be a big job and one that cannot be hurried." Fine worked particularly hard on the deep blues:

> In the search for a key as to what hue to paint the deep blue areas, as they occur in the bits of colored paper in the original, I first looked for the deepest hue in blue that was actually painted somewhere in the canvas. I found one such plane just below the second yellow rectangle on the lower left half of the painting....This deep blue has caused me some concern and I have repainted some areas as many as eight to ten times, but when the blues functioned in relation to the other colors, it was always because they had the purity and depth of color but no blackness in them. *This is one of the most important discoveries of pure plastic painting.* Color is never given more or less *light attraction* through the use of *white* or *black* but through *change of hue* in relation to the other colors of the canvas.[8]

All the extra effort made Fine an acknowledged expert on Mondrian, and one of the few artists in the world who understood how revolutionary "Victory Boogie-Woogie" truly was. Fine discovered that Mondrian had entered "'upon a new and fuller conception of color," away from using only the primaries red, yellow and blue on which he had relied almost exclusively to give spatial dimension to his canvases. In the "Victory" he used gray, a shade he had not used for many years, to communicate a calm, ethereal movement toward the corners, and the multiple hues of white to create what Fine called "a straight into depth," while small black planes functioned as staccato notes. The overall musical impression was of a complex, insistent beat, moderated by slow, almost elegiac passages.

Furthermore, in "Broadway Boogie Woogie," painted prior to "Victory" in 1942, Mondrian had used a single motif, what Fine called his "box within the box." But in "Victory" he had used at least four motifs, which Fine explained as "making for a fuller symphonic conception and this without any loss in achieving an equivalent of the opposing forces, which are, on the contrary, magnificently integrated."[9]

Fine's interpretation toured the country with The Miller Company exhibition that was entitled "Painting Toward Architecture" in homage to Mondrian. Eventually it hung in the company's board room while the original hung in the Tremaines' living room in New York City. Two other works by Fine, "Midnight" and "Climax," were also included in the highly regarded tour, which interspersed paintings and sculpture by acknowledged European and American masters (among them Juan Gris, Férnand Leger, Picasso, Alexander Calder, and Stuart Davis) with that of lesser known American painters and sculptors, including Irene Rice Pereira and Mary Callery. Furthermore, the people involved in putting together the exhibition and its catalog were of the highest caliber including: Henry Russell-Hitchcock, art historian; Alfred Barr, director of the Museum of Modern Art; Vincent Scully, a young art historian at Yale University; Mary Chalmers Rathbun, who had been working at the Addison Gallery; James Thrall Soby, an influential modern art patron; and Chick Austin, who had left the Wadsworth Atheneum to assume the directorship of the John and Mabel Ringling Museum of Art in Sarasota, Florida.

The fact that Fine had literally lived with "Victory Boogie-Woogie" — studying it for days on end, spending hours mixing a single white tint — put her in a unique but not necessarily advantageous position. In the late 1940s, admiration for Mondrian's purist approach was turning to hostility in some artistic camps. Fine's own style was very different from Mondrian's. Critics had compared her work to that of Miró, even on occasion to Klee, but not to Mondrian. In an interview with Irving Sandler several years later, Fine said that for her, "expression through color and through an emotion about the color had become so necessary to express that it simply wasn't enough to do a painting in an absolute vertical-horizontal, black, white and red thing."[10] As

Fine's painting *Midnight*, her copy of *Victory Boogie Woogie*, and *Climax* were in the "Painting Toward Architecture" touring exhibition which opened at the Wadsworth Atheneum, Hartford, Conn., in December 1947. (L. to r.): Beatrice Kneeland, Henry Kneeland, Fine.

Jean Franklin had written in the pages of the *New Iconograph,* Fine's paintings were beautiful because of "delicate colors, varying effects of light, subtle complexities of formal and spatial relationships," not red-blue-and-yellow linearity. When the phrase Abstract Expressionist finally came into use, Fine would define her style as being within its amorphous boundaries. She was not attracted to pure geometric abstraction, preferring at this point in her career to work with "forms in space." Even other artists did not see her as a Mondrian devotee as indicated by a cartoon that Ad Reinhardt (who was known for his acerbically prescient cartoons about the peccadilloes of the art world) drew in 1946 for the Sunday supplement of *P.M.,* a New York newspaper. At the center of the cartoon stood a huge tree, its branches covered with leaves on which were the names of more than 200 artists (not including a few he buried unceremoniously in a corn field beside the trunk.) The leaf on which Fine's name appeared was on the middle abstract branch near the names of Norman Lewis and Melville Price. Other groupings on the same branch included Hofmann, Pollock, and Motherwell. Reinhardt did not place Fine among the artists he considered to be influenced by Mondrian, including Albers, Blaine, Glarner, Greene, and Holtzman.[11]

Nonetheless, Fine's willingness to defend Mondrian jeopardized her reputation as an incident at the Wadsworth Atheneum in Hartford, Conn., made clear. In 1946, someone vandalized a painting by Mondrian, drawing a circle on it and scribbling "Kilroy was here," the ubiquitous graffiti phrase that Americans loved to write on out-of-the-way or inappropriate locations and objects. Subsequently, *ARTnews* ran an article on the defacement in its January 1947 issue, but instead of expressing anger, the writer treated it as a joke in which "a pristine surface" was benignly sullied. He likened it to Jan van Eyck testifying to his own presence at a marriage ceremony by inscribing "Johannes de Eyck fuit hic" on his 1434 painting of the event. Angered by the dismissive tone of the article, Fine fired off a letter to the editor charging that their report was "in the height of bad taste," and that it would "only serve to encourage more of the same." *ARTnews* was unrepentant.[12] Its attitude was indicative of a shift in the perception of Mondrian only two years after his death. No one doubted that he had been an important pioneer of abstraction, but Mondrian's simplest compositions were deceptively complex and most artists did not totally comprehend what he was doing. He was also a European who had painted in a highly controlled, seemingly unemotional way, often reworking a painting for several years, striving for elusive perfection. This was very different from art being the automatic expression of a natural or unconscious impulse, the diametric opposite to, as one art critic put it, the "American fury" of Pollock.[13] To compound matters even further, he was a theosophist at a time when many New York artists had lost interest in arcane eastern-oriented philosophies, considering them irrelevant to a world haunted by the atomic bomb and the accelerating arms race. Instead many of them chose to embrace Existentialism with its emphasis on meaninglessness. Essentially, Mondrian's style was perceived of as the polar opposite of where certain critics, specifically Clement Greenberg and Harold Rosenberg, thought American art should be going. So thoughtful and meticulous was Mondrian's approach to painting that anyone who tried to follow his precepts ran the danger of being derivative. However, no one could quibble with Mondrian's integrity, and this meant that a wholesale overthrow of his principles and his work was virtually impossible.

In an article about a memorial exhibition of Mondrian's art at the Museum of Modern Art in March 1945, Maude Riley wrote for *Art Digest*:

> What may appear empty canvases at this point, frigid and abstemious to the casual observer (the work of the 1920s and 30s) are, on longer acquaintance, really remarkable paintings. No one can imitate them, no matter how simple seem the rules that direct them. For Mondrian was surely no less sincere and intense than Cézanne, another who notably cannot be copied and who painted searchingly and with concentrated reasoning, however painful and exacting.[14]

Every artist and critic of the era had to struggle to determine his or her position in regard to Mondrian. The artist Peter Busa believed that American artists were fascinated by Mondrian to the point of idealization, but that his formalist concepts were "in terms of the Americans' development much more strict than our own temperaments would allow." Busa considered the "graphic inventiveness of Picasso" to be more influential on Americans; unfortunately, this "clouded" for many years the understanding of Mondrian's concepts.[15]

Fine admired Picasso as much as she admired Mondrian and had worked out for herself the aesthetics that bound them:

> These artists on the surface are completely different, surely, but where Mondrian's intention is so manifestly clear, Picasso's intention is, on the other hand, not always so. Every painter makes as many problems as he chooses to make for himself. When Picasso did what appeared to be non-representational work, it was certainly extremely beautiful, and when he was painting Analytical Cubism, it too was very moving, very beautiful. Every phase of his work, without any symbolical connotation, has extremely beautiful examples in it. As an artist, I'd say they are beautiful because Picasso is cognizant of the elements that Mondrian demonstrates so purely, that he used these elements as well as other elements and played with them as a virtuoso, not as a novice; played with them and was often motivated by them in his purer phases, and surely was, and is, guided by them all through his work. Certainly a painter with the courage to plunge headlong into completely unexplored territories with only his and Mondrian's "compass" as a guide and direction will, of course, not always do masterful work, but the level of both of these painters is so high that there is no question of the genius of either.[16]

Barnett Newman was bedeviled by Mondrian, struggling to escape from his philosophy, which he considered to be sterile dogmatism. In fact, Newman's painting "Euclidean Abyss" was so named to confront what he considered to be the problem of geometry. Yet he himself was also routinely accused by critics in the late 1940s and early 1950s of aping Mondrian. In a review of his 1949 exhibition, published in *Art Digest*, Judith Kaye Reed wrote, "His pictures demonstrate what happens when art becomes an intellectual game instead of an adventure in communication. The majority of his large rectangular canvases are covered with a single flat color and divided into two or more areas by one or more lines in one or two colors. This is the kind of *reductio ad absurdum* art that may have refreshed some people and shocked many others back in the days when no advertising man had heard of Mondrian. Today, however, it is rather shocking for another reason: that a presumably serious and well-trained painter should find absorbing material in so sterile and played-out a game is surprising."[17]

Because his work was frequently compared to Mondrian's, Newman truculently tried, again and again, to distance himself: "I would say that Mondrian was definitely related to the theory of nature: his horizontals and verticals moved in relation to, you might say, platonic essences about the nature of the world. The things in a sense reflect a utopian idea about the nature of life. And this has had a powerful influence on all forms of culture. My position was very strongly against Mondrian in that sense. I respected him very highly, but I felt that I had to confront his notions."[18]

Ad Reinhardt and Robert Motherwell had similar difficulties determining how their styles related to Mondrian's, although Reinhardt did not see Neo-Plasticism as a dead-end and chose to continue with his own austere explorations. In 1942, Motherwell wrote in an article for the publication *VVV* that Mondrian's art was "clinical" and "a failure." Yet, Motherwell was uncertain of his own critique, admitting: "one wonders if this judgement of Mondrian is not too harsh." He concluded almost wistfully that "despite the arbitrariness of new self-imposed limitations, despite all this and more, a definite and specific and concrete poetry breaks through his bars, a poetry of constructiveness, of freshness, of tenacity, of indomitability, and, above all, of an implacable honesty, an honesty so thoroughgoing in its refusal to shock, to seduce, to surprise, to counterfeit, that in spite of one's self, one thinks of Seurat and Cézanne. Beside Mondrian the other abstractionists seem dull and grey."[19]

Art critic Clement Greenberg disliked Mondrian, contending that he functioned as a brake on true innovation. Greenberg had also begun to rail against the Museum of Non-Objective Painting and the American Abstract Artists. He hated geometric abstraction, finding it intellectually cold and sterile, therefore, he was opposed to everything Hilla Rebay as well as the AAA were trying to accomplish. To him they were deadwood that had to be gotten rid of. For example, about the 1947 annual AAA exhibition, Greenberg declared that "not a single important new impulse has manifested itself, since cubism and abstract post-cubist art, Kandinsky, Klee, and Mondrian, laid down a position almost thirty years ago. . . .Painting has had in the interim to content itself with intensifying its occupation of territory conquered long since." He attacked Judith Rothschild and Fine for "fruitless energy" in their paintings, and concluded that not one artist in the show "is bold, extravagant, pertinacious, or obsessed." Greenberg was familiar with Hofmann's ideas and often insisted that a painting should not be a window on a wall and should not have "holes" in it, but his attacks on the AAA indicated incomplete understanding of what it meant for a picture to be "behind" or "in front" of the frame, for which he was taken to task by George L. K. Morris, one of the founding members of the AAA. While he saw himself as a formalist, Greenberg chose to champion Pollock precisely because his work appeared to be uncontrolled and wild — "obsessed" — whereas Greenberg considered the AAA artists as being "mortally afraid of making fools of themselves" and overly influenced by Europe.[20]

What would increase Greenberg's power was his great gift of words, which he was not shy in strewing about in print, his overweening confidence in his opinions — he was known to stride through galleries, assessing the art almost on the run — and his role as an extraordinary promoter of the artists whom he considered worthy of carrying the mantle of greatness. Unfortunately, the converse was also true: he hindered artists he did not like, in some cases making it difficult for them to get dealers. Writing in *Partisan Review* and *The Nation* during the 1940s, his criticisms reached beyond the painters to literary people who were interested in what was happening in art but who were uncertain as to how to respond to pure abstraction and were looking for guidance and interpretation. No one wanted to walk into an Abstract Expressionist exhibition and look foolish by either chortling when one was supposed to frown or frowning when one was supposed to chortle. Greenberg may not have been clear in his articles, and there were jarring inconsistencies between his aesthetics (which changed over time) and the painters he championed, but he was passionate about his likes and dislikes. He was a zealot, and a zealot, even a disdainful one, is always more entertaining to read than an academician, especially when he has the ability to reach a broad range of readers. Until his arrival, there had been almost no overlap, and very little cross-fertilization, between music, dance, literature and the arts. In March 1946, Alfred M. Frankfurter, the editor of *ARTnews,* had bewailed such separation: "One really serious deprivation art must suffer in America is that it has so pitifully few advocates outside its own ranks. We have always lacked, and never more desperately than now, the cohesion of all the arts which in France has allowed painting and literature to flourish interrelatedly side by side."[21] Greenberg had many detractors, but he also had many readers beyond the narrow borders of art, so his influence was greater than might have been expected.

The real American painter, as Greenberg perceived of him, would be a male who did not feel the dead hand of the past on his shoulder but would assert a "new independent personality."[22] This theme, forcefully presented, showed up in many of Greenberg's reviews and articles on a wide range of artists, not just those associated with the AAA. At various times, he backhanded Georgia O'Keeffe by saying her paintings were no better than "tinted photographs," labeled Mark Rothko a "clinical paranoid," and called the paintings of Barnett Newman and Franz Kline "boring." In reviewing Gorky's 1945 exhibition at the Julien Levy Galleries, Greenberg asked whether his longstanding interest in Picasso and Miró meant Gorky lacked "masculinity of character."[23] According to Greenberg, any artist who was influenced by European painters was tied to the past (hence, not free) and feminine in character.

Fine saw nothing to be gained by returning to an America-first position in which anything remotely European was denigrated. That had been Benton's furiously defended position before the war. It was also, on closer inspection, artificial: Alexander Liberman, Louise Nevelson, and Mark Rothko (having changed his name from Marcus Rothkowitz) were Russian; Josef and Anni Albers and Hans Hofmann were German; William Baziotes was Greek; Willem de Kooning was Dutch; Hedda Sterne was Romanian. And Gorky, who committed suicide in 1948, hanging himself in his Connecticut studio, never was able to cast off his Middle Eastern world-view, riddled with the horror of the Armenian massacre. However, the jingoistic drumbeat, played with increasing fervor by Greenberg, had begun, although he himself would have strongly denied it. To him, the United States had become a political and military super-power. Therefore, it was only to be expected that it would also become an art super-power.

The irony is that artists and critics alike were caught up in Existentialism, the most European of philosophies. De Kooning remarked that "it was in the air." Suddenly it had become meaningful to be meaningless and artistically tragic. Existentialism was also right for the politically uncertain times when *iron curtain, cold war,* and *nuclear power* were disturbing new phrases in the international lexicon, for its emphasis was on the realization and development of the individual human being who was trying to live fully in an absurd world. It seemed as if everyone had a copy of *The Stranger* by Jean-Paul Sartre stuck in their pockets. They dropped the names Simone de Beauvoir, Jean Genet and Samuel Beckett, and inserted the words *angst* and *void* into their conversations. Fine's own words in a lecture she delivered in 1950 show the Existential influence: "It is the very precariousness of what is happening to an artist that holds my interest in him; and it is when he ceases to be troubled and to despair that my interest in him wanes and gradually disappears."[24] So also, Greenberg's language indicates his fascination with Existentialism, for example, his insistence that the painter free himself from over-reliance on the past, which could not provide meaning or guidance. Mark Rothko reiterated this Existentialist idea in his "Statement on His Attitude in Painting," published in *The Tiger's Eye* in 1949: "As examples of such obstacles, I give (among others) memory, history, or geometry, which are swamps of generalization from which one might pull out parodies of ideas."[25] Even the names of exhibitions and other art-connected events had Existentialist ties. For example, in 1949 Samuel Kootz presented at his gallery an exhibition titled "The Intra-subjectives," the title coming straight from the Existentialist idea of subjective perception. So also did the name of the short-lived school established in 1948 called The Subjects of the Artist. The word *intra-subjectives* did not catch on as a title and was eventually replaced by Abstract Expressionism and the more generic sobriquet the New York School, but only after an appropriately Existential battle over the irrelevance of choosing *any* name.

It is paradoxical, given the popularity of Existentialism, that some artists and critics would demand an American art free from European influence. The painter Nell Blaine, who was a member of the AAA at the same time as Fine, recalled that following the war a schism began to form between the artists who retained an open appreciation for the work of Europeans and those who appeared to break from it. To her the first group valued continuity while the second group valued fissure: "We weren't unfresh or lacking in the 'American Spirit,' but…this talk of 'American art' as superior and cut off from European was not only a distortion but also silly." There was growing hostility between the two groups which culminated for Blaine in the early 1950s when the European Max Ernst was invited to speak at The Club and was peppered with belligerent questions. Blaine was appalled at the treatment he received. "The idea was America the Great. I thought this view was destructive. But I suppose it's the same as with any minority group: American artists had had such an inferiority complex they needed to feel a sense of independence and at the same time create their own heritage. But I never wanted to break with the past."[26]

Neither did Greenberg, Pollock and the others desire as much of a break as they sometimes truculently demanded. Like a son who longs to surpass his father but also wants to be seen as his worthy heir, American artists were pleased when compared to Europeans. In fact, when an Italian critic writing about the Venice Biennale in the summer of 1950 wrote that Pollock's painting made "poor Pablo Picasso" look like a "quiet conformist, a painter of the past," Pollock was overjoyed. [27] No comparison to an American painter would have pleased him as much.

Harold Rosenberg, who along with his arch-rival Greenberg would become a major polemicist for Abstract Expressionism, was perturbed by rationality in art. Already he was formulating his idea of the man of action — the painter who didn't live a stale life of the mind, over-intellectualizing his canvases, but who made bold gestures with his brush which were marks of freedom.[28] This "action painter" who acted in the face of the absurd, creating meaning in the doing, was closely related to the Existentialist heros of Albert Camus and Jean-Paul Sartre (who often stayed at Rosenberg's home when he was in America). Rosenberg himself had a larger than life quality. He was over six feet tall, had dark hair and a heavy mustache, and was barrel-chested. He was not just physically big but psychologically big, making himself the center of attention whenever possible. If dramatic conversation was not taking place at a party or social gathering, he was not averse to dramatic monologue. He could talk all night and still be going strong in the morning. In a way, he was his own "action" figure, believing in spontaneity and improvisation as a means to be authentic. His writing style had the same bravado. Unfortunately, sometimes his articles sounded wonderfully profound on first reading but did not hold together logically on second reading.

In 1947, the image of the lone cowboy hero in a white hat single-handedly taking on the black-garbed bad guys with only a six-shooter had not yet reached mythic proportions in American culture. Certainly, the cowboy image had not been arrogated by the American artist, but it was coming. In its vanguard was the frequent use of the word "frontier" by art critics, which is where new art was supposed to be located. In fact, the title of Samuel Kootz's 1943 book was *New Frontiers in American Painting*. What was not verbalized was that the impetus for the elevation of the cowboy image was a need to look thoroughly American and not effete, essentially not to look like a Bolshevik. In the fuzzy thinking of middle-class Americans, New York intellectuals and artists looked like "sissies." There was a strong suspicion outside of New York City that all of them were either Socialists or closet Communists.

Another reason why the image of the lone cowboy became valorized so rapidly was that it was able to balance on the razor's edge between individualism and anarchism, and between good alienation, which was creative, and bad alienation, which was destructive. The cowboy didn't see himself as alienated, merely alone, and he liked it that way. If there were bad guys to be dealt with, he did so by himself with the help of his six-shooter. Furthermore, the cowboy was not only a loner — he also had an unspoken (since he was a man of few words) disdain for culture, particularly for Easterners with all their artificial airs.

One of the reasons Jackson Pollock became the first Abstract Expressionist to win broader public acceptance was that he looked like a hard-drinking ranch-hand in blue-jeans who instigated barroom brawls. Fortuitously, he had been born in Cody, Wyoming.[29] No one else fit the part as well, certainly not heavy-set Mark Rothko, Barnett Newman who liked to sport a monocle, or Robert Motherwell, who was too upper-crust, having graduated from Stanford University and pursued his doctorate at Harvard.

While there are many reasons why Fine was not included in the inner circle of Abstract Expressionists, certainly one of them was the stress she put on the importance of underlying aesthetic principles that an abstract artist needed to know. These were not to be strictly enforced in one style, such as geometric abstraction, as her admiration for Matisse, Cézanne and Picasso made clear. On the contrary, individual expression mattered greatly. Without it, Fine insisted the result was "sterile imitation." She wrote that Mondrian "himself was often heard to urge artists to work out their experiences in their own way."[30] Essentially she was a classicist at the point when artists were not overly fond of the word. As Pollock put it, "I am nature." To which Fine would probably have retorted, "but even nature has underlying laws."

She was not the only painter who brought to Abstract Expressionism a classicist approach. Gorky and de Kooning had been known as "painter's painters" since the 1930s. In fact, they tended to be impatient with artists who were not knowledgeable; both could discourse at length on theory, and neither eschewed figuration. De Kooning took a long time on each painting, often erasing work but not entirely, until his canvases became palimpsests. Hofmann was certainly in agreement with Fine, evident not only in his words but in his work. Nor was she the only one to defend Mondrian. Reinhardt did. Motherwell did reluctantly. But she was one of the few who openly took the position that the best purely abstract painting was in fact classical. She would have agreed that painting could be a form of self-disclosure in which the artist himself was the subject, as Pollock and Rothko maintained. (Newman went even further, insisting that artists spent their entire lives painting a single portrait of themselves.) However, Fine would have added that a painting must first be a form of aesthetic disclosure. To her, there was such a thing as beauty that was independent of figuration, did not arise from psychological necessity, and yet was humanist in the sense that it hinted at a deeper potential in humankind.

Twice in 1949 Fine vehemently made her case. The first was a long letter to the editors of *ARTnews* published in January 1949. She wrote in response to the content of the December 1948 issue: the editorial, four articles on classical art and one article on abstract art, all of which had been spurred by the recent publication of *Aesthetics and History in the Visual Arts* by Bernard Berenson, the internationally known critic and scholar, whose studies of Italian art shaped generations of art historians. In his editorial, Frankfurter stated that Berenson's thesis "is that there *are* standards, and that values can be arrived at" and that a spectator must have a "trained mind." Berenson's conclusion, as quoted in the editorial, was "that nowadays we are in the midst of a decline which, like all cultural declines, ignores its symptoms and euphorically imagines that it is revolutionizing the world when it is merely playing the infant, kicking, screaming and smashing, or daubing and kneading with paint and clay." The four articles, accompanied by nineteen photographs and spread over eight pages, were followed by a two-page article "The Whitney; exhibit Abstract" written by Thomas B. Hess, then managing editor. Hess criticized George L. K. Morris's "Unequal Forces No 2." included in the Whitney Annual as a complete failure: "The whole problem of fitting colored shapes into an interesting arrangement is here reduced to a pseudo-scientific laboratory level." On the other hand, he praised "Wood of the Holy Cross" by Rico Lebrun as showing old methods of abstraction used in new, personal ways. However, Lebrun's painting, reproduced on the page, was clearly of the cross, even to the inclusion of the mocking sign nailed to the top.[31] Fine's letter was blunt: "Sir: Why is there such a discrepancy between the quality of your articles on the Classical...and the 'Abstract,' such as the one on the Whitney exhibition? Why have your reviewers been so lax on even the most basic elements concerning abstract art?" Referring to Berenson's statement on the need for trained minds, Fine charged that "for the first time in the history of art, the spectator is called upon to come to modern painting with some background and some sound knowledge of painting in order to enjoy and later, perhaps, to judge the work. It assuredly follows that the reviewer should have at least this background to be able to report what occurs." These were fighting words, for Fine was calling Hess uneducated. Unfortunately for Fine, Hess was on the verge of becoming one of the arbiters of taste during the height of the Abstract Expressionist period and beyond. But she didn't stop there:

> To call the LeBrun an abstract painting is an absurdity, for every element which goes to make an abstract painting is lacking in this one: *color, determined form* in *determined space,* tensions between these forces, two-dimensionality and its ensuing reciprocal action, concentricity, etc. On these bases, it is the LeBrun rather than the Morris which should be called the retrogressive since it shows not the slightest break with the photographic sort of painting that is sometimes called the academic. Half-close your eyes and you will see nothing more than a photographic image in the Lebrun. The Morris, on the other hand, is far more progressive primarily because it stems from the neo-plastic idea of pictorial life within the canvas.[32]

She closed her letter by stating that such a lack of understanding might be expected of lesser art publications that "have no caliber, no sensitivity, no erudition," but that "one hopes for more in *ARTnews*."

One month later, LeBrun wrote a reply to *ARTnews* in which he defended Hess: "I don't believe he needs to be instructed through the statement of Miss Fine." Derisive of Mondrian, LeBrun took umbrage at the implication in Fine's letter that his approach lacked courage:

> One can with honor and fully aware responsibility, be dedicated to the making of images carrying within them the sum total of a visual tradition so vast, so ancient and multi-faceted as to be anonymous. To accept this challenge does not indicate lack of intellect nor courage. It is precisely because of the avalanche of pretentious, futile revelations of the so-called "plastic elements" that the latest efforts in painting point to a collective will to forge identified substance into the framework of design....Conservatism dies hard, even when the barricades are as carefully spaced as a Mondrian.[33]

Ripples of this acrimonious debate over pure abstraction, objectivity and realism continued over the next year. For de Kooning especially, who was a friend of Fine's, the implication of her disagreement with Lebrun over his painting of the crucifixion loomed large, because de Kooning was already working on "Woman One," the first of his series of gargantuan and brutally fierce figures, profoundly identifiable as female. Already considered to be one of the leaders of the new movement (Pollock being the other), de Kooning was in many ways the antithesis to both of the models of the Abstract Expressionist hero as put forth by Rosenberg and Greenberg. He was Dutch, spoke with an accent, embodied a European tradition, worked and reworked his paintings, and never rejected figuration. As a participant in the three-day conference called the Artists Sessions at Studio 35, which took place from April 21 to 23, 1950, de Kooning alluded to the argument between Fine and LeBrun and the role of Mondrian after a comment was made that Motherwell painted stripes:

> If we talk in terms of what kinds of shapes or lines we are using, we don't mean that and we talk like outsiders. When Motherwell says he paints stripes, he doesn't mean that he is painting stripes. That is still thinking in terms of what kind of shapes we are painting. We ought to get rid of that....Mondrian is not geometric, he does not paint straight lines. A picture to me is not geometric — it has a face....It is some form of impressionism....We ought to have some level of professionalism. Some part of painting has to become professional....What is called Mondrian's optical illusion is not an optical illusion. A Mondrian keeps changing in front of us.[34]

From the drastically edited transcript of the sessions (which is all that remains), de Kooning then said: "I wonder about the subject-matter of the Crucifixion scene — was the Crucifixion the subject-matter or not? What is the subject-matter? Is the interior subject-matter?" It is as if his statement about Mondrian and the need for a level of professionalism led him inexorably to the dilemma of objectivity as exemplified by the LeBrun painting.

The second time Fine defended classical principles occurred in early September 1949 when she gave a speech in Provincetown as part of the Forum 49 series, held each Thursday in late summer at Gallery 200. She began humorously, saying that to explain modern art was a perilous undertaking especially before an audience filled with artists, critics and teachers: "So there will be a brief pause while all those who wish may turn a deaf ear this way." Then she drew a rectangular plane on a piece of paper and talked about the difference between depth and perspective and the attainment of equilibrium through the "direct play of rhythms and counter-rhythms." She ended by encouraging artists to see "*better* composition, *better, purer* color, *clearer* forms," which, when followed by "*intelligent analysis* and *use* of the knowledge we have today will bring about some really great painting." But she closed with a sharp barb: "Out of the 10,000 artists working in New York today, there are perhaps no more than 10 who understand and employ this knowledge."[35]

Therese Schwartz, then a student of Fine's, remembered the lecture well, although she recalled the final number as different:

> During this time when abstract expression was still fighting to gain a foothold, many of the discussion panels sponsored by the Provincetown Art Association pitted the artists against the most articulate of the summering Freudian psychiatrists (present in great numbers). Most of them thought ab-ex an aberration and indicative of an unresolved personality. Perle Fine was a frequent panelist, able to speak her mind and defend the principles of this new movement. She was greatly respected by the other artists, mostly male, but her uncompromising personality did not make her a favorite among the men. Once, appearing on a panel, and in defense of her strong post-Mondrian principles, she said that there were probably no more than 10 people in the United States who understood the basic tenets of visual abstraction and in that room there was but one.[36]

Whether the number was ten in the United States, ten in New York City, or only one, the point was the same. And no one in Gallery 200 that evening had to ask who the one was.

CHAPTER SIX

THE TURBULENT DECADE

In 1948, Fine had her first solo exhibition at the Betty Parsons Gallery — a gallery that was up-scale, urbane, and heir to Peggy Guggenheim's mantle although it did not possess the zany mystique of Art of This Century. On viewing the fifteen paintings in June 1949, Robert Coates, art critic for the *New Yorker,* was so overwhelmed by their quality that he felt compelled to write Fine a personal letter of congratulations: "I must say I thought the pictures looked, well, stunning, they were so strong, assured, and powerful."[1]

In the hushed, white-walled atmosphere — so different from the good-natured maelstrom at Nierendorf's or the surrealistic glitz of Guggenheim's — hung "Poem Without Words #1" and "#2," "Variations on a Theme #1" and "#2," "Spinning Figure," "Summer Studio #1" and "#2," "Theme Blue," "Iconic Mutations," "Turning and Twisting," "Pure Myth," "Bicycle Forms," "Figuration in the Shape of a Diamond," "Pink Harlequin," (also titled "Pink Troubadour,") and "Progressively Affluent." Fine wrote in the catalog: "I like to light up a canvas with color. I like to make it shout or whisper; I like to make it spin — or make forms melt softly over the whole picture." Howard Devree wrote in his *The New York Times* review that not "all the paintings were judged to be successful in bridging the gap between innovation by the artist and comprehension by the observer, but those that were successful displayed a breadth of vision, organic construction, and a distinctive spatial sense that conveyed a remarkable movement through the painting as a whole."[2]

"Bicycle Forms," a gouache on paper, is an excellent example of Fine's ability to convey a sense of complex motion punctuated by points of stillness (see color plate). Strongly angular, the focus is not on the circularity of the wheels but on the triangular patterns made by the spokes, shot through with the glint of sky-blue, sun-yellow, and dirt-brown, bounded on the periphery by blue and black. It is not a painting of a bicycle (without the title, a spectator would make no association with a bicycle at all) but of the impression of movement across a summer landscape seen through turning parts. The only horizontal plane is deep blue and juts from the right edge toward the center as if it were the ocean providing a stable horizon line.

Judith Kaye Reed, the conservative critic for *Art Digest,* was one of the few critics who were equivocal about the exhibition. During this period, Reed struggled to understand what non-objective art was communicating, a struggle she shared with many others. Reviewing Ad Reinhardt's exhibition a few months after Fine's, she took him to task for painting "personal solutions to problems that do not hold the same challenge or interest for the observer." Her criticism of Barnett Newman's exhibition was similar: "His pictures demonstrate what happens when art becomes an intellectual game instead of an adventure in communication." About Fine's art, she raised the same issues. Referring to Fine's statement about making color shout, whisper, spin and melt, Reed wrote in her review titled "Canvases Lit with Light": "All these things Miss Fine does remarkably well — along of course with considerably more. But whether her personally exciting adventures in paint are always of much communicative value to the observer is a question not always answered in the affirmative."[3]

Taken as a whole, the reviews from both conservative and liberal critics were favorable and encouraging. It appeared as if Fine were on the verge of success. Indeed, the next five years were highly productive for her, with two more solos at the Betty Parsons Gallery in February 1951 and December-January 1952–53, and participation in numerous group exhibitions, enriched by the daily interchange of ideas with other artists. However, the association with the Betty Parsons Gallery ultimately proved to be frustrating for a multiplicity of intertwined reasons, chief among them being, paradoxically, the improving economy. Following World War II, the U. S. economy had gone through a sluggish period. Few artists working non-objectively were financially secure, not even Pollock, unless they were independently wealthy or had other sources of income. The painter Jon Schueler, who came to New York in the early 1950s, remembered de Kooning's laconic reply to being asked what he earned from the sale of his paintings: "Well, two years ago I wasn't selling them for $400 and now I'm not selling for $800."[4] With the chances of success being remote, competition between artists was somewhat dampened, there being no money, no fame, and no prizes for which to compete. Then as the 1950s picked up momentum, the economy finally took off, the standard of living began to rise, and competition became stiff. Between 1949 and 1956, the GNP jumped 4.7 percent, and people were spending not only on consumer durables but also on luxury items. Art was selling again. Wealthy collectors, who had the financial ability but not the aesthetic nerve, were emboldened by the emphasis that was beginning to be placed by art critics and museum curators on Abstract Expressionism (the name that finally trumped non-objective, which with its oblique reference to Buddhism was too obscure for almost everyone but Hilla Rebay). It was also becoming acceptable to buy American, not just European. In her book *Prestige, Profit and Pleasure: The Market for Modern Art in New York in the 1940s and 1950s,* A. Deirdre Robson explains the escalation in the prices that resulted as the decade progressed:

> Although the remarkably high prices fetched by Pollock's work in the late 1950s undoubtedly owned a good deal to his "nonliving" status, the prices of the other Abstract Expressionist artists also rose substantially in these years, as their critical and commercial standing became more assured from the early 1950s onward as a result of greater critical coverage situating them within the development of twentieth-century modernism, institutional exposure in both temporary exhibitions and permanent collections, and their appearance, like Pollock, in prestigious promoter-validator galleries such as [Sidney] Janis's.[5]

Robson does not analyze how these changes affected women artists specifically, but it is clear that the increase in institutional acceptability of Abstract Expressionism worked to the detriment of women, as did their under-representation in what Robson calls "the promoter-validator galleries," in which category she lists those of Janis, Kootz, and, at a slightly later date, Leo Castelli. Pointing out the shift in collecting patterns that was occurring at this time, Robson maintains that "the arts were gradually thought of less in terms of being part of the 'female' realm and more as an interest suitable for a hardheaded and successful businessman."[6] When collectors began buying art not only for aesthetic pleasure but as a business investment, long-term appreciation in value became important, which meant that the name on the canvas mattered as did the gender attached to that name. Rarely did collectors admit that financial gain entered into their purchase decisions. But in terms of eventual re-sale, they would have admitted that it was more prudent to buy a painting by Jackson Pollock than one by Lee Krasner, or a sculpture by David Smith instead of one by Dorothy Dehner.

The GI bill, which paid college tuition for servicemen following the war, exacerbated this trend because it enabled a large number of young men to enter art history programs. Prior to the war, a degree in art history was pursued only by a small upper-class group generally at select universities, Harvard being one of the foremost. But after the war, college programs expanded exponentially as did the number of students enrolling. By 1950, there was an influx of young impressionable male art historians — degrees freshly printed — into New York City. They helped to fuel what Thomas Hess called the institutionalization of Abstract Expressionism that took place in the 1950s:

> As soon as a painting was finished, museum and university trainees would accept, classify and tag its look. Sainte-Beuve's dream of a Botany of Intellectuals had come true. The social protest inherent in modern painting — its essential aspects that shock or startle or disgust at first sight — was muffled in a "big yes" of specialized professional taste (that only de Kooning's "Women" have been able to contradict since). And if a painter like de Kooning made some pictures that were a bit too difficult to be understood immediately, his followers diluted the concept and made it readily available in a matter of weeks.[7]

By 1950, Emily Genauer of *The New York Herald Tribune* and Peyton Boswell of *Art Digest* were disturbed by the speed at which the paintings of certain artists were entering museums. Because it took time to determine quality, they contended that works entering permanent collections too rapidly had not been properly and painstakingly vetted. On learning that the Museum of Modern Art owned four works by Motherwell, had just purchased yet another work by Gorky (bringing the total to three) and a second by Pollock, having purchased the first from his initial one-man show at Art of This Century in 1943, Genauer criticized the museum for being selective and subjective. "If the Modern Museum does indeed believe that the highly controversial Jackson Pollock and Robert Motherwell are among the greatest artists of our generation, should it not attempt to explain why to a bewildered public?" Genauer was particularly bothered by the attention being paid to Motherwell. "As a conscientious critic eager to receive new ideas and forms in art with understanding and sympathy, I have been increasingly concerned with my inability to go along with the small but influential group of collectors and museum officials who have been extolling Motherwell to the skies." Boswell agreed: "My personal opinion is that Pollock, Motherwell, Gorky & Company are as far from being the Vermeers of our generation as I am now from the town of Delft." In the next issue, he wrote another editorial in which he added to the reasons why the museums were acting unwisely in canonizing certain artists: "Aside from the speed with which most bad abstraction can be turned out, here is the enervating factor of the fashionable adoption. A museum director who buys at the right time to influence a small but powerful group of patrons greatly aids the imitators of the New Academy along the road to temporary fame." In other words, by purchasing too fast, museums were giving a false imprimatur to these artists, thereby encouraging imitation of what should not be imitated.[8] Over time, this process tended to solidify the reputations of the artists dubbed "the Giants" by Betty Parsons. Their work was seen more frequently because it was owned by museums and well-known collectors who were willing to lend the works for numerous exhibitions and retrospectives. Soon a storm of paper began to swirl around this small group of painters as art historians and graduate students focused on it. Conversely, this meant that significant paintings and sculpture that had been erroneously, and all-too-rapidly, judged to be of lesser quality were consigned to the ignominy of storage, were lost, or even destroyed, so that no further assessment — no fresh look — could easily occur. It happened to men as well as women, and left some of them bitter for the rest of their lives.[9]

Not surprisingly, an artist's chances of being selected as a member of the mainstream increased if he had a hyperbolic personality, either in person or in print. The composer Morton Feldman who knew the Greenwich Village artists very well, drinking with them in the neighborhood bars and visiting their studios, told art historian Dore Ashton that it was crucial for a painter to have charisma. According to Ashton, Feldman "arrived on the scene soon after Gorky's suicide, and remembers that he heard nothing about Gorky's work — only about the man." He also heard anecdotes about Hofmann, de Kooning or Pollock but seldom anything about their art.[10] Bombast was also useful because it was repeatable and made good press copy. For example, Barnett Newman wrote of his painting "Vic Heroicus Sublimis," shown at the Betty Parsons Gallery in 1951: "What is to be pitied is love of impotence…fear of the creative man…man spelled masculine.…No matter how many it takes to tango it takes only a real man to create a work of art."[11] Clyfford Still often spoke in language equally god-like, stating that his freedom was "absolute," and that his artwork was one of the "truly liberating concepts mankind had ever known."[12]

In such a frenetic atmosphere heated by charged rhetoric, Fine was an anomaly. She was not a hermit but neither was she overly social. Always polite, she was never ingratiating. Robert Richenburg, her friend and fellow artist, described her as reserved: "She had a unique style. There was a soft mystery to it. Her paintings were always well-composed. I liked her but she was quiet and remote, off in her own cloud — and very beautiful."[13] However, even if she had been flamboyant and her paintings visually outrageous, it would not have made a difference. There were larger cultural forces at work that would bring about Fine's eclipse even as she was beginning to be noticed. Despite her stellar solo exhibitions, she never made a single sale directly through the Betty Parsons Gallery. More than five years of effort yielded nothing. Yet at the beginning of her relationship with Parsons, Fine appeared to be in the right place at the right time.

In the contract dated May 1948, Parsons was entitled to one-third of the selling price on all sales of pictures and commercial assignments. If a sale were made by Fine in her "studio to clients outside the gallery's clientele," Parsons was entitled to 15 percent. While Parsons was responsible for promotion, all additional expenses including cata-

Betty Parsons, in front of *Pink Harlequin* at Fine's 1949 exhibition, was an artist herself and was respected both for her abilities and her sensitivity toward the painters she represented (See color plate).

logues and photographs were Fine's responsibility. It was a standard contract, but because the few paintings that were purchased during this period were handled by Fine through her own studio or occurred because of her inclusion in group exhibitions (for example, the sale of "Submarine" to The Whitney Museum of American Art following its inclusion in one of the annuals), all Parsons ever earned was the 15 percent commission.[14]

Still, the Betty Parsons Gallery was the place to be. Compared with that of the other major dealers promoting Abstract Expressionism — Kootz, Janis, and Charles Egan among the most prominent — Parsons's stable of artists was large, heterogeneous, and prestigious. Although she was not an aggressive marketer, she was respected for her integrity and the fact that she was willing to showcase art that was aesthetically challenging, hence difficult to sell, for example, Newman's "zip" paintings. She championed a troublesome Pollock (hesitantly taking on his contract after Peggy Guggenheim had moved to Venice), put up with the demanding personality of Clyfford Still, and endured the oddities of Richard Pousette-Dart. In some ways she was the scion of Guggenheim, but the two women could not have been more different. Parsons wore her dark hair in a trim page-boy that accentuated her high, rounded forehead. She dressed in trim suits appropriate for a business lunch. Conversely, Guggenheim attempted to personify the avant-garde. (At the opening of her gallery Art of This Century, she wore a miniature mobile by Calder in one ear and a surrealist earring by Yves Tanguy in the other.) Parsons was also willing to promote women, representing at various times Buffie Johnson, Lee Krasner (albeit only one solo exhibition), Anne Ryan, Ethel Schwabacher, and Sonya Sekula. Guggenheim cared nothing for women artists and, in fact, poisoned her relationship with Krasner when, on a visit to see Pollock's paintings, she noted a painting by Krasner and screamed "Who's L. K.? Who's L. K.? I did not come up here to look at L. K.'s paintings!"[15] Parsons was an artist herself, having had periodic exhibitions at the Midtown Gallery beginning in the late 1930s and continuing throughout her life, and so was aware of how deeply such slights could cut. She was also a collector who moved easily through upper class society, which was important from the standpoint of gallery clientele. According to Lee

Hall, her biographer, "As a consequence of Betty's social connections, she enjoyed the interest and support of rich friends who, in turn, had rich friends who could be enticed into the gallery. Betty claimed always that she had no talent for or interest in 'hype.' In actuality, she put her gallery in the news and kept it there. For the most part, she attracted attention in a good-mannered fashion, setting out to interest friends in her work and her cause."[16]

On the other end of the dealer scale was Sam Kootz who had been marketing aggressively to the burgeoning upper middle class since the end of the war, putting himself in the position of an arbiter of taste. Kootz did not wait for a customer. Without Parsons's wealth, he had to hustle, which he did by means of new marketing techniques and unrelenting salesmanship. For example, in June 1946 he presented an exhibition that sounded like an article for *House and Garden,* "Modern Painting for a Country Estate: Important Painting for Spacious Living." In 1950, he mounted an exhibition in which he asked five architects to supply plans for buildings that were large enough to display murals, then he asked five artists (Baziotes, Motherwell, Gottlieb, Hofmann, and Hare) to supply "decorations which would fit." Such exhibitions were not as upper-crust as Parsons's approach, but they were more effective in attracting a new group of potential collectors to his gallery. In reporting on the Kootz show, Doris Brian wrote that "dealers in contemporary art are beginning to create brand-new markets for their boys."[17] Her use of the word "boys" was apt. According to Motherwell, Kootz "liked strong, masculine, semi-abstract artists" in his gallery.[18] The first group exhibition at his gallery to include women, "Talent 1950," in which Nell Blaine, Jane Freilicher, Helen Frankenthaler, Grace Hartigan, and Joan Mitchell took part, was curated by Clement Greenberg and Meyer Schapiro, not Kootz. He could also be extremely callous, injuring the reputations of artists in whom he had lost interest, the most egregious example occurring in 1951 when he sold off works by Byron Browne and Carl Holty at Gimbel's Department Store, as if the paintings had no more worth than discounted dry goods.[19]

For Fine, the atmosphere in the Betty Parsons Gallery was not affirmative as it had been at Nierendorf's and Willard's. "It was the custom

About her 1949 solo at the Betty Parsons Gallery, art critic Robert Coates wrote to Fine: "I must say I thought the pictures looked, well, stunning, they were so strong, assured and powerful."

in the gallery for the male members to be supportive of one another and to help in the mounting of each other's shows," wrote Therese Schwartz. "Fine's exhibits went unsupported by the others — hanging her show was not a group activity — and left her with a feeling of loneliness. Although her work firmly belonged in this group, personally she felt an outsider." [20] Buffie Johnson, who was in the Betty Parsons Gallery at the same time as Fine, knew the feeling well, finding the men "dismissive of women." She felt that the only reason she received better treatment than the other women was because she was married to the writer Gerald Sykes with whom Newman was very impressed. According to Johnson, Sykes wrote "the most cruel reviews in *ARTnews*. I ameliorated those."[21] Therefore, her presence in the gallery was tolerated.

Yet for her part, Fine attempted to be supportive of the other artists in the gallery. For example, when Rothko exhibited his soft rectangular canvases of diffused, glowing color — which were for him a religious experience both in the creating and in the seeing — at the gallery in January 1950, Fine tried to calm him down and encourage him after the show opened. "He was very nervous and excited about it. He saw me on the street and we went and had a drink together and he talked about his work....He was completely uninhibited by any of the moods, you might say, that I set for myself or anything like that, which was a great help to him."[22] While Fine felt that both of them were working with "quiet complexes of color," their objectives were different. For one, while she often used the word mysterious to describe her art, she did not interpret that word as indicative of sublime transcendence with which Rothko was concerned. Nor was she motivated by myth, as Rothko had been in the 1940s when he had painted "The Sacrifice of Iphigenia" and from which his new paintings were descended by means of simplification and emotional compression. Fine explained:

> I seemed always to be concerned about the thing itself. The thing made the problem for me....And yet in quite a few of my paintings I realize that the paintings that had a sense of myth in them were the more successful ones. Which is another way of saying that the ones that depended more largely on the design, say, were less successful even though the problem set wasn't simply a matter of design....Sometimes just the way the paint was handled would give you a kind

> of a sense of mystery in what appears to be a perfectly flat design, and another wouldn't do it at all. It's very strange that it worked that way....It has to do with everything that's there — and what isn't there as well.[23]

In 1949, Fine rented a larger studio at 90 East Tenth Street (the area that was quickly becoming the hub of the Abstract Expressionist world) while keeping her walk-up apartment at 51 W. Eighth St. "I don't know whether I was frustrated, but I knew that I was completely disgusted with the commercialism of art. And I didn't care whether I ever showed again or not," she said. "I just wanted to be among artists. I wanted to see artists and I wanted artists to see me." Although the studio was "a terribly beat-up place" with barely a roof, its location was superb, surrounded as it was by artist studios, including those of Willem de Kooning, Esteban Vincente, Landes Lewitin, and Milton Resnick. In all respects, it was a wonderful place to work. "There was a certain release there that I didn't get anywhere else. And I think it had to do with these people dropping in who I found were *real* people."[24]

While the give-and-take of ideas was energizing, Fine knew that she was working in a different frame of reference from the artists around her. At one point, she tried the kind of complete psychological release that artists, such as Pollock, were employing, which gave her the feeling of having gone through a "session with a psychiatrist." However, there was always an underlying structure in her work:

> I couldn't paint a picture that was a scribble.... All the pictures appear to be very free but as you look at them you see they still have this very strong basic structure. And the complexes of color are very subtle....But in all of them after I did them, I would automatically sit down and study what I did and make a diagram, a plan. And it would have the same expression as all the other things I did except there was a kind of very free handling and excitement about it.[25]

Other artists were using a thin, almost calligraphic, line at the time, but Fine preferred to work with a thin line only in drawing, not in painting. Instead, she began to use "a larger brush and did a bolder stripe," to give it more substance. At that point, she realized it became a plane of color again, much like what had happened when, during her student days, she had experimented with "Seurat's dots," making them larger and larger until they too became planes of color. "In a sense, history repeated itself for me."[26]

As did Pollock and Rothko, Fine tried using house paint, learning tricks from other artists as to how to keep the colors and the whites true. "We all used house paint. It was Nicolas Carone who told me about one that did not turn in color and which was very good, particularly if the white was mixed with a little color — very little — so it still looks like white. It won't turn. It hasn't turned. It's a small trick that house painters know." Occasionally Fine used house paint essentially as a glue for "embedding" in her canvases pieces of aluminum foil, which she found did not tarnish as did metallic paint. "I embedded the foil in the color and painted over it and just let a little of it shine through." Initially she had tried using artists' paints for the purpose, but they were not as effective as house paints. "That was the only way to get the brush to flow in a certain way and to get enough pigment in there.…Also I used sand in some areas and such things."[27]

One of the most important places where artists gathered to discuss their work and share tips about technique was known simply as "The Club," which was formed in the fall of 1949 in Ibram Lassaw's East Eighth Street studio. The initial membership was 20 and was supposed to be exclusively male, but by the end of the first year there were 80, among whom were several women, including Elaine de Kooning and Mercedes Carles Matter. Fine joined at the invitation of de Kooning. "I met Bill on the street. He started to talk about the beginning of The Club and would I join? I said I'd be delighted to."[28] One of the artists who did not join was Pollock, the reason being, according to Harold Rosenberg, that he "didn't like doing things with coffee."

The atmosphere in The Club was sometimes hostile, with polemical arguments carried on far into the night, petering out toward dawn. At one of the Friday evening sessions, Fritz Glarner, a geometric abstractionist, was lecturing and had brought several of his paintings to illustrate his points. "Someone in the audience became very incensed and said 'what has this got to do with the [Korean] war and suffer-

It was Willem de Kooning, with whom Fine had been friends since the 1930s, who invited her to join The [Artists'] Club.

ing and just about everything else?'" Fine recalled. "He said, 'It's all there!' Which was really true. He had a difficult time." Nonetheless, Fine found the Club to be a place that filled both social and aesthetic needs, allowing her to get to know artists individually in a relaxed atmosphere, the occasional argumentativeness being part of its charm. "We all wanted a place to go to," said Fine. "It wasn't always the best thing to go to someone's studio for one reason or another."[29]

It was at The Club that she came to know Ad Reinhardt personally, although both had been members of the American Abstract Artists for several years. Impossible to pigeon-hole, Reinhardt did for the Abstract Expressionists what he had done for the Neo-plasticists, which was to force them away from narrow definitions, denying them hegemony. There was something compelling both in his art and in his personality that meant critics and artists could not ignore him even when they were befuddled by his unclassifiable work. It also helped that Reinhardt had a sardonic sense of humor, enabling him to rib artists who were becoming too grandiloquent. "I felt that he was very brave in his attitude and it was an inspiration to me that he carried out his ideas," said Fine. "He was doing his big fields of color. Reds and blues. Very brilliant. It was shortly afterwards that he started to do the black series but not so black that you couldn't see the crosses."[30]

Fine also liked Franz Kline although it was his personality and off-kilter wit that most impressed her, not his powerful black-and-white canvases. "Kline was lots of fun. He was quite a hero to all of us because he was the one who stuck his neck out and let people take potshots at him. He had a language which was very strange." For example, one evening at the Museum of Modern Art, he talked about Shredded Wheat eloquently for five minutes.[31] Kline also had the ability to handle difficult people with a combination of tact and humor, often defusing dangerous situations at The Club and at the Cedar Tavern. Frequently baited by Pollock who at various times threw beer at him, poured soup on him, snatched his hat and threw it on an out-of-reach shelf, and wrestled with him in fights part real and part ruse, Kline could quiet him down. "Franz would say something amusing," recalls Mercedes Matter, "and this grin would come on Jackson's face, this adorable grin, and all the menace would disappear."[32]

However, it was not all seriously argumentative. Fine recalled that they frequently got into arguments merely for the absurdity of it about whose studio was the largest. "Milton Resnick had the largest studio in the neighborhood. I think it was one inch larger than Elaine de Kooning's, or it might have been the other way around. There was all that kind of discussion and it was a lot of fun. People were painting for the fun of it."[33]

Helen Frankenthaler, only in her early 20s but already beginning to make a name for herself by staining unprimed canvas with poured oil paints achieving a watercolor-like effect, also perceived of the period as positive and the constant arguments as productive. "Hindsight is always easy, of course, but it seems to me now those days were fruitful, and we were all living in the young, lively, active nucleus of an 'art family.' It was lucky and wonderful to be in one's early twenties, with a group of painters to argue painting with."[34]

The Club, as well as Studio 35, another gathering spot only two doors away (best known for its three-day roundtable discussion on the Subjects of the Artist in April 1950), revealed that the Abstract Expressionists had both the desire for organization and the planning capability and geographic density to bring it about, although they didn't like to admit it. Not only did the artists need to see each other's paintings but they also needed to talk about them deeply and theoretically. The dialectic set up between Harold Rosenberg and Clement Greenberg created a charged atmosphere. "It was really a very exciting time for me because they [the artists] would drop in, and I would love to have them," said Fine. "And everybody was very frank about my work. [Landes] Lewitin, I remember, told me to do the smallest paintings I could possibly do if I wanted to be a success."[35] Oddly, Lewitin had voted against Fine's entry into The Club, a fact he himself took perverse pleasure in telling her at the first meeting she attended. Robert Richenburg, who was already a member, described Lewitin as "a very obnoxious person. He was always trying to manage The Club, very unpleasant."[36] As to his advice about size — which was peculiar in light of the fact that the canvases of the Abstract Expressionists were getting larger and larger — throughout her entire career, Fine did not feel compelled to paint either large or small. However, several years later, referring to the large painting "Tournament" in which each diptych was 57" x 66," she said, "I don't feel that it's necessary to get a painting that large to have impact. I think that, with the control of whatever the medium is, you can get it, I always say, in a postage stamp size."[37]

The Club hosted weekly roundtable discussions, lectures, and symposia, often organized by the sculptor Philip Pavia and announced by postcard mailings to the members each week. The list of speakers was long and varied, from Hannah Arendt on philosophy to John Cage on avant-garde music. It hosted parties for Alexander and Louisa Calder, who were returning to Europe, and another for the poet Dylan Thomas, who was visiting from Wales. Art critics of all stripes, including Harold Rosenberg, Thomas Hess and Robert Goldwater, always attracted large audiences and fired up debates. The artist Alfred L. Copley (known by his painting name Alcopley), one of the original founding group, remembered an evening when The Club was so overcrowded "that some people present, among them Sidney Janis, who was a volunteer fireman, were scared stiff that the entire building would collapse."[38]

The biggest most persistent debate carried on at all functions was the attempt to define the new art. B.F. Friedman, collector and author, recalled:

> Much of the talking that went on at The Club seemed aimed at a definition of the newly emerging art. However, such a definition was as much resisted as sought. There was never agreement as to the rightness of any label but more to the wrongness of all; Pavia called Abstract Expressionism "The Unwanted Title." There was never a manifesto or an official program or exhibition. What there was has been well summarized by Robert Goldwater: "The consciousness of being on the frontier, of being ahead rather than behind, of having absolutely no models however immediate or illustrious, of being entirely and completely on one's own — this was a new and heady atmosphere."[39]

Fine took an active part in these debates. In a talk she gave during this period (either at The Club or as part of the Provincetown summer lecture series), she agreed that most artists were incorrectly labeled but that it made very little difference whether they were called "Abstract

Expressionists, Expressive Abstractionists, Unexpressive Expressionists, or even Expressive Unabstractionists." There was too much emphasis on style and as a result a danger of falling into imitation "in an effort to stay in style." Personally she was pleased there was disagreement among the artists. "I think it is a very healthy thing," she insisted. "I hope I have convinced nobody of anything. It is only in Complete Agreement that Real Danger Lies."[40]

Besides the issue of labels, there was sharp disagreement among artists over the vast exhibition "American Painting Today-1950" at the Metropolitan Museum of Art in December of that year in which 307 works of art were exhibited in 17 galleries on the second floor of the south wing. The list of artists whose paintings had been selected by jury was long and diverse, including Romare Bearden, Isabel Bishop, Charles Burchfield, Lyonel Feininger, Karl Knaths, Rico LeBrun, and Yasuo Kuniyoshi. It was this exhibition that led to the publication of a photograph (subsequently to become famous) of dissenting artists in *Life Magazine.* The chain of events began the preceding spring when Barnett Newman drafted an open letter, signed by 18 artists and 10 sculptors, to the president of the Metropolitan announcing their intention to boycott the upcoming exhibition. In the letter, Newman contended that Francis Henry Taylor, the Met's director, and Robert Beverly Hale, the associate curator, were hostile to advanced art and had chosen a jury in line with their contempt. It was a curious protest given the fact that the Met, trying to counter its conservatism, had tried very hard to be even-handed in picking the juries. Not wanting to favor New York artists or one style, Taylor and Hale had set up a two-tiered system, wherein paintings were submitted first to regional juries that then sent their choices to the national jury. Aware of the disagreements over the terms Abstract Expressionism and non-objectivity, they chose instead to title that section of the exhibition "Advanced Art," the title Newman himself preferred for the new movement. None of which made any difference to Newman, who took his letter to the city desk of *The New York Times* in order to publicize the protest. Fortunately for the signatories, he handed it in on a light news day, and the editors decided to write a front-page article with the headline "18 Advanced Painters Boycott Metropolitan; Charge 'Hostility to Advanced Art.'"

Genauer at *The New York Herald Tribune* dubbed the group "The Irascibles," because she thought the criticism of the Met was unjustified, even a little silly with which Paul Bird at *Art Digest* agreed, writing that the bias was "imagined" and that the protestors were probably fearful of their paintings "being lost" in the welter of similar work. Museum protests being commonplace, all of this would have blown over and become a footnote in art history except that *The New York Times* story caught the eye of the editors at *Life Magazine* who decided to take a photo of the group. At the time, *Life Magazine* was one of the most popular publications in the United States. With television in its infancy, it provided its readers with the still-photography equivalent of the evening news, spicing up national and international coverage with articles on glamorous Hollywood celebrities, sports events, and what the editors considered culture, hence their interest in Jackson Pollock, who was featured in an article titled with the ambiguous question "Is He the Greatest Living Painter in the United States?" in August 1949. Copies of *Life* could be found everywhere: on the coffee tables of suburban homes to which it was mailed weekly, and in stacks at barber shops and hair salons. It was perused in doctors' waiting rooms. In classrooms, its pictures were cut out and tacked on current events bulletin boards. *Life* was so popular that if someone appeared in its pages, it was tantamount to having been installed in a cultural hall of fame. So it was for the eighteen men and one woman (Hedda Sterne) in the photograph printed in the January 15, 1951 issue. Fine had not been a signatory of the letter and, therefore, was not included in the photograph for a simple reason: the Metropolitan jury had selected one of her paintings for the Advanced Art section.[41]

Another locale where controversy often ruled was the Cedar Street Tavern, a nondescript neighborhood bar on University Place filled with cigarette smoke and the smell of beer. But unlike at The Club, Fine never felt comfortable there, nor did many other women artists. It was totally a male haunt of hard drinking, chain smoking, occasional fist fights, and frequent arguments. Women were welcome only as dames, as broads, never as equals. Lee Krasner recalled that "women were treated like cattle" at the Cedar Tavern. "I loathed the place," she said.[42] She loathed it even more because she could not keep Pollock from returning to it. Friedman in his biography of Pollock recounted how Krasner would struggle to get him back to The Springs after a mid-week visit to the city which invariably meant a visit to the Cedar Tavern. According to Krasner, "when he's with those cronies of his at the Cedar, it's not easy. I never know when he's going to show up on Wednesday. One in the morning, Two, Three, Noon. Afternoon."[43]

The notoriety of the Cedar Tavern was a fact of life that Fine resented because, unfortunately for the women, it was also a place where art business was transacted informally, contacts were made and ideas shared. According to her, the Cedar Tavern helped make the reputations of a number of artists, none of them women. Knowing its low-life aspects and concerned for her safety, Fine's husband did not want her to go there, but it was a hard place for her to avoid entirely. "Maurice did not want me in that milieu," Fine said. "But once I did go and stayed until 2:00 a.m." When she returned to their apartment, he confronted her angrily: "Well, if you come back this late, why bother to come back at all!"[44]

Berenice D'Vorzon, then a young painter finding her way in the New York art world who eventually became a close friend of Fine's as well as a neighbor in The Springs, remembered many arguments and fights at the Cedar. "Once Bill de Kooning was upset at Clem Greenberg's statement that Abstract Expressionism was dead. 'I'm not dead' he screamed across the bar at Clem. Then another man yelled 'I agree with Bill. I love emotional work.' At that moment Pollock pulls in and bangs the door so hard he breaks it. And there I am trying to figure out how to get out of the place in one piece. Now Perle, who became like an older sister to me, was a lady. She didn't go there. Lee Krasner was a different matter. She hated the Cedar because she would see Pollock get crazy, but Lee herself was aggressive. Eventually Lee became bitter. Perle didn't."[45]

Regrettably, the mystique of the Cedar Tavern became part of the mythology of Abstract Expressionism: Pollock ripping off the men's bathroom door in a drunken rage; Pollock attacking Kline repeatedly until Kline punched him in the gut; dames and more dames. It all fed into an image of maleness. The Abstract Expressionists were the ones who went to the Cedar, hence the real Abstract Expressionists were obviously men. In his book on Pollock, Friedman admitted that "there were hardly any women" at the Cedar, then went on to state that "during the fifties it was the one place everyone went; students, established artists, artists from out-of-town and from abroad; there one could make contact with New York, with where it was happening and the men who were making it happen." In other words, the art world was at the Cedar Tavern and there were no women in that world.[46]

Fortunately, there were signs of positive change, albeit small. One was the arrival on the Tenth Street scene of several women artists who were assertive on their own behalf, not on behalf of their husbands as were Lee Krasner and Elaine de Kooning. Jon Schueler recalled a panel at The Club in which he and Joan Mitchell, then in her mid-twenties, participated:

> She was one of three very aggressive women — Grace Hartigan and Helen Frankenthaler were the others — who fought to become known as artists rather than "woman artist." She was a good painter, an aggressive painter. One night we were to appear on a panel together at The Club to discuss the woman artist. Before the eve of the panel, I remarked that the creativity of woman was in the womb — and all hell broke loose. Joan got Grace and Helen to join the panel, and they raked me unmercifully.[47]

Fine dealt with the prejudice at the Betty Parsons Gallery, the Club and the Cedar Tavern by refusing to be shunted aside and by immersing herself in her painting, being, as she often phrased it, "severe with myself." According to Ernestine Lassaw, the wife of the sculptor Ibram Lassaw, "Perle was forceful about her art. She was very ambitious, Perle never let anything interfere with her art. Never!"[48]

For her February 1951 exhibition, Fine had begun to work toward the edges of the canvas. "It is kind of interesting that at one point I found myself doing peripheral painting almost entirely. I remember that it was Gottlieb who used that word. He came to the exhibition I had and he said 'Oh, everything is taking place on the edges, isn't it?' And I thought — well, that's a strange criticism. But I took it as a criticism. And today everybody is doing peripheral painting."[49] By the use of the words *edges* and *peripheral,* Gottlieb and Fine were referring not to the sides of the canvas per se but to peripheral vision, in which the eye focuses on one thing while out of its corner, it sees other things. In terms of art, the word *peripheral* indicated shifting foci in a painting that resulted in movement of the eye. Efforts were made to explain this phenomena in terms of the unconscious (as in things sensed but not seen) but for Fine it came down to a concern with use of the entire picture plane. In his review of her 1951 exhibition, Devree noted the strong emphasis on the periphery in Fine's art:

> She has effected a quite striking fusion of the suggestive, the sensuous and the cerebral in these nonobjective canvases. A black canvas with white linear organization gives a clue to her procedure of working from the outside in toward a center of gravity....There is nothing haphazard or automatic about these paintings. One feels that they have been worked in a fashion of a lyric poem or a musical composition from some shadow deeply underlying emotion translated into color-forms that play together and are occasionally more obviously united through a looping meandering line-form. The suggestion is never to be specifically tied down more than in music but to a greater or lesser degree it is there in surely emotive and personal statements.[50]

In several paintings of this period, Fine used black and white extensively but rarely exclusively. Her dynamic painting titled "Thor," 1951, enamel and gouache on paper (see color plate), is evocative of the power of the Norse god of thunder. Black and gray ribbons of medium density tangle into clusters within which is open space. Along some of the ribbons are knots of paint as if it had suddenly congealed and then became liquid again. Some of the lines trail off the four sides of the canvas. There are centripetal and centrifugal forces at work, pulling each other into balance on the white picture plane. Several Abstract Expressionists were using black and white: Pollock with his drip technique on unsized canvases; Kline with his huge enveloping swaths; Motherwell with his "comma" forms. Fine's use of black in "Thor" is unlike theirs. It explodes outward in a controlled blast, then plunges inward. Nothing shatters and nothing is lost. The light arises from the darkness, and darkness arises from the light. By naming it after a storm god, Fine played with the idea of a mythic space. Similarly, about her use of black in the painting "Que ce soit Songe ou Pas Songe" (from the Jean Cocteau poem "Dos D'Anges," translated as "whether this be dream or not dream"), she wrote, "again the paint, the color, coal-black, and handling of the line which one moment appears and then seems to disappear as in a dream, all this insistence is intended to make quite real a dream world."[51]

Fine never limited herself to black and white. In fact, there are several narrow canvases painted the same year as "Thor" in which she used a broad range of hues — a sandstone-brown, a flesh-tone verging on cream, a smoky gray (almost smudge-like) interlaced with purple, blue, yellow, teal-green, and a rusty red — with an intricate white line overlaying all. Of these untitled paintings, Robert Goodnough wrote in *ARTnews,* that she had "reached into a lighter and vaster world in her recent paintings, at times coupling twirling forms suggesting Chinese calligraphy, and again using areas of close values in over-all effects....Painting No. 4 is more involved with writing symbols achieved by curling the brush over the canvas and avoiding concentration of interest."[52]

In an attempt to sever for the spectator any connection to reality that might be suggested by a title, Fine numbered her paintings in the 1951 exhibition instead of titling them, but she gave up the practice shortly thereafter, finding it unsatisfactory. For example, "Submarine" as a title might call up images of the ocean, nudging the spectator to perceive of a gray ellipsoid as a shark, or a wavy green line as seaweed. Frank O'Hara, a poet and critic, wrote that the widespread practice of numbering was in tune with the "spiritual climate" of the New York School: "Most of the painters involved in it simply used numbers for identification of canvases, though many had previously used titles and would return to them again, as did Pollock."[53] In his review of Fine's exhibition, Devree wrote that numbering the canvases was a smart decision on her part, and then underscored the nature of the problem which was to interpret Abstract Expressionist canvases as analogous to landscapes and seasons: "[Fine] has wisely avoided titles, but if she had employed them "No. 21" with its yellow-greens might well be considered to suggest spring; another in orange-reds with touches of green might well have been worked out from a sense of midsummer or Indian summer; and "No. 4" surely was conjured up by a feeling of underseas depth." Certainly, the use of a number for a title was non-descriptive, but it was also confusing, even for Fine who had to resort to color descriptions on the list of paintings she sent to Parsons: Oil #7 was described as "large yellow (predominant), grey white, brown, deep green." Oil #13 was "all pinks, greys, cream, soft greens, no frame."[54] Fortunately, Fine was skilled at coming up with titles that were evocative but not specific, for example, "A Feeling of Becoming," "Sequel to an Afterthought," "Tyranny of Space," "Astraea," "Colloquy," "Unfurling," "Sudden Encounter," "Swift Plunge," "A Timelessness," and "Prescience." Even when a title referred to something in nature, the reference was oblique: "A Radiance at Noon," "A Soft and Silent World," and "The Moment of the Wind." She also continued to favor musical terms such as "Polyphonic," "Vivace," and "Accelerated Rhythm" because they were non-visual.

About the time of the exhibition, an incident occurred that was extremely hurtful to Parsons as well as Fine. One evening, "The Giants,"- Pollock, Rothko, Newman, and Still — gathered for a meeting in Parsons's studio, at their behest, supposedly to discuss the future of her gallery. Actually, they had come to deliver an ultimatum. They demanded Parsons get rid of all the other artists in her gallery except themselves. If she refused, they would defect to Sidney Janis. She refused. According to Parsons's biographer Lee Hall:

> Betty resented being cast exclusively in the role of handmaiden to the Giants; she, too, wanted recognition as an artist. Therefore, when the Giants assembled in Betty's studio and proposed that she chuck out all of the other artists in the gallery and concentrate exclusively on them, she was offended. "We will make you the most important dealer in the world," she recalled Barney's telling her. "But that wasn't my way. I need a larger garden. I always liked variety." Her verdict assured the defection of the artists, one by one. Sidney Janis…"just took them away," Betty recalled.[55]

Parsons was stunned and wounded, feeling rightfully that she was the one who had made their success possible. "Where would they have been if they hadn't been able to show with me? No one would have known about them." Word of the meeting soon got out. "Well, I had to go on," said Parsons. "I couldn't just sit and complain."[56] As for the Giants themselves, the rupture with Parsons did not bring them the short-term financial success they had anticipated. Newman did not have another show until 1958 when he was given a retrospective at Bennington College. Pollock was drinking heavily again and could not handle the stress of changing galleries. Clyfford Still, ever disdainful of all artists but himself, thereafter refused to show his paintings unless he had total control over the environment. Only Rothko made the change to Janis relatively unscathed. Fine occasionally alluded to "the incident" at the Betty Parsons Gallery, which she considered personally damaging, but she was too polite to name names or go into details. Neither did she hold grudges, even against Newman, with whom she occasionally agreed particularly about rejecting symbolism in art and the importance of the "pure idea." There was too much painting to be done to waste precious time and psychic energy on self-pity and bitterness, although she occasionally admitted to close friends that she had to fight hard to ward them off. Years later, one friend recalled that while his primary impression of her was graciousness, his secondary impression was of a person with such strong convictions that she could withstand a great deal of negativity. "One had to look up to her," he said in admiration.[57]

Besides her solos and her inclusion in several Whitney annuals, one of the more provocative group exhibitions in which Fine's painting appeared was titled simply "Nine Women Artists" at the Bennington College Gallery in Vermont, March 20-April 2, 1953. Just a few months before, Bennington College, known for its avant-garde stance on the arts, had hosted the first retrospective of Pollock's work. He attended the opening with Krasner, the artist and art collector Alfonso Ossorio, Greenberg, and Frankenthaler (who had attended Bennington). The "Nine Women Artists" show was equally far-sighted, including Fannie Hillsmith, Alice Trumbull Mason, Hedda Sterne, Sonya Sekula, Pennerton West, Helen Frankenthaler, Linda Lindeberg, and Joan

Mitchell. Fine's painting was "Tyranny of Space No. 4." In the exhibition catalog, Eugene C. Goossen, only 32 years old but already making his mark as an art critic and teacher, wrote that: "Perle Fine is the boldest of all, and is willing to risk everything (the prime quality needed for success in the romantic approach). Beginning with no other elements than paint, color, and canvas and indeed, an exceptionally clear idea of what a painting should do, she comes out with a certainty of statement we are accustomed to find only in classical art."[58]

Fine was one of 24 artists who took part in all six of the "New York Painting and Sculpture Annuals" from 1951 through 1957 (there was no annual in 1952). The idea for the first annual germinated at The Club. Held in a former antiques shop that was slated for demolition at 60 East Ninth Street, it was called simply the "Ninth Street Show." "I remember the artists carrying their work into that vacant building," said Rae Ferren, the wife of John Ferren, one of the organizers. "Some of the paintings were still wet. It was work no one had seen before. It was memorable and important because this was what the artists were doing — what they wanted shown." To make the long and narrow space presentable for the exhibition, the artists themselves whitewashed the walls, then covered them, floor-to-ceiling, edge-to-edge, with paintings. Hess wrote: "An air of haphazard gaiety, confusion, punctuated by moments of achievement, reflects the organization of this mammoth show which, according to one of the organizers 'just grew'...but such hit or miss informality and enthusiasm has resulted in a fine and lively demonstration of modern abstract painting in and around New York — or more properly Greenwich Village."[59] However, competition between artists almost spoiled the show for Fine. After she had hung her painting and gone back to her studio, Conrad Marca-Relli, one of the original founders of The Club, took it down and hung his painting in its place. On her return, Fine was so offended that she ordered her painting to be withdrawn from the show. Ferren interceded, Marca-Relli's painting was moved to another spot, and Fine's rehung.[60]

Two years later in 1953, the Stable Gallery, owned by Eleanor Ward, began to host the annuals, at least in terms of providing the space. The selection of who would be invited to submit remained with the committee (on which Fine served in 1954 and 55), which was comprised of artists who had participated in the prior exhibition. It was this self-selective aspect that made the New York annuals historically significant because they were a venue for painting and sculpture that the artists themselves deemed important. The 1954 show took up three floors of the Stable Gallery, crowding the walls as they had at the Ninth Street location, with the sculptures in front, the whole conveying a feeling of dizzy excitement. To Hess, the exhibition indicated that the New York art world had coalesced: "Of their own accord, some artists dropped in, others out; in a few weeks the whole Salon was set. It was easy because it was inevitable, it could not have been stopped; invitees could only refuse on the grounds of protest against the collective, like a son often protests against the fact of family. In other words, the historical moment or spiritual climate or ambiance or Zeitgeist or whatever is in the air made the issue, as it was made for the Impressionists or the Fauves. And the basic standard is the individual's sensitivity to and sympathy with the group."[61]

With the increase in artists, there came the need for more gallery space — a need which was partially met by the opening of several artist cooperatives. The one with which Fine became closely associated was the Tanager Gallery formed in 1952 by Angelo Ippolito, Charles Cajori, William King, Lois Dodd, and Frederick Mitchell. At first it was located in an empty barber shop on Third Avenue at East Fourth Street, but a year later Fine informed the group that a large room with a good-sized shop window, located in front of her studio, was going for less than what they were paying. So the Tanager Gallery and Fine's studio became contiguous. The name referred to the bright color of the window-trim at the first location that reminded one of the artists of the scarlet tanager. Artists had to pay for their own exhibition catalogues but were not charged a gallery fee, and initially paid only 25% commission to the gallery for sales. Unfortunately, sales were usually low, but at least artists could count on an audience, for the Tanager also filled the role of a kind of community center; one writer referred to it as similar to a parish hall.[62] Mitchell remembered that on the opening nights of exhibitions "traffic was completely blocked and the street just packed with people....It was marvelous."[63]

In an unusual pairing of painting and print, Fine had dual exhibitions at the Betty Parsons Gallery in December 1952-January 1953 and the Wittenborn Gallery; at the first were paintings and at the second lithographs of those paintings. "My paintings, like my lithographs, deal not in definition, but rather with the art of evocation and suggestion," Fine wrote for the Wittenborn catalog. "I arrive at a certain simplicity by cutting away all the non-essential elements, and whatever calligraphy remains is only that necessary to qualify the forms and render a purer deeper emotion." Another unique aspect of the Wittenborn show was that two other artists participated, Stanley Twardowicz and Maurice Berezov. Larry Campbell wrote in *ARTnews* that: "Husband Berezov and wife Fine make speleological trips into themselves. Berezov's lithographs describe the cave itself, and Fine's, the marks on the walls made by the smoke from the candle. The most striking is her two-color "Whither-Within" in yellow, black and white. ($10–18.)"[64] There were sixteen paintings in Fine's solo at Parsons, among them "Tyranny of Space," "Yellow Ambit," "Cleavage," and a series titled "Prescience," ranging in price from $350 to $1,250. "The pictures called 'Prescience,' of which there are several, succeed the best," a reviewer commented. "There is typically a large space of blue, or red or yellow, or mixed colors, whose depth comes from the thought and care, the variety and subtlety in the surface, and the time that was necessary to achieve all this; and around the edges another color, often white, comes in, in places overlapping, in places overlapped, in others embedded, deliberately making an artificial object, in which time plays a role. But she does not count on time doing some of the painting for her; she intervenes herself to do what time might fail to do. The weight of time taken plus their worked out simplicity makes these paintings very quiet. When she works quickly, weight is lacking, and the effect is transitory."[65]

This exhibition prompted Fine to send a statement to *The New York Times* (which was not published) in which she defended herself against the common charge that Abstract Expressionism was out of touch with reality:

> It is true my paintings do not represent anything. They do not

> delineate anything, that is, in the sense of accepted imagery. For me Color is enough — Color has its own palpable reality — Color has its own validity. Through Color, I create something which, through its own innate beauty, moves one to feel something. Many people have asked me to explain my paintings. It would be as presumptuous for me to tell them what they ought to feel about them, since *feeling* is what we are involved with, as it would be for me to tell them what they should *feel* when listening to music, or poetry or drama.[66]

For all of her seeming success, Fine was becoming disillusioned with the art world. A level of gritty competitiveness had set in on Tenth Street exacerbated by the arrival of a second generation of Abstract Expressionists jockeying for gallery space and press attention. There was also the increasing tunnel vision of some of the critics and the perception (whether right or wrong) that there were two dominant stylistic — and warring — camps: Pollock's and de Kooning's. Everything was becoming a battle. James Brooks recalled that the swelling commercialism and the fact that some artists were selling while others weren't began to split the Greenwich Village community in two. "There wasn't quite that much of a community anyhow. But it did have to exist then, and it was very pleasant. When it disintegrated, it was expected, I think, but it was sad."[67]

On looking back on this period, Motherwell said in an interview: "I think the 'expressionist' part of abstract expressionism had to do with a certain violence native to the American character; I do not think it was the result of aesthetic considerations."[68] Fine was aware of the undercurrent of violence in Abstract Expressionism. In an interview conducted years later, Fine succinctly identified her problem in a statement both simple and profound: "I couldn't be aggressive. I'd have to do aggressive work to be aggressive."[69]

The end of the era for Fine came in the form of a letter from Parsons dated February 9, 1954: "You have been very patient with me these many years and I feel that I have done practically nothing for you. I have never made a sale so it would be wiser for both of us to part company. I have always enjoyed showing your pictures and hope that you will have better luck somewhere else. Affectionately, Betty Parsons."[70]

L to R: Ruth Kligman, Bill de Kooning, Perle Fine, The Springs, 1958

CHAPTER SEVEN

THE SPRINGS

Cast adrift by Parsons with little hope of finding another dealer, in 1954 Fine gave up her Tenth Street studio in frustration and decamped to The Springs, a rural section of East Hampton, Long Island. Prior to the move, Fine and Berezov had often visited with Krasner and Pollock who had settled in The Springs in 1946 after purchasing an old farmhouse with a ramshackle barn that Pollock had converted into his studio. It was there that he spread out his canvases on the floor, moving around them with the grace of a dancer, holding a can of house paint in one hand and a stick for dripping and flinging in the other. For her studio, Krasner had to settle for a small upstairs bedroom. Still, for both of them The Springs was a peaceful place that provided a measure of solace within which to paint — just the atmosphere Fine longed for. "It was through Lee that we decided to come out here on the East End," explained Fine. "Lee was always talking about how wonderful it was, how much she and Jackson enjoyed it. We found this lot in the woods. The road wasn't opened, but it was marked on the county map, so the telephone company had to put in poles. The banks were not interested, either, because they thought a studio-house had poor resale value."[1] Ernestine Lassaw, who with her husband the sculptor Ibram Lassaw had also settled in The Springs, remembers Fine was very determined to build despite the obstacles. "When Perle found Red Dirt Road on the map, she went to the town and had them bulldoze it. They went up to where the driveway was going to be, and no further."[2]

It was the opportunity to be by herself and to paint without distraction that most attracted Fine to The Springs:

> I was really totally alone out there. My husband was in the city. The city had got me down: the air; the fact that I couldn't live where I could paint and couldn't paint where I had to live; and all that kind of thing. So we built a little one-room studio house out there in the woods. And it was pretty rough. The road wasn't even a road; it was just a firebreak through the woods. But after putting up a shell I wouldn't come back to New York. And I didn't for eight

> years. I stayed there summer and winter. And it was very rough. At first there was no heating system and the house was not insulated. So my husband said, "If you're determined to stay here I'll show you how to insulate it."...So I worked there. And I worked very well during all that time.[3]

Fine was not the only artist to make the decision to settle in East Hampton. In fact, at the time of her move, the town was once again becoming a major center for painters. In the late nineteenth and early twentieth centuries, the area had been a popular summer art colony attracting the painters George Bellows, Winslow Homer, and Childe Hassam among many others, but eventually its popularity had waned, although it still could boast of the Guild Hall Art Museum, Ashawagh Hall, the Parrish Art Museum located in Southampton, and several seasonal art galleries. During World War II, some of the European artists in exile spent summers there. However, not until the arrival of Pollock and Krasner did artists begin returning in appreciable numbers with many settling down permanently, among them Baziotes, Carone, and Zogbaum. One commonality of this group was that they were in their middle years, and most of them had made their mark, to a greater or lesser degree, in the New York art world already. They no longer needed, at least not to the same measure, the constant interplay of ideas and mutual psychological reinforcement that Greenwich Village provided. The creative but brawling give-and-take that had attracted them to the city when they were in their twenties had begun to wear heavily on them as they entered their middle years. However, for all their insistence on individuality and freedom, few of the artists were hermits, which explains why most of them chose to live within a ten-mile radius of each other in the East End, a term that designated the entire area from East Hampton out to the lighthouse on Montauk Point, including The Springs and Amagansett.[4]

Illumined by a clear, high, watery light, The Springs had many attributes that were attractive to artists. It was sparsely populated, the air was clean and salt-scented, and farm fields and woodland intermingled. East, south or north, the ocean was not far, but neither did it dominate the landscape as it did in Provincetown. Sea birds, shore birds, and land birds were plentiful. Scrub oak grew abundantly in the sandy soil allowing sunlight to filter down to the forest floor. In the winter after the other trees had lost their leaves, the oaks tenaciously held onto theirs, tingeing the woods a rusty brown.

The year-round inhabitants of The Springs, many of them farmers and fisherman, were cordial even though they did not care much about art. There was little socializing among the artists and the locals, but neither was there animosity. "The artists live in The Springs, within village limits but without village involvement," wrote a reporter. "For the most part, the artists are loners, more articulate with their canvas than their words, and their roots are sunk only lightly despite many years in residence."[5] Fine was certainly a loner, but she did not feel distant from the residents whom she found to be "good people, hard working and tolerant."[6] In fact, it was their tolerance that made East Hampton welcoming to artists, for the McCarthy hearings had cast a heavy cloud of suspicion over everyone associated in any way with the arts. Several other art colonies and schools far from the sheltering anonymity of the city felt unwelcome, even threatened, by the communities in which they were located. (This was especially true of the Black Mountain School in North Carolina.) But the "Eastenders" had lived with artists for over 70 years and had learned to be non-judgmental about their unusual lifestyles and mores.

The other attribute of The Springs was a practical one: it was connected by train and highway to New York City approximately two hours distant, allowing artists the privacy and space they craved as well as the convenience of returning to the city to visit the galleries and museums. For Berezov, the train was his link to Fine, and he rode it every weekend until his retirement in the 1960s. In turn, she rode it into the city every few weeks to exhibition openings. "Our ties to New York City were still strong," she said. "The trips kept us in touch with our close friends."[7]

For all these reasons, the choice of East Hampton over Provincetown as a permanent residence was obvious. Provincetown was becoming overcrowded, the congestion on the roads too great, and the competition for studio space too intense. The artist Tony Vevers wrote that

Summer was a time of socializing in East Hampton. For Fine, winter was the season of unhindered work when she was totally alone. (Left: sitting facing front Josephine Little; in front of tree: Balcomb Greene, Syd Solomon, Perle Fine; behind Balcomb: Carlos Baseldoa; standing, from right: Frederick Kiesler, John Little, Mike Goldberg, Ernestine and Ibram Lassaw, Conrad Marca-Relli; seated in front: Anita Marca-Relli and Lucia Wilcox (on her knees); couple in center unidentified.

just getting to Provincetown was a challenge: "You had to undergo the tortuous, unmarked passage of Providence, and then on to the Cape via Taunton and Wareham....One could easily spend 8 to 10 hours driving from New York to P-Town."[8] Some artists, including Motherwell and Bultman, chose to make Provincetown their year-round residence, but many found it inconvenient.

However, in one respect East Hampton's accessibility was a drawback, for in the summer it attracted hordes of tourists and vacationing artists, swamping the year-round residents, and crowding the beaches. "In the summer all kinds of activities mounted to a feverish pitch, then leveled off again in the fall," said Fine.[9] Summer was the season for socializing and play, winter was the time for work. It was then that The Springs came into its own as a place perfect for painting. "After my husband and I purchased property here, I was surprised to find that Perle was living here all the time," recalled Rae Ferren. "The Springs was very country-like then, very underpopulated. It was very rare to stay the winter."[10] According to one reporter who interviewed Fine, it was only after the summer visitors had returned to New York, "snuggling into their barstool hustles, trading summer wishes for winter dreams," that she really got to work:

> In the winter, the East End is left alone. The potato crops are carpeted with crop cover and vacuumed by the north wind. Hardly anyone walks the beaches. Desolation/Isolation. Quietude/Solitude — pick any, or all. The signs of the season say it all. At motels, "Vacancy." At art galleries, "Closed." At some shops and restaurants, "See you in April." The rhythm of winter is a slow, sagging jog, and the East End moves like an old man, with its head down and its shoulders stooped.
> In the winter the East End belongs to the committed, to the romantics, not the romancers. Artists and writers hunker down for the siege, hoping to emerge in springtime with some masterpiece, some butterfly to show for the cocoon months. Under the surface, it's a time for creativity, for hard work in hard times. This is the frontier, and it carries its own special strength....Perle Fine knows that feeling as well as anyone.[11]

Fine was stating the truth when she described her combination of house and studio as merely a shell standing alone in the woods without another residence in sight. One winter she chopped down a large tree to heat the place, feeding it little by little into the raised brick fireplace that separated the living-studio area from the kitchen eating area. She slept on a daybed that did double duty as a sofa. The deer routinely ate her ivy. There were occasional hurricanes and fierce winter storms, but it was exactly what she wanted. "I love working here. It's so quiet. I can work on and on, without stopping for anything," she said. "Sometimes I work around the clock." She had no desire for a suburban style home. She wanted a live-in studio in which she could wake up in the morning and the first thing she would see were her paintings and the second thing was the light flooding through the windows unblocked by high-rise buildings. Space and light were essential; comfort was not. "It's the possibility of my being completely free of social obligation, free to work without interruption. Sure, I get cabin fever once in a while. So I go to New York and see a show, and you know? I can't wait to get back again."[12] Not until 1959 did Fine and Berezov add a second room, what Fine called the "happy room." In a postcard sent to Berezov, she told him that construction was just about done. "The heater hasn't come yet, but that's a separate job anyway. And it is beautiful, and HAPPY. Sunny, clean, everything I/we hoped it would be."[13] But until then, the basic structure was just that: basic. A reporter who visited Fine and Berezov described the place as follows:

> An up-and-down winding drive in The Springs is the approach to Perle Fine's studio and house. The weathered shingles and seemingly pitched roof give the appearance of a typical Springs Fisherman's cottage, from dado height to the ceiling, and I realized that this part of the house was a studio with a shed roof. White painted rafters were exposed both inside and out. "We really wanted a modern house," Maurice explained, smiling. "But our local contractor-carpenter said that that type of construction would not withstand the storms here on the East End. So we went along with the carpenter's ideas, and this is what he built. It is a shell, really. There was a hurricane last year, and the carpenter came by right after, to see how the house fared. He was pleased to find that there was no structural damage."[14]

Unlike many other painters of the period, Fine was not driven by personal demons, being very level emotionally. Her fissure with Betty

Fine and Krasner, here at the Ashawaugh Annual Fair in The Springs, remained friends throughout their lives, although they also competed with each other. It was Krasner and Pollock who encouraged Fine to move to The Springs.

Parsons stung, but she did not retreat sullenly to East Hampton to express her bitterness and frustration in her paintings. She was not like Louise Bourgeois who admitted that when her work was on view, she felt as if she were "invading" the domain of men, therefore, she was only comfortable when her work was hidden. Neither was she drawn to suicide or to alcohol as were several women painters. Abstract art was a totally separate world for her. And in that world, stylistic change was inevitable and good, but it did not arise from a personal need. Instead, it arose purely in response to aesthetic questions and was, therefore, a logical progression. "Every change in my work has always arisen from a deep-rooted need, a *pictorial* need, never any need to express or to limn or to define anything that I do…it's a need within the painting itself to express more."[15] In her personal life, Fine may have been buffeted by political and cultural winds of change, but she did not allow a zephyr to reach the surface of her canvas. For her, art was a spiritual sphere "above reality," yet it had the power to penetrate reality. Emotion was essential; without it, a painting was "purely intellectual," hence dead. However, emotion had to be tied directly to aesthetics: "My preoccupation throughout my career has been with the ideas that make a work of art. Though the final irrevocable statement eludes one, one knows that the emotional state that exists in the field of aesthetics must be at the base of the answer to this problem, that anything less than profound feeling is only an approximation of feeling — documentary, anecdotal, nostalgic." Even when Dorothy Seckler tried hard to pin her down in her interview for the Archives of American Art (Smithsonian) as to the social and environmental stimuli that affected her work, asking whether radical changes in the world or even "outer space" (as Seckler put it) impinged on her forms, Fine turned the question back to art and only art: "It's an awareness of what is happening to, let's say, just a piece of white paper. When you do something to that white paper, when you put one or two forms on that white paper, that simple sheet of white paper can become one of the most beautiful things in the world if those forms are put in there in such a way as to involve every inch of that, from top to bottom and from left to right."[16]

Given her laser-like focus, what Fine needed from The Springs was nothing more than solitude, and that it could provide abundantly particularly in the off-season. It offered her "a wonderful undisturbed freedom for creativity."[17] But she was never reclusive, remaining close friends with other artists and writers who had moved to the area, among them Harold Rosenberg and May Tabak Rosenberg, the Lassaws, Ad and Rita Reinhardt, and Rae and John Ferren, looking forward in late spring to the arrival of those who came only for the summer. According to Berenice D'Vorzon who was a neighbor, "every year when Perle would see the lights go on in my house, she'd call up and say 'you've finally come!' It was like having an older sister."[18] Fine also remained friends with Krasner, helping her through the difficult period after Pollock died in an automobile accident — dead drunk and depressed — on the night of August 11, 1956. However, their friendship eventually became strained because Krasner, afraid of being by herself in the farm house at night, kept pleading with Fine to stay. According to Ernestine Lassaw: "After Pollock's death, Lee hated to be alone so she would have Perle come over and babysit her. But after a while Perle got tired of it. Perle was very friendly with Lee but it was a competitive friendship."[19]

Nor did Fine sever her ties with the New York-based art organizations, the Federation of Modern Painters and Sculptors and the American Abstract Artists. The latter had loosened up stylistically under the leadership of George L. K. Morris. In fact, it hosted some international exhibitions (in which Fine took part) at a time when the Tenth Street artists were focusing almost entirely on themselves.[20] Fine also continued to serve on the selection committee for the New York Annuals, a task that required her to be aware of what was incubating in the studios, not just the galleries. The annuals were not juried; instead the committee decided whom to invite, then left it up to each individual artist to select the painting or sculpture to include. That being the case, it was essential for the committee to be broad-minded. As Ferren described the committee's working relationship, "the urge toward qualitative judgments wanders into its picking and then promptly wanders out again. It is, most accurately, a state of friendship." In 1955, Fine was on the committee with the painters Ferren, Brooks, Carone, Kline, Elaine De Kooning, Marca-Relli, and Tworkov and the sculptors Lassaw and James Rosati. That year, Abstract Expressionism was still at the core of the exhibition, but not completely. Ferren wrote: "If Abstract Expressionism is the largest vortex, the antithesis, the rejections, the yet unmade developments are also there. Why? Through involvement. A simple unintellectualized decision. 'He should be in,' meaning, 'He is involved somewhere in the tensions and polarities of our thinking, and through his work, he made us see it.'" But even Ferren sensed that the energy level of the annuals was beginning to drop, although the art of 30-year-old Robert Rauschenberg and 33-year-old Richard Stankiewicz was certain to "titilllate" the sophisticated spectator. (The previous year Rauschenberg had included one of his "combines" of moss, dirt, and ivy, which had to be watered to keep the ivy alive.) Humorously, Ferren wrote: "The de Kooning whiplash line, whose speed I estimate at, roughly, ninety-four-and-one-half miles per hour, is seen here and there but is being used within the speed limits."[21]

Besides the New York Annuals, Fine had yearly solos at the Tanager Gallery that were always well-reviewed, and she took part in its group exhibitions, coming in from The Springs to assist in hanging the paintings. These shows had their own panache of which one component was a heartening openness to art, even the most extreme: Stankiewicz showed his sculptures (some with the whimsy of the Tin-Man from the Wizard of Oz) welded from pieces of junk; Philip Pearlstein and Alex Katz found an audience for their sharp-focus realism; and at the 1955 group exhibition, an unknown young painter named Jasper Johns showed a work that Fairfield Porter likened to a "music box."[22] The Tanager may have been small with even smaller sales, but throughout the 1950s it remained a place of good will, different from the competitive fervor of the commercial galleries. In fact, Porter preferred the Tanager annual exhibitions to the New York Annuals held at the Stable Gallery. "If the Stable is the Salon of the Secession, then this exhibition is a secession from the Secession. At the Stable exhibitions the artists express their competitiveness: it is an exhibition for the exhibitors. And though this show contains many of the same exhibitors, it is an exhibition for people to come and look at what is being done; it is for the spectator."[23] On occasion, the Tanager also presented shows around a theme, but it was never heavy-handed in forcing artists to comply. For example, for the exhibition "The Private Myth" in Septem-

Fine's woodcut *Wide To the Wind* was exhibited at the Wittenborn Gallery and at the Brooklyn Museum in 1955 where she demonstrated how it progressed from a sketch to a print. She produced several versions. (See color plate.)

ber, 1961, twenty artists were asked to submit a statement not about mythology (which Philip Pearlstein, writing about the exhibition for *ARTnews*, said was a misleading word because it conjured up gods and nymphs) but about the relationship between visual forms and intangible ideas. To Pearlstein, the Tanager Gallery wanted to make clear that "some contemporary work seems to radiate an urgent message." It was not trying to define a trend. Fine wrote in response to the question on myth: "For me, true reality exists in the aura of the unknown. The spell-binding quality, the one that beckons and holds, the unpremeditated, the nameless, touched off perhaps by some transcendental experience but guided by a poetic and creative hand — these are the things hidden beneath the surface. What we see with our eyes, on the canvas, is but a small portion of an audacious system of symbols and concepts and is truly incapable of rationalization."[24]

One of Fine's more unusual group exhibitions was at the Brooklyn Museum in November, 1955, showcasing 14 artists, each represented by three paintings and three prints. Eleven prints were chosen for purchase awards, Fine's "Wide to the Wind" among them (see color plate). The previous June, the evolution of this particular woodcut had comprised a show in itself at the Wittenborn Gallery in which Fine had demonstrated the ten stages of its development from a gouache sketch to a six-color print. One critic wrote, "Since it is a well-planned abstraction, the stages are interesting to follow; it becomes quite clear that the white spaces are as actively designed as the printed areas. They interlock with fragmented forms (greyed in their different hues) and a dark mass to create an effect of lightness, of the free sweep of air across a landscape of mountain and plain."[25] Concurrent with the Brooklyn exhibition, photographs of "The Moment In and Out of Time" and "On a Theme from T.S. Eliot's Four Quartets" were published in a feature article in *Arts* providing Fine with major exposure, but it also marked the end of her printmaking, because instead of moving her forward she saw it as pulling her backward. Yet it was the same forethought and totality of vision that were essential to produce an exceptional print which would undergird her oil paintings and powerful collages of the late 1950s.

Despite her solos at the Tanager Gallery and her inclusion in important group shows, Fine's old problem continued unabated: there were few sales. Unable to find a new gallery and financially strapped, she applied for a $10,000 Ford Foundation grant in 1958, which was to be awarded via a competition. Financial need was supposed to be a factor in the judging, but when the winners were announced, it turned out that several were not poor. Riling the waters even more was that at the same time the Carnegie prizes, which were given to artists participating in its Pittsburgh International Exhibition (in which Fine took part), had all been awarded to Europeans, a fact that stirred Reinhardt to write a tongue-in cheek letter to *ARTnews* signing himself as a member of the "Society for the Protection of Our Artist Friends," an organization that had been very "busy these days handling cases of artists needing protection from themselves." Reinhardt asked why the prizes were awarded "to third-rate foreign artists when there are so many good well-known second-rate American artists in the show."[26] Fine, however, was not in a mood to laugh, at least not at first. In fact, she was furious about the flippant treatment she received from the Ford Foundation. She had not even been extended the courtesy of being told she had been turned down, finding out by accident. In pure disgust, she wrote to her husband:

> a.m. Darling. This is a sad tale of a fool who refuses to stop hoping. It's all over. The chagrin, the mean madness of waiting, then — no ANSWER! What an awful way to let you know you've lost. Yes, their brochure says "If you don't hear from us by Dec. 8th — pick them up, or we'll fine you." To hell with them!...And the damned Carnegie prizes all going to the Italians & foreigners. Think I'll join the D.A.R. and be really revolting.

Berezov calmed her down and in her next letter to him she expressed her resolve to get back to painting: "You are right. The only thing that matters is work!!! So with nose to the grindstone, eyes on the ball, feet together and arms straight, you can play a pretty good game of golf. Thanks for being in sympathy with me. NOW that's that. All my love. P"[27]

Fine's painting "Astraea," (see color plate) which was not only included in the 1961 Pittsburgh International Exhibition but printed on the

Many of Fine's paintings in the late 1950s were very large and included elements of collage as well as embedded pieces of foil.

publicity poster, is a large starburst of black that explodes on the right side of the canvas, yet it does not overwhelm the thinly painted flesh-tone space to the left. As the title indicates, Fine perceived there to be a loose affinity between her painting and nature (in this case to a star) that intensified after her move to The Springs. She felt that the country environment encouraged her to be free with color and form, and that her paintings were "more open and more relaxed" than those she had done in the city, which she described as "more cerebral."[28] "A Ceremony of a Kind" (1955), (see color plate) for example, is a duality of light and dark color, with white and light gray predominating. Lines, both heavy and attenuated, swirl around a darker core in which two curvilinear shapes evoke violins. In its entirety, it achieves an airy solemnity, like an adagio played softly at high noon. In "Black Waterfall" (1957), Fine used color sparingly, almost as shadows of her strong but fluid black-and-white brush strokes (see color plate). Because of its underlying structure of planes, it projects a serene force, the opposite of chaos. However, the title is appropriate, for there is about the painting an evocation of falling water. So also in the collage "The Roaring Wind" (1958) (see color plate) pieces of aluminum foil glint through a vortex of black as if actual scraps had been caught up by a gust and were whirling around. When, however, de Kooning remarked during a visit to her studio, "But this is all out of doors. It's what you see out here, isn't it?" Fine disagreed. Her reply was politely equivocal, masking her strong dissent, "Well, yes, I guess so, if you say so."[29] But then she insisted that he had the order of perception wrong. "I *first* painted the pictures and *then* saw these forms, the black trunks of the trees in the vertical, and the horizontals of the panorama of the landscape all about me. The paintings then as now were truly abstract paintings — with aesthetics the only goal."[30] According to D'Vorzon, Fine did not want her work to have any relationship to the real world. "While de Kooning, who used to go over to her studio and sit and rock, may have been painting the land, influenced by what he saw, Perle was not. Her work was pure, really pure. It was also incredibly peaceful. Space was always organized."[31]

Despite Fine's assertion about total abstraction, the reviewers of her solos at the Tanager Gallery also noted a connection to nature. John Ashbery, reviewing for *ARTnews*, said of her 1958 exhibition that her paintings offered “abstract intimations of nature — bare twigs, wind, ice, split-rock — rendered by tan, white, and silver cris-crossed by forked black lines.”[32]

This perception was reinforced when Fine was included in “Nature in Abstraction: The Relation of Abstract Painting and Sculpture to Nature and Twentieth-Century American Art,” an exhibition of the Whitney Museum of American Art that opened in January 1958, then traveled to the Philips Gallery, the Fort Worth Art Center, the Los Angeles County Museum, the San Francisco Museum of Art, the Walker Art Center, and the City Art Museum of St. Louis. The previous spring John Baur had written to Fine inviting her to take part in the exhibition. However, because she had no dealer in New York City, there was no place for him to see her paintings to make a selection. Unable to make the trip to East Hampton, he asked her for suggestions and in response she shipped him several. “Your paintings arrived yesterday and I am delighted with them!” Baur immediately wrote back. “It is difficult to choose, but my preference is slightly in favor of “The Storm Departs” and I believe that, for this particular exhibition, it would be the best selection.”[33] Baur had designed the exhibition on a three-fold theme: “The Land and the Waters”; “Light, Sky and Air”; and “Cycles of Life and Seasons.” “The Storm Departs” was in the “Light, Sky and Air” section.[34]

Fine’s own words, printed in *It Is: A Magazine for Abstract Art* published by the sculptor Philip Pavia, give evidence of the surface connection between her art and nature. At the same time, they point to the interplay between seeing and feeling as the primary impetus for her paintings:

> First Session Clear day, vivid-bright, almost too bright to see color. The canvas, pure and taut, beckons, yet frightens. Look around the studio. The canvas — not quite. Through the studio window, the green-black trees sharp against the other bank of trees a hundred, maybe two hundred yards away. One color, one hue against another hue, not another shade, but another hue, another color. Blending yet distinguishing, forming, always forming. Through seeing, feeling. Through feeling, seeing.

> "Tell me, what do you think of when you paint? Do you paint what you see? What is it related to? Through seeing, feeling, through feeling, seeing. Which comes first, the chicken or the egg?" The better question, how deeply do you feel about what you see, and how did you get that way? One thing is certain, only when it came to expression in my own language, through my own variety of experiences, both subjective and cumulative, did it sharpen my perception, and apperception.
>
> Action, feeling, surging, demanding action. Mixing the color. What demands that makes on time, fleeting time. Plenty of color, for broad bold strokes. Landscape is panoramic, canvas is not. Across, across; it heaves — and thankfully, it holds. Now, against and through, back and forth, color against color, color through color, changing and modifying, as the heavy cloud, which has just blotted out the sun, hovers overhead, and at once softens and pulls together the masses of the trees. Its singleness is — now. Walk away, far across to the end of the room. Turn, Dare to look.
>
> It has passed the first test — it has life, pulsating, meaningful.[35]

Two immense diptychs, "Flood Cloud" (1960), and "Tournament" (1959), (see color plates) dominated Fine's 1960 solo exhibition at the Tanager Gallery, taking up much of the exhibition space. To the art critic Helen De Mott, both paintings were aptly named. "Flood Cloud" was "a devouring monster rushing across a white horizon." "Tournament" gave the impression of mounted knights, bright pennants, and gayly dressed spectators, all gathered on a clear day to celebrate an event that could best be described as controlled conflict. In her glowing review, De Mott wrote that in "Tournament," "Large, natural forms push and move against each other, suggesting combat; black and dull reds are broken by matted stretches of color and collage."[36]

Besides their scale, the paintings of this period made vibrant and intricate use of collage. Overcoming its inherent static quality, Fine imbued collage with what one critic called "a breathing, animated nature." She interwove jagged scraps of paper, slanted spears of gray or black, a tracery of pencil lines, heavy paint-laden brush strokes, and glints of embedded aluminum and gold foil, often slashing horizontally across a white field. She never used photographs, cut-outs from newspapers, or detritus in her collages as a form of cultural commentary as did Rauschenberg; instead the paper and foil were true to themselves as material, adding a sculptural dimension, what De Mott called "a textured impasto." Somehow, for all the dynamic power of the collages, they were "essentially anchored, typical of the artist, almost her signature," commented Edith Burckhardt in *ARTnews*.[37] Martica Sawin wrote in *Arts*: "The handling of several media simultaneously while preserving the fluidity and spontaneity of the whole is no inconsiderable achievement, especially when there is also a delicacy of nuance as well as purposeful structuring of the ensemble. Other artists have been content simply to establish a complicated space through similar means, but in this work there is the enrichment of an emotional and visually connotative shape imposed on the whole."[38]

Because of the compelling aura of her collages, Fine was invited to take part in the major exhibition "The Art of Assemblage" in the fall of 1961 at the Museum of Modern Art. William Seitz, associate curator, wrote in the catalogue that an assemblage was "made by a process of dismemberment and rearrangement." Like Robert Rauschenberg's combines, an assemblage aggressively pushed beyond collage, as indicated by Seitz' use of the word "dismemberment." In actuality, the exhibition of 251 works was wide-ranging, paying heed to everyone from Picasso and Fine (to whom the word "dismemberment" was not applicable) to Rauschenberg and Jasper Johns (to whom it was); in fact, Johns's "Target" incorporated disembodied faces and plaster casts of body parts, including severed hands and an ear.[39]

As this exhibition was going on, Fine was painting a series of much more austere works, their force reliant solely on the placement of a simple form and color. "For some time I had been searching in painting for the powerful confrontation of the image that I had experienced in collage. Yet, I wanted to be more direct, not to fuss around with collage," she explained.[40] She did not show these experimental paintings to anyone but Berezov, for she was dissatisfied, finding most of them to be too "pretty," too "pleasant," and lacking intensity. "I think pleasantness was the thing I was trying to destroy, so that something could be said by elimination."[41] The breakthrough came in the early 1960s, when she was preparing a show for the Graham Gallery, the first gallery to represent her since her break with Parsons.

> I had a whole exhibition ready to go out. And I decided it was not going to go....I destroyed every painting there. I said, “well, it’s good but it’s not good enough.” I learned more from that experience with no one there to say “save this one; don’t do this.” I just had the feeling — and it was a very important feeling — that nobody cared really. Only *I* had to care enough to do this and to know that I could do better. And I had to destroy it in order for it not to exist. But I learned more from that experience than from anything that ever happened in my life...that feeling was the basis of everything that I had to do...if [a painting] didn’t have that depth of feeling, that intense degree of depth of feeling, it would have absolutely nothing....If I’d had a psychiatrist he couldn’t have done any more for me than just that. It was through the painting that I discovered what it was I had to do and that I could then really face coming back to the city and going to teach. . . .And I went out with such confidence because I knew what I was talking about. And I have that feeling today, that I can face anything because I know what it’s based on.[42]

From hereon, Fine’s paintings took on an ineffable yet compelling quality that she felt she had never achieved before. “It’s a very strange thing that it should have had to happen that way,” she said. “But there was no one to stop me.”[43]

Harold Rosenberg wrote that Fine's art had an intelligence that was beyond concept. During the 1960s he worked with Fine and Berezov on a manuscript about Hofmann.

CHAPTER EIGHT

PAINTING IN THE SHADOW OF THE GRID

Harold Rosenberg who had written voluminously about many artists finally wrote sincerely and succinctly about Fine in 1958: "A painter who keeps at it within the changing art movements develops an intelligence in work that is beyond any concept. This intelligence cannot be pushed the way an idea can — a fact obscured by the crowd that likes to collect in the empty lot at the end of the line. Perle Fine's paintings have that intelligence which comes from working into ideas and out of them. Free of the obsession of The Last Word, each represents an accumulation of thought that by this time cannot help but be original."[1]

The late 1950s had been a solitary time of profound reflection and reassessment for Fine, preparing her for the early 1960s and her reentry — intelligent, calm, and original — into the maelstrom of the New York art scene, although she continued to live and paint in the serenity of The Springs. She brought with her a series of paintings called "Cool." Of these, she wrote: "Out of revelation, which came about through endless probing, came revolution."[2]

In Manhattan, there were many more galleries, rising from approximately 100 in 1950 to 150 in 1960 and then jumping to 250 in 1965. And these galleries were showing many more styles — the foremost being Pop and Minimalism which, as the decade progressed, clashed, merged, and blurred with Op, New Realism, Color Field, Conceptual, Earthworks, and Performance Art. There were so many new artists that *ARTnews* had been forced to expand its venerable Reviews and Previews column adding a section titled "New Names This Month." About the entire culture, there was a manic-depressive quality, with extreme highs and lows. Pop was certainly the manic part with its garish colors and mechanical processes of reproduction such as silk screening. Its endless imagery of consumer culture (e.g. hamburgers, movie stars, comic strip characters) appealed strongly to young people who wanted to be "with it" and who found the new art much more accessible than Abstract Expressionism had ever been. Pop was a bell-bottomed, love-beaded, flower-child happening in which "the media is the message," as Marshall McLuhan proclaimed. But, paradoxically, Pop was also the depressive part; Warhol's silkscreens of an electric chair and grisly automobile accidents testified to its darker side.

At the opposite extreme was Minimalism with its strong reductionist strain. As a style, some critics maintained that it superceded Abstract Expressionism in a neat historical progression, and that its theoretical underpinnings were as solid. The critic Michael Fried made the point that the Minimalists "read Greenberg, valued the same recent art, but saw in it a development that projected literalness….It was as if [they] were the ones who really believed the Greenburgian reduction — that there was a timeless essence to art that was progressively revealed."[3] Like Pop, it had a mechanistic component in which the creative presence of the artist or sculptor was downplayed or, ideally, eliminated often by the use of purchased materials or recycled items, for example, Carl Andre's neatly aligned firebricks and John Chamberlain's battered car parts.

Pop and Minimalism were perceived by other critics to be reactions against the gestural paintings of the Abstract Expressionists in which the souls of the artists were supposedly poured/dripped/slashed onto the canvases, or bent/hammered/torched into the sculpture. But many young artists were convinced that their work was without historical precedent or influence, arising sui generis. For example, Roy Lichtenstein pronounced that he was "anti-experimental, anti-contemplative, anti-nuance, anti-getting-away-from-the-tyranny-of-the-rectangle, anti-movement, and light, anti-mystery, anti-paint quality, anti-Zen, and anti-all those brilliant ideas of preceding movements which everyone understands so thoroughly."[4] But Fine, having seen many art styles and their intermeshed world views come and go since the 1930s, knew differently: "I think the whole art scene is conditioned by what's shown, whether we like it or not. And the minimal art, for instance, the minimal sculpture, we certainly can't look at sculpture the way we did before, because minimal art exists in sculpture. It makes some of the most quiet sculpture look baroque." She expressed concern that minimalist artists "may be limited in how far they can go" but that nonetheless what they were doing was important. "The fact is that it does convey a pure feeling about rhythm and distance and cadence and movement and all that kind of thing."[5]

For all the endless talk of the "artist as subject" ten years before, now the talk was on art as object. Frank Stella, a prominent Minimalist, pronounced "what you see is what you see," a statement with which Andy Warhol would have agreed. When asked why he painted Campbell Soup cans, Warhol replied with arch innocence that he really liked Campbell soup. The quest of the Existential hero for meaning was reduced to the acquisition of green stamps, reproduced in a grid pattern. Even Jasper Johns's flags could be interpreted not as paintings per se but as objects that filled the entire canvas with the repeating motif of stars and stripes, muted with white, or replicated in reverse order of perspective, thereby undercutting any oblique reference to patriotism.

Along with the new styles, there was a major reassessment and realignment of Abstract Expressionism. Rothko was still painting his amorphous and glowing cloud-like forms, only now they were very dark and brooding, culminating in the deep austere canvases eventually displayed in the Rothko Chapel in Houston, Texas. Kline was experimenting with color with varying degrees of success, and de Kooning was still skillfully and inventively turning out de Koonings as were a host of young imitators. Newman, whose work had never sold but whose proclamations remained as strident as ever, began to be noticed by a new generation of art students, particularly those exploring Color Field and Minimalism. His 1958 retrospective at Bennington College had prompted Eugene C. Goossen, curator for the exhibition, to declare that "Vic Heroicus Sublimis" was of equal quality to the large pictures of Picasso, Matisse, and Monet. Such lavish praise sent Newman's star on an upward trajectory. Then there was Reinhardt who by 1960 had reached the apotheosis of reduction with his five-feet-by-five-feet canvases, divided into nine squares with a cross used not as a religious symbol but as a kind of axis mundi. He was in many ways the precursor to Stella and the other Minimalists, having been transfixed by austerity since the late 1940s, although he would have eschewed the title of Minimalist as he had all the other titles that had been proffered him.

There had also been an enormous shift in cultural perception, so much so that paintings that had seemed violent when first shown in the late 1940s now seemed almost quiet. This called into question the interconnection between the psychological profiles of the Abstract Expressionists and their art as well as the true nature of change. In discussing Pollock's innovative use of scale, Frank O'Hara made a telling observation:

> No wonder, then, that when these paintings were first shown in the Betty Parsons Gallery the impression was one of inexplicable violence and savagery. They seemed about to engulf one. This violence, however, was not an intrinsic quality of the paintings, but a response to Pollock's violation of our ingrained assumptions regarding scale. So impressively had Pollock expounded his insight into the qualities dormant in the use of scale that when seen only a few years later at the Janis Gallery or in the Museum of Modern Art the violence had been transmuted into a powerful personal lyricism. The paintings had not changed, but the world around them had.[6]

Abstract Expressionism would continue as an important style, however, it had lost much of its impact. Not long before Kline's death in 1962, Jon Schueler spoke with him at a party held in the lavish apartment of a wealthy collector. On the walls were paintings by Rothko and Pollock as well as a few by Kline. "They're not the same paintings that we painted," Kline forlornly told Schueler. "We had a force and a rebellion in us. We were angry and we wanted the paint to be sloppy and we wanted to break everything apart, and now look at it! It has become polite and refined and cultured. I don't recognize it anymore. The painting is not the same."[7]

Another major change was that women who had been painting and sculpting since the 1940s began to receive some belated recognition, among them Nell Blaine, Louise Bourgeois, Lee Krasner, and Alice Neel. For the first time in an interminable 17 years of neglect, Louise

Nevelson tasted critical success when she showed her "Moon Garden Plus One" sculptures at Grand Central Moderns in 1958. About her show at the Herbert Gallery two years later in January 1960, a critic wrote, "Miss Nevelson has 'arrived' now, so needs no critical panegyrics jammed with wisdom after the event, but everyone should see this show."[8] Her arrival was indeed a long time coming and was by no means complete. Nor was it for the other women artists, who moved fleetingly in and out of the blind spots of the critics' eyes. Henry Geldzahler wrote an illuminating mea culpa several years after the fact about excluding Bourgeois from the important "New York Painting and Sculpture 1940–1970" exhibition at the Metropolitan Museum of Art, an exhibition which became infamous among women artists because he had chosen 41 men and one woman: Helen Frankenthaler. About Bourgeois, he admitted: "My inability to deal with women on certain levels, I understand now, interfered with my ability to see what she was doing."[9] Geldzahler's inability to see was a chronic disease among museum curators. When in 1969 the Whitney Annual included only eight women among 143 artists, the museum was picketed by angry women. Slow to learn from their New York brethren, the curators of the Corcoran Biennial in Washington, D.C. included no women in 1971, which lead to the museum being picketed a year later while the selection process was underway for the 1973 show.[10]

Turning 60 in 1965, Fine did not participate in these demonstrations although she was in complete sympathy with them. "I started so long ago. I was one of the few women painters of the time. It's always a fight, and I always thought, 'Well, it should get easier.' But it never gets any easier, though it does remain very exciting. I'm not myself at all when I'm not in the studio. There is life there."[11] But at least she had a dealer again, the Graham Gallery on Madison Avenue, with solos in March 1961, April 1963, March 1964, and February 1967. The Graham was not among the galleries that were considered influential — among them being those of Leo Castelli, André Emmerich and Sidney Janis, as well as Richard Bellamy's Green Gallery — but it was a good one, and Fine's affiliation meant that collectors once again had the chance to see her paintings.

It was in preparation for her 1963 show at the Graham Gallery that Fine destroyed the entire exhibition, painting instead her "Cool" series. Eliminating what she considered irrelevant, she placed on strongly vertical canvases simplified monochromatic horizontal bands, some sharply defined, others softly lapping, as if they were "at sea at some eternal doorway," as an impressed art critic described them.[12] "Cool" was one of the most popular words of the era, signifying a sophisticated but knowing detachment. Irving Sandler took it to mean a deadpan art "devoid of signs of emotion." Another critic defined it as nihilistic.[13] Fine chose the word "Cool" to convey "a quiet kind of nothing," via a limited motif and subdued color, that still had an expressive quality, a serene excitement. "The [paintings] have a clarity that rings a bell, like an awakening." (See color plate.) Fine was open to the Minimalist idea of a painting being an object in and of itself; that idea had been inculcated in her during her student days with Hofmann. Where she differed with the Minimalists was stopping there. Writing about the "Cool" series for the German publication *Das Kunstwerk,* which had requested permission to reproduce one of the paintings, Fine stated: "There is more than meets the eye here. These simplified works do not intend to be hard-edge or soft-edge; the expression is more than merely chemical or optical — it is metaphysical."[14]

In a radio interview, Sandler point-blank asked Fine if the "Cool Series" was a reaction against gestural painting, to which she replied, "It isn't really a reaction. It's more a growth," and while it appeared to be different from her Abstract Expressionist paintings, "it wasn't really." He then asked if they had any symbolic meaning, to which her answer was a flat no: "The paintings are *really* abstract. I think for the first time in my life I'm painting abstract painting. And I think I was really shoved into this — a *necessity* to do this through Pop art. Because Pop art went so completely in the other direction which was so super-super-real, I felt that — well, why not be super-abstract or super something or other? In any case, that was the direction I was going, and I felt clarity was very, very important for me to achieve."[15]

The "Cool" exhibition prompted reviewer Lawrence Campbell, writing in *ARTnews*, to use the words "radically different," although he warned that the work should not be tumbled into a file marked "Hard-Edge," because they retained Fine's own quality of lyricism:

> For [Fine] the wave of New Realism and Pop Art has cleared the air and brought doubters off the fence. The hardening of the ranks should frighten off the painters who have found the avant-garde an asylum for the untalented. To her it seems more important than ever to clean up the aura of garbage which is clinging to art, and to paint works which will express life-affirming, idealistic feelings through the construction of ordered color-spaces.... The force of the relationships and the quiet eloquence of the colors triumph here. And the more "confusing" expression in her earlier paintings was perhaps less mysterious than these spaces which seem to sway or bend at the command of invisible forces.[16]

In retrospect, Fine felt that her "Cool Series" was ahead of its time. Critics praised it, but collectors, razzle-dazzled by Pop, didn't buy. Yet she did not regret the effort it took. "It was a kind of nerve-wracking thing to do and yet a marvelous thing to live with, that at the end of the day you could really enjoy looking at a painting like that."[17] The series provided her with a sense of peacefulness similar to that which she experienced in The Springs. "It is a strange world for an artist to be untroubled, and this period of painting gave me a strange feeling of elation, like breathing good clean air."[18]

Fine was also aware that her change in style could lead to charges of inconsistency. This charge was the bugbear of many artists including Picasso who masterfully went through period after period. Its opposite — doing the same thing in the same way, thereby developing a signature style that collectors and curators could readily identify — was equally onerous, as if serial working methods had sunk into the marrow, forcing the artist into replication. In the early 1950s, Pollock was skewered by critics for changing his style and skewered by his own psyche for not changing. O'Hara wrote only a few years after Pollock's death that culture is capable of entertaining more than one truth simultaneously in a given era: "Few artists, however, are capable of sustaining more than one in the span of their activity, and if they are capable they often are met with the accusation of 'no coherent, unifying style,' rather than a celebration."[19] So too, when Stella abandoned

Minimalism for a garish bas-relief that practically exploded off the wall, he was pilloried by the critics.

It was the problem of stylistic change that prompted Fine to write to her friend May Tabak Rosenberg, the wife of Harold Rosenberg:

> When one is committed to working in the abstract, there is more of a necessity to follow through in the pictorial sense; aesthetics rule here, and where aesthetics dictate, means often change; and a new look seems to have been created. When an artist no longer lives, there is never a lack of unification in the body of his work. One can look back and see the whole idea much more easily; but there is an uneasiness while the artist is still alive, and the possibility that he may continue to move disconcerts many people. We learn that every great movement of art in history — surrealism, impressionism, dadaism, to name a few, affects all artists in one degree or another. Why not, then, the art of today? We can discard the pop in pop-art, but the clarity of expression cannot be overlooked; certainly surrealism abounds in the art of today, although it is 50 or 60 years old already. It may not always be apparent, because that single nameless thing that belongs to each artist takes precedent over all the influences around him, unifies his ideas and his life.[20]

If Fine had been forced to categorize her art in its entirety, the set (or label) she would have chosen would have been "pure abstraction," for within it were the subsets geometric, biomorphic and expressionist. Metaphorically, change was analogous to the progression of wheat from the grain to the seedling to the mature stalk, all outwardly different but inwardly the same; and empowering all was a mysterious force, as real in art as in nature.

Fine would have agreed with O'Hara that celebration, not censure, was in order when an artist's stylistic change was motivated by integrity (which she would have identified as a call towards expressive wholeness and clarity) and not by a need to please an audience of dealers, collectors and curators, nor by the need for the adrenalin-rush of novelty. Once when she was asked whether being connected to a gallery brought about a change in her painting, Fine was adamant: "I don't even think of the gallery, or anything that's the outside world, because it stands in the way. If you think of a gallery, you have to think of a particular gallery. Let's say you are thinking of going into the Pace Gallery or the Marlborough. Then you have to think about what they might like. I can't think of that. I concern myself only with the elements that make a work of art. Are you interested in changing your light concept? Should it absorb or should it reflect more light? Do you want more and more?"[21]

However, her own ability to focus so thoroughly did not preclude her paying close attention to the changing aspects of the avant-garde. Just as she could see the value of Pop art and Minimalism, so she saw Conceptual art, that began to develop in the late 1960s and gained impetus in the 1970s, as an intriguing aesthetic movement that would enrich the whole "world of painting." According to Fine, up to that point, there had been "two major polarities" in art: abstract and representational painting. She considered Conceptual art to be an entirely new and distinct third polarity. Using italics for emphasis, she wrote: "Although it is an extension of the *abstract* idea, it has become so interesting and diverse as to warrant its own category. This is a world *outside* of painting — a world of ideas, the new, the shocking, the philosophical, the intellectual, the ecological, etc. As such, it should be called something that would separate it from the art of painting, which is, strictly speaking, a pictorial art."[22]

It was her openness to new ideas and her broad knowledge of the art world that worked in Fine's favor when she decided she had no choice but to seek a teaching position to alleviate her on-going financial difficulties. While she had no degree to qualify her for teaching in college, she had her work and her long experience in the art world to recommend her. "Perle, by making her home in New York City, has the opportunity to be at almost every opening of significance, meet critics, museum directors, and other artists," wrote an art professor in a recommendation for her.[23] In 1961, she was a visiting critic and lecturer at Cornell University from which came the offer of a permanent position. At the same time, Hofstra University approached her with an offer. Located in Hempstead, Long Island, between The Springs and New York City, Hofstra was ideal for Fine because her appointment would not require her to relocate. She told Hofstra that if they could match Cornell's offer, she would take it. They did match the offer, and Fine immediately became an associate professor. "I was dead broke before then," she said. "That was the equivalent of a grant."[24] While she had taught privately both in New York City and Provincetown, her position at Hofstra, from 1962 to 1973, was her first and only academic one. At the very beginning, she was uncertain how to teach undergraduates in the formal sense: "I didn't know what I should say or lecture on until somebody said, 'Take the attendance.' So I took the attendance."[25] She soon discovered that she liked teaching undergraduates, no matter the course, whether it be abstract or academic, figure or still-life, drawing or painting. "I had always been an anti-person person. I kept away from too much social involvement because I felt that I needed the time to be alone to work out my ideas, but when I began to teach I discovered to my surprise that I enjoyed people. I took teaching very seriously but found that it drained most of my energy. Teaching is a creative commitment."[26]

Hofstra was not renowned for its art department and, therefore, did not attract students who were intending to make painting their lifework. As a result, many students entered the studio never having taken an art class before. "They didn't know how to sharpen a pencil!" Fine recalled with dismay.[27] Challenged to come up with ways to motivate the students, at one point she wrote to her friend John Cage, the avatar of musical silence and the composer of random sound, about the difficulty:

> I might add that we talk a lot about your work in my classes and when it is most difficult to penetrate young minds about pure painting, I often resort to discussion of pure music and the beauty and expression innate in pure sound and its analogy to pure color penetrating the canvas. It is difficult to teach out there where mediocrity is the norm, but I think it is all the more rewarding when it succeeds in awakening these flaccid souls.[28]

Despite her insistence that she was primarily a "painter among painters," instead of a teacher among students, she was very strong in her ideas about how students should be taught, going back to her days with Nicolaides and Hofmann. For example, she thought that contour drawing misled students. "It is more important to know the various axes of the figure: the upper part of the figure takes one direction, making one axis; the pelvis takes another, creating a second axis; the head, if turned slightly, takes another," she explained. Contour drawing as masterfully practiced by Matisse was markedly different than that done by students. "Matisse did these magnificent drawings in maybe four or five lines in which he included the forms that he knew, the space they were going through, and so on, which made such extremely satisfying drawing," explained Fine. "But the way a student would do it would be to follow it around the outside edges, flattening it out and not including the space in which it occurs, which would make all the difference between a good drawing and a bad drawing."[29]

"I was quite a severe task master," she said. "I overheard a student say 'I don't like her very much but I certainly respect her.'"[30] Fine enjoyed telling the story about a member of the football team who signed up for her course to earn what he thought would be "a few easy credits." One afternoon, his work incomplete, he requested that he be dismissed for football practice whereas Fine told him it wasn't going to make any difference if he missed practice because she was about to fail him, so he wouldn't be on the team much longer. He began to pay attention and get his work done, eventually becoming one of the art department's best students.[31]

In 1965 while teaching at Hofstra, Fine came down with a severe case of mononucleosis that lingered for many months. "I had the worst case of it. My throat closed right up. It really was very painful."[32] Too tired to paint standing before an easel and with doctor's order to be "quiet for a while at home," she undertook a series of collages made out of pieces of wood, which she spread out on the floor of her studio. The first ones were as large as five feet square and employed curvilinear forms and high relief. They were painted a vivid blue, which Fine mixed herself so that it "came forward and receded," emitting as much light as it absorbed. For her, this "color had a kind of shocking feel" especially in the daytime when the light hit the sides of the cut-out forms.[33] These collages became a bridge to her next set in which the forms were superimposed on a white wood surface painted with the traces of a grid. Writing in the catalog "Perle Fine: Major Works 1954–1978," David Deitcher, curator at Guild Hall in East Hampton, wrote of this group: "The cut-out forms often pictorially warp the grid, as if the space has been subjected to some powerful gravitational pull. The passages of color act almost musically, endowing these images with rhythms, sometimes contrapuntal, sometimes almost staccato. Seen from certain angles, light hits the edges of the raised surfaces and further activates the image.[34] When the collages were shown at the Graham Gallery in February 1967, a critic also picked up on their musicality, likening them to "scores for instruments not yet invented, notations for hot jazz passages in a foreign scale, or if you are space-minded, of architectural models of a city on Mars, where buildings and boulevards are bathed in clear blues and sharp black and whites....Is it real? It is a real object produced by the intricate processes of the imagination and a completely controlled technical skill. And it's right there before you."[35]

Fine moved from the "Cool Series" to the bas-relief collages on the basis of a challenge to herself: "Could I get as much satisfaction from paintings that had a more tactile surface, something in which the surface itself is more exciting? Could I then get that same kind of sense of mystery? Could I get something perhaps with a stronger motif and still have some of that mystery, something that was a little more brilliant...not so much in color but in surface quality?"[36]

For the first time in her career, Fine's exhibition was not only a critical success but also a financial one. In a draft of a note to the Pennsylvania Academy of the Fine Arts regarding their invitational exhibition, Fine wrote in Oct. 30, 1967:

> If invited, I shall be happy to exhibit one of my new wood collages. Very few are available from my show early this year. Most of them are taken, four by the State Department for tour and exhibition in Australia and elsewhere, one acquired by the University of California at Berkeley for their permanent collection, several sold, etc. But this summer I completed two which I consider to be handsome and important works. Thank you very much for getting in touch with me.[37]

William Seitz, then serving as director of the Rose Art Museum at Brandeis University in Waltham, Mass., was so impressed by the collages that he wanted to acquire one for the collection. Having no acquisitions budget, he proposed to Fine that he trade "Moment of the Wind," which had been donated to the Rose by Fine's parents, for a collage. But the difference in value was too great, nor did Fine want to offend her parents, so she declined. "Perhaps sometime in the future, if funds should become available, you will be able to acquire the collage for your collection," she wrote to him in response.[38] Other universities were more fortunate. "CrossCurrents" went to the University of California, which was in the process of establishing the Hans Hofmann archives and was collecting paintings by his former students. "Unequivocably Blue" went to Cornell University. "Blue Streak Blue" and "Blue Anyway" were sold to Westinghouse. Guild Hall in East Hampton acquired "Blue Anyway #5." In 1969, at the personal request of the architect Philip Johnson, she donated "Blue Chip Blue #1" to be auctioned off by Parke-Bernet for the Israel Relief Fund. (See color plates.)

Yet Fine was not totally at ease with the wood collages because she felt that "the object was taking over" although they were completely abstract. "As they became more and more beautiful, they also became objects — *Icons* — and they got farther and farther away from painting. I knew then that I must return to painting — that in painting only could I find the means to express what I felt. A concept of *inward* called for a somewhat different form than I had been using — the frontal, holistic form, with a clearly stated surface which had to exist in order to implement the idea."[39]

That call to painting and only painting, doing nothing else, led to her decision to retire from Hofstra in 1973. In her letter to the head of the art department, she wrote about the burden of teaching and her need for total immersion in her work:

> I accepted the position at Hofstra when I found myself almost completely out of funds to continue my work and to pay for a studio. I was not young when I took the job, but did not realize what it would entail. It meant getting up at 5 a.m. and leaving my door while the moon was still high in the

> sky, and the weather was often bitter cold. When I returned, it was dark. Thus, these days were completely lost as far as my painting was concerned. What was worse, I needed the following day to recuperate from this strenuous work — in a word, the job of teaching (since I was very conscientious) was completely debilitating and useless as well, since all my energies went to earn money to pay for a studio that I could not use, because I WAS WORKING, A COMPLETELY VICIOUS CIRCLE. The only answer then was to ask for a leave of absence. This I did and was denied. This is where I stand now, and at 67, I feel that I can no longer divide my interest and my energies, not to mention the fact that it endangers my health....My painting in the last couple of years is of a subjective nature. It is my answer to the violence, noise and strife rampant in our world today. It is non-gestural, it is a whisper in reply to a shout. It demands constant uninterrupted performance. I must lose myself in it for it to have any meaning beyond what one sees with one's eyes. I feel that it is crucial to give my work all my time, for anything less than the full utilization of it jeopardizes its complete realization toward which I have been working all my life.[40]

In February 1974 following her retirement, she was given a ten-year retrospective at the college, the centerpiece of which was the unusual "Quinquepartite," a single work comprised of five canvases, each over 5 feet square. It was so named because it consisted of five equal, interrelated, and individual parts in which the unity arose from the warmth and "the weight of its color," its breadth and its openness, and "through its non-gestural commitment."[41] She called it an "evocative rather than an evincive work — that is, a work that one experiences with the senses, rather than one that is merely seen." Fine's selection of the word "weight," was intentional; she also frequently used the word "gravity" in reference to her paintings of this period, as if she were working with force fields, the result being not heaviness but energy.

That same year, Fine was inducted into the American Academy of Arts and Letters and the National Institute of Arts and Letters. Membership in these two groups (which would merge two years later into the American Academy and Institute of Arts and Letters) was honorary, and was extended to a limited number of notable artists, composers and writers. Along with Fine, her friend the sculptor Ibram Lassaw

In 1969, In Fine and Berezov spent Thanksgiving with her family in Malden, with whom she had always been close. L to R: Robert, Perle holding her niece Tania, and Melvin. Artistically precocious, Tania eventually became a graphic designer and an artist.

was inducted as were the artists and sculptors Richard Fleischner and Nancy Grossman. Fine's reaction to the formal induction ceremony was contained in a letter to her brother Melvin and his family in which she enclosed a souvenir program: "Dear Kids, I thought you might get a vicarious kick out of this program. It was almost as much fun as a Bar Mitzvah. But I am afraid I was guilty of 'gape mouth' at the proximity of all the celebrities."[42]

Even with the honor, doors still did not swing open easily unless she leaned on them, and often that wasn't enough. When The Whitney Museum of American Art was organizing "Abstract Expressionism: The Formative Years," Fine wrote to the curators twice, convinced that she had a rightful place in the exhibition. Receiving no response to her September 22, 1976, letter, she wrote again, "I feel strongly that I should be included here." But it didn't help. Krasner was the only woman among the fifteen chosen, and her inclusion in a show which was supposedly devoted to the "formative years" was peculiar because she did not begin to concentrate on her own work and to show until after Pollock's death.[43]

In the mid-1960s, following Berezov's retirement, Fine built a separate studio, at which point the house was dedicated primarily to living space, although Berezov used it for painting as did Fine in the winter. The studio was barn-like in construction, similar to the house, with unpainted vertical wood boards on the outside and a large bank of windows to the north over a barn door that could be slid open on warm days to flood the space with light. Smaller windows to the west and south provided cross ventilation. A loft at the south end provided a two-story storage area for her paintings. It was neither insulated nor heated because according to town code the installation of a heating system would have classified the structure as a house. Therefore, in the winter she worked in the house, using the studio on warm days only. Despite that one draw-back, the studio was the most wonderful space for painting that Fine had ever had, allowing her the luxury of spreading out her large canvases and showing them to visitors under optimal conditions. For example, one day she hosted a class of art students from Southhampton College who had seen only slides of her art.

"Someone pulled out one of the paintings of this group, and somebody else said 'let's see another.' Before we knew it we had a whole exhibition of them there in the studio. And the students were amazed that it was only by having a number of them around that they could get the idea. They had to see them all, one in contrast to another to see what a pink and, let's say, a tan and a green would do, and what it evoked as opposed to some other color or combination of colors."[44]

She was always very encouraging, telling students to "just keep on painting or sculpting no matter what happens," but at the same time, she was honest. During one of these studio visits, a mother of one of the Southhampton students who had accompanied the group cornered Fine:

> "I want to ask you this question: Can my daughter make a living at this?" And I said, "I'm sorry to say, no." She said "Well, that's terrible, I wish you hadn't said that." I said, "I wish I didn't have to say that, but it's true. If she does, she is very lucky, and if she sells, in all probability the work is mediocre, and might sell more because it's mediocre than it's good." Everybody knows mediocre does sell better than good work, and she said, "Well, I heard what de Kooning made." I said, "Ah that's the trouble. How many people are making what de Kooning makes? There might be eight or ten people in the whole country and the rest make less, they don't make anything, because people either buy or they don't buy."[45]

After her show at the Graham Gallery in 1967, there was a hiatus until 1972 when she had a solo exhibition at the Washburn Gallery, followed by three solos at the Andre Zarre Gallery in 1973, 1976 and 1977. Fine won Best-In Show at the 39th Annual Guild Hall Artists Members' Exhibition in 1978 in which 190 artists participated. The judges were Cynthia Navaretta, Betty Parsons, and Ray Prohaska. The award was the retrospective "Perle Fine: Major Works 1954–1978" at Guild Hall, covering a 24-year span, beginning with "A Broken Stillness" and extending through "Accordment Series #55: A Roseate Innocence," which Fine had just completed.

Generally, a retrospective is considered the culmination of an artist's career and codification of her role in the mainstream. That being the

Fine built a new studio down the hill from the house in the mid-1960s.

case, the most important retrospectives are at major museums, such as the Museum of Modern Art, the Guggenheim, or The Whitney. Merely on the basis of being a regional museum, Guild Hall didn't meet such vaulting criteria, but it didn't matter to Fine. She didn't care about retrospectives anyway because to her they looked backwards and she preferred to look forwards. "I'm always troubled when somebody says, 'I want to have a retrospective of your work.' I'll say, 'From when on?' because I feel that I was born anew doing this."[46] The 'this' to which she was referring was her masterpiece series, the "Accordments," so named because the word meant to her "an acceptance, serene, tranquil, evocations of being in tune with nature and the Universe."[47] Her vision — hinted at in the austere linearity of the "Cool Series" — now fully embraced the grid. Of the first paintings in the series, shown at the Andre Zarre Gallery in 1973, Edgar Buonagurio wrote in *Arts Magazine* that "these are gentle paintings of near unspeakable beauty." With wavering bands of close-valued mauve, pink, and ocher that suffused the canvases in what he described as "an elusive ethereal light," Buonagurio compared the series to Monet's "Waterlilies" "somehow boxed up and gone structural."[48] Other reviewers were equally laudatory, echoing Buonagurio's sentiments.

The use of the grid and serial working methods had become major components of art and sculpture beginning in the late 1950s, partially because they eliminated the difference between figure and ground, as well as emphasizing the flatness of the picture plane, as exemplified in the work of Johns, Larry Poons, and Agnes Martin, whose first grid paintings were shown at the Betty Parsons Gallery in 1961. But Fine approached the grid with a totally different mindset, predicated on her study of Mondrian in the 1940s and her prodigious skills as a colorist. She felt indebted to Mondrian whose theory of equivalences informed her painting, essentially enabling her to achieve an equilibrium in the midst of chaos. "He freed every artist," she said, "and everything I do is based on the plane. Our universe is right there on the canvas and color is the binding medium....My aim is to make it more beautiful."[49] In line with his metaphysical ideas of a fundamental reality intimated by painting, Fine attempted to express something unnamed and unnameable. This was diametrically opposed to how the grid was being used by artists such as Sol LeWitt who saw it as providing information on nothing but itself. "The serial artist does not attempt to produce a beautiful or mysterious object," he wrote, "but functions merely as a clerk cataloguing the results of his premise."[50]

Close in age and in temperament, Fine and Martin shared many similarities, one being that their art was routinely described by critics as "atmospheric" and "classic." But to the artist Mary Abbott, who knew Fine beginning in the early 1950s, Fine's grids were "tougher" than Martin's, which reflected her demanding approach to all her work: "There was no baloney, no horse-shit — tough thinking throughout."[51] Fine admired Martin, considering her to be a "very vital artist" whose grid paintings held a sense of mystery, "a quality that is more than just a flat design."[52] In her own paintings of this period, Fine was intrigued by how something that appeared to be flat could take on distance, a quality she found compellingly strange. Unfortunately, the two women did not know each other well, having met only a few times during the 1960s when Martin lived in New York City before returning to New Mexico. They appeared together in only one group show, "Geometric Abstraction in America" at the Whitney Museum of American Art in 1962, in which Fine's 1941 grid work "In Staccato" had been included along with Martin's 1961 work "The Islands," twenty years separating the paintings.

When Fine's grids were shown at the Andre Zarre Gallery in 1976, Peter Frank, art critic for *The Village Voice* who wrote the exhibition text, went to great lengths to make clear that "Fine no more apes Martin than Martin does Fine. Fine sees the precisely-drawn grid not only as a beautiful formation, but as a gorgeous one — that is, a formation that benefits from lush treatment." Her brushwork was very sensual, at times not only underlying the grid but surrounding it and "preventing it from reaching the picture's edge."[53] The hand-rendered lines, fluctuating in intensity, and the alternation of color longitudinally set up "color-rhythms" that were asymmetric, creating a rolling syncopation.

Fine's unique strength was, and always had been, her use of color. She had the capacity to combine cool and warm hues in a way that made

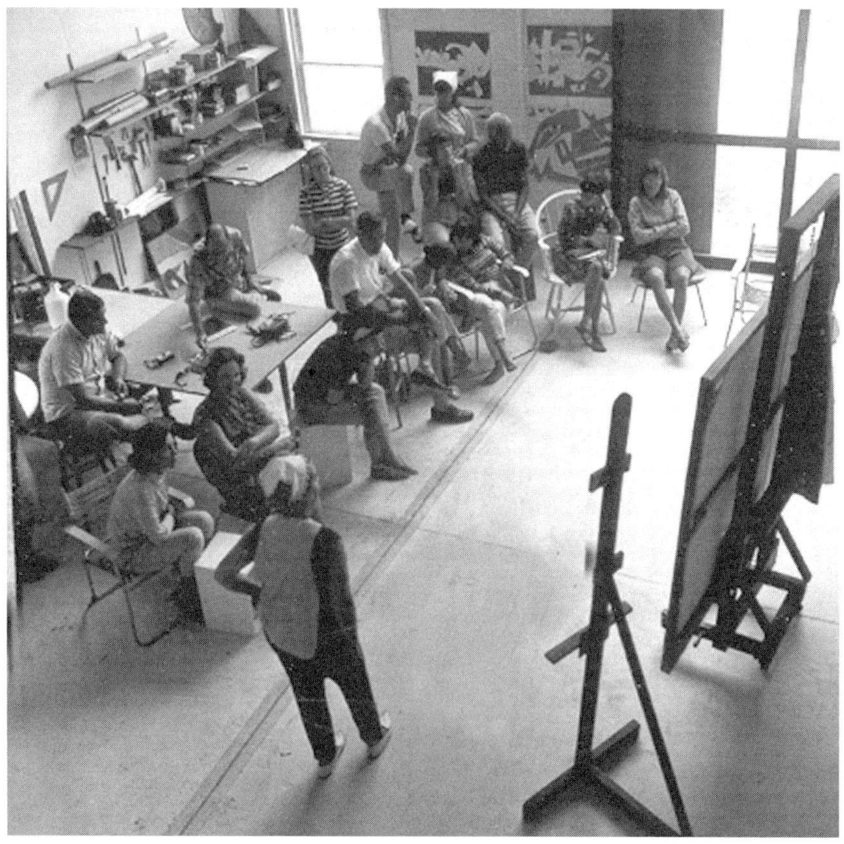

Art students from Southhampton College were frequent visitors to Fine's studio. Once she pulled out so many paintings for them to look at that the session turned into an impromptu exhibition.

them luminous. Finding the paintings to be a "provocatively beautiful interplay," Marjorie Welish was almost at a loss for words in an article in *Art in America*:

> Pale but tantalizing, Fine's color generally hovers around poles of pink and blue, but it is sometimes so subtly determined that it seems only to allude to namable hues. In the vertical stripe painting "A Woven Warmth," smooth brownish-pink bands alternate with scrumbled, nearly-white pinks and blues, the pink fading out entirely at the sides of the canvas, the blue growing more saturated as it approached the bottom edge — a subtlety of means so much more blatant in the telling than in the seeing. The best paintings are the ones where a range of brushwork enters into the low key — almost subliminal — interaction between structure and color.[54]

For an exhibition in 1977 at the Freedman Art Gallery at Albright College in Reading, Penn., Andre Zarre had been asked to write some text for the catalog, which he first sent to Fine for her review: "Miss Fine belongs to a generation of painters that has come up through the many facets of the art world of the '50s and '60s to a plateau of translucent calm and repose." Fine made only one change: she crossed out the word "translucent" and wrote in "imperturbable."[55]

It was ironic, and for Fine bittersweet, that in 1979, as her career was coming to an end, she received a $10,000 grant from the National Endowment for the Arts given on the basis of "the quality of the applicant's work and record of professional affiliation." Fine was 74 year old. The first signs of Alzheimer's had appeared.

EPILOGUE

In Fine's letters and papers, there is a scribble on a yellow legal pad made with a fine-point marker. On the bottom of the page in Berezov's handwriting are the words: "Perle Fine 4/10/87 at the Southhampton Nursing Home." After a lifetime of painting that began with crayon drawings on the walls and ceiling of her childhood bedroom, this was the last one — the paper carefully set before her and the marker placed in her hand by her husband who sat patiently by her side as she attempted to draw yet one more time.

The signs of Alzheimer's disease — cruel and irreversible — had begun to show at least seven to ten years earlier. Margie Kerr, who moved to East Hampton in 1980 with her husband Robert Richenburg, saw the evidence right away:

> Perle and Maurice used to come to parties here. She was very sweet and kind. I remember that she came into the kitchen once after almost all the food from the party was gone and she said to me, "Margie, if this were Provincetown, the artists would just open up your cabinets and eat whatever is there. By the end, the cabinets would all be empty." But already she was becoming forgetful. Once she came and was very apologetic, "I've forgotten I had a present for you. I've forgotten."[1]

Fine had two solos at the Ingber Gallery in April 1982 and 1984, and was included in several group shows, among them: "Modern Masters, Women of the First Generation" in 1982 at the Mabel Smith Douglas Library, Rutgers University, New Brunswick, N. J.; and "Some Major Artists of the Hamptons Then and Now: 1960s — 1980s," at the Elaine Benson Gallery in Bridgehampton, but the paintings in all of these were done in the 1950s and 60s. Despite her increasing infirmity, she continued to paint. In one of her last published statements for the group exhibition "Women Artists of Eastern Long Island" at Guild Hall in April-May, 1979, she wrote: "I propose to push forward beyond the known boundaries of art that evokes, rather than defines. These involvements become gravitational, emotional, and have, of necessity, their own logic. I want to find and paint a significant extension which is beyond known knowledge."[2]

Until 1985 when Fine was admitted to the Southhampton Nursing Home, Berezov tried with great difficulty to care for her by himself, not telling close friends and family how serious her condition really was. Particularly difficult to handle was her increasing paranoia that Berezov confided to Rae Ferren had started well before the memory loss. He first became aware of the problem one day when Fine picked him up at the railroad station in East Hampton. As they were walking to the car, she said to him, "We have to be careful. There has been someone sitting in the back seat." D'Vorzon remembered that Berevoz tried to hide even from his nearest neighbors how bad the situation was becoming. Once she stopped in unexpectedly and Fine began to talk about terrible things she thought were happening in the woods. "Maurice looked mortified. He did not want anyone to know."[3]

"As the Alzheimer's advanced, Maurice had a very rough time," said Kerr. "Perle was fearful for periods; then there were periods of anger; periods of suspicion. He absolutely adored her, and it was very hard on him. Once we saw them at a local restaurant. She wasn't really herself anymore, but Maurice was loving and gentle." Finally the burden of her care became too great. Kerr's mother was admitted to the Southhampton Nursing Home about the same time as Fine, so she often drove Berezov to visit. "I got to be very close to him during that period for he would tell stories as we drove. He had lived in Paris as a child and I had been born there, and it was like being with family when he told his stories about it. But Maurice would be in rags after he had visited with Perle."

Fine died of pneumonia on May 31, 1988, at the age of 83. Berezov died the following year. They were buried in the Green River Cemetery in East Hampton, the resting place as well of Willem and Elaine de Kooning, Lee Krasner, Jackson Pollock, Harold Rosenberg, and many other friends. In a eulogy written for the local paper, gallery owner Elaine Benson, who had known most of the artists in The Springs for many years, wrote that Fine was a strong and sensitive painter and a key figure in the New York School. “Perle was an eclectic artist, whose various phases demonstrated an intellectuality and search that placed her in a special category of committed painters whose works went beyond talent or craft.” Benson remembered her fondly as a small, pretty woman, who “was a dynamo of energy and commitment.”[4]

Fine had continued to work on her “Accordment” series until her confinement. For her, pure abstraction was like a beautiful unexplored country, the entry to which even Alzheimer’s could not seal off. Years before, Fine had listened to a recording of James Joyce reading from “Anna Livia Plurabella” from *Finnegan’s Wake.* Struck by the way Joyce made more than one thing happen by means of a single word, she wrote:

> Where words come out slower and slower, you sense the river flowing, the women washing, falling asleep, turning to stone. Those abstract words are grouped into a universe in which there is the feeling of movement of everything. I have been aware of trying more and more in painting to invest every form with many possibilities of meaning.[5]

In her last years, Fine’s own words had come out slower and slower, the river flowed around her as she fell asleep and turned to stone — fulfilled in her art and in accordment.

East Hampton artists at a beach picnic, 1962. Standing, left to right: Buffie Johnson, Lester Johnson, Howard Kanovitz, Fairfield Porter, Syd Solomon, Frederick Kiesler, Norman Bluhm, Emanuel Navaretta, and Perle Fine. Seated, left to right: unidentified, Lee Krasner (back to camera) Al Held, Mary Kanovitz, Balcomb Greene; middle row: John Little, Elaine de Kooning, James Brooks, Rae Ferren, Charlotte Park, Louis Schanker, Sylvia Stone, Ibram Lssaw, Theodore Stamos, Jane Wilson, Jane Freilicher, Robert Dash; left from front center: David Porter, Adolph Gottlieb, John Ferren, Lucia Wilcox. Photo: Hans Namuth

ENDNOTES

PROLOGUE

1. Terenzio, Stephanie, ed., *The Collected Writings of Robert Motherwell*, (New York: Oxford University Press, 1992), 167.
2. Quoted by F. Kaufmann, Thomas Mann, *The World as Will and Representation* (Boston, 1957), 272.
3. Benjamin Baldwin, "Perle Fine," *Arts & Architecture* (May 1947), 20–21. Jewell letter, Berezov Archives, Nashville, TN. Edgar Buonagurio, "Perle Fine," *Arts Magazine* (February 1973), 29.
4. Robert Richenburg interview with Housley, March 2003. Charlotte Fine interview with Housley, January 2003.
5. Alexander Russo, *Profiles of Women Artists* (Frederick, MD: University Press of America, 1985), 52.
6. Ann Eden Gibson, *Abstract Expressionism: Other Politics* (New Haven: Yale University, 1997), 80.
7. According to the Berezovs, the unnamed gallery owner was Samuel Kootz. However, in her interview with Russo, Fine implied it was Leo Castelli. Russo, 53.
8. Ibid., 50.
9. Miriam Schapiro, *Woman's Sensibility* (Valencia: California Institute of the Arts, 1975), 20.
10. Philip Pearlstein "The Private Myth," *ARTnews* (September 1961), 42.

CHAPTER I: ART FROM THE DAY SHE WAS BORN

1. Interview with Charlotte Fine, conducted by Housley, Jan. 2003
2. Sholom and Sarah appear as Simon and Sadie in some records. Leo's first name was Israel. The area of Russia from which the family emigrated was reconfigured into Poland following the First World War. Danzig is now Gdansk, Poland.
3. Website for the Town of Malden. Http://cfweb.smartedu.net/maldencity/welcome/landmark
4. Perle Fine interview conducted by Dorothy Seckler in 1968 for the Oral History Program, SI N/735, Archives of American Art (AAA), Smithsonian Institute, 1.
5. Russo, 52. Also Seckler, 1.
6. Housley.
7. Seckler, 21.
8. *Blue and Gold* (Oct. 11, 1923), Vol. XIII No. 13, 1.
9. James Brooks interview conducted by Dorothy Seckler, June 10, 1965, AAA, 2.
10. Seckler, 3.
11. Seckler, 2.
12. Ibid.
13. Henry McBride, "New York Season," *Art Digest* (Mid-December, 1927), 13.
14. W.P.A estimation, cited in Dore Ashton *The New York School: A Cultural Reckoning* (New York: The Viking Press, 1972), 45.
15. Seckler, 6, 8.
16. Seckler, 2, 3.
17. Seckler interview Brooks, 3.
18. Perle Fine videotape interview (n.d.), conducted by Hermine Freed and Miriam Schapiro. Copy in Pollock-Krasner Center, East Hampton, N.Y.
19. *The New York Times* (September 2, 1930), 1.

20. David Berezov interview conducted by Housley, March 2002. Russo, 51.
21. "Grosz and Sloan," *Art Digest* (15th April, 1932), 4.
22. Seckler, 4.
23. "New York Season," *Art Digest* (Mid-March 1930), 16. "Benton Depicts America Aggressively for the Whitney Museum," (15th December 1932), 5.
24. www.wellesley.edu/DavisMuseum/wwwmcgibbon.html.
25. "Woman Question," *Art Digest* (July 1928), 13.
26. *ARTnews* (Oct. 11, 1930), 14.
27. *ARTnews* (Nov. 15, 1930), 14.
28. Seckler, 5.
29. www.wellesley.edu/DavisMuseum/wwwmcgibbon.html.
30. Seckler interview Brooks.
31. Seckler, 5.
32. Seckler, 5, 21.
33. Russo, 46
34. Seckler, 6. Matisse, 1972, 84n, as quoted in Roger Lipsey, *An Art of Our Own: The Spiritual in Twentieth Century Art*, 30.
35. Ibid.
36. Russo, 50.
37. Seckler, 23–24.
38. Perle Fine interview conducted by Karl Fortess, July 1976. Berezov Archives, Nashville, TN.
39. Seckler, 24.
40. Russo, 46.
41. Berezov Archives, undated.
42. Lipsey, 255, hm ecrits 258, the name of Matisse, translated by Lipsey.
43. Berezov Archives, undated. Fine's remarks also echo those of the American painter Macdonald-Wright who with Morgan Russell formulated Synchromism in Paris around 1912. He wrote that he attempted to divest his art of all anecdote and illustration and to purify it to the point that the emotions of a spectator would be wholly aesthetic similar to listening to music. Macdonald-Wright, whose paintings had been exhibited by Stieglitz, returned to figurative painting around 1920, so Fine may not have known of his abstract work and his theories.
44. Because it was expensive to hire models, and Fine was not using them, Berezov bought a camera and took a series of photographs of their favorite model, a beautiful woman who one day, to their surprise, married a French count and abruptly left for Europe, leaving her image behind in several early paintings still owned by Fine's relatives. Then he worked from the photographs for his illustrations. It was the beginning of his interest in photography.
45. Housley.
46. Fortess.
47. *ARTnews* (Oct. 3, 1931), 3, 13.
48. *ARTnews* (April 15, 1930), 14.
49. Berezov Archives.
50. Perle Fine, "Mondrian: An Artist's Observation and Comments on His Work," 10. Tremaine Archives, Emily Hall Tremaine Foundation, Meriden, CT.
51. *ARTnews* (April 19, 1930), 1–6,
52. William Seitz, *Arshile Gorky: Paintings, Drawings, Studies*, (Garden City, New York: Doubleday & Co., the Museum of Modern Art, 1962), 7.
53. Edwin Denby, *Willem de Kooning*. New York: Hanuman Books, 1988, 61.
54. Vytlacil interview conducted by Susan Larsen for her dissertation, *The American Abstract Artists Group: A History and Evaluation of Its Impact Upon American Art*, (Ann

Arbor: Xerox University Microfilms, 1975). The quote about Miller is from *American Art 1934–1956, Selections from the Whitney Museum of American Art* (Montgomery: Montgomery Museum of Fine Arts, 1978), 18.
55. Hofmann had been coming to the United States to teach summer courses at the Chouinard School of Art in Los Angeles since 1930. He had taught briefly at the Art Students League just prior to launching his own school. *The Teaching of Hans Hofmann*, unpublished manuscript written jointly by Fine and Berezov. Berezov Archives
56. Russo, 45.
57. Fortess, 1976.
58. *Art Digest* (15th Nov.1938), 27.
59. Munro, 265.
60. Berezov Archives.
61. Ibid.
62. Eleanor Munro, *Originals: American Women Artists,* (New York: Touchstone Book, Simon and Schuster, 1979), 110.
63. Seckler, 13.
64. Seckler, 4, 6.
65. Fortess.
66. Seckler, 10.
67. Carone interview conducted by Paul Cummings, AAA, May 11, 1968.
68. Berezov Archives.
69. Freed/Schapiro.
70. Randy Rosen and Catherine C. Brawer, *Making Their Mark: Women Artists Move Into the Mainstream, 1970–85* (New York: Abbeville Press, 1989), 30.
71. Freed/Schapiro.
72. Ibid. Hofmann applied the word lyrical to himself as well, saying at a Studio 35 session in 1950 that it was in his nature to have both "a lyrical as well as a dramatic disposition." Motherwell, *Modern Artists in America, Vol. 1,* 21.
73. Audiotape on teaching, n.d, or interviewer, Berezov Archives.
74. In 1966 when the University of California at Berkeley was setting up the Hans Hofmann archives, Fine sold or donated a wood collage and wrote the quoted text. Berezov Archives.
75. Cummings, AAA.
76. Fortess.
77. Housley.
78. Freed/Schapiro.
79. Berezov Archives.
80. Denby, 57–58, 62.
81. The precursor to the W.P.A, the Public Works of Art Project began in 1933 and lasted one year.
82. Seckler, 7.
83. Ibid., 2.
84. Munro, 30.
85. Ibid., 128.
86. Ibid., 245. Also Charlotte Streifer Rubinstein, *American Women Artists from Early Indian Times to the Present* (Boston: G. K. Hall, 1982), 268–69.
87. Rubinstein, 269.
88. For a full discussion of the founding of the AAA, see Larsen dissertation.
89. *Pioneers of Abstract Art: American Abstract Artists, 1936–1996.* Sidney Mishkin Gallery, 8.
90. Ibid.
91. *Art Digest* (April 1939), 19.
92. *Art Digest* (15th March 1939).

93. Denby, 44–45.
94. *Art Digest* (15th Jan 1938), 22.
95. "Pioneers of Abstract Art," Mishkin, 9.
96. Russo, 46.
97. "The Fortnight in New York," *Art Digest* (15th Jan, 1st Feb, 1st March, 1938).

CHAPTER II: THE WAR YEARS

1. "Nazism and Art," *Art Digest* (1st August, 1934).
2. "Famous Modern Canvas Goes to Minneapolis," *Art Digest* (April 1, 1942), 21.
3. "The Digest Interviews Karl Nierendorf," *Art Digest* (Feb. 1, 1944), 10.
4. Russo, 47.
5. *Art Digest* (Feb. 1, 1944), 10.
6. "The Passing Shows," *ARTnews* (Nov. 15–30, 1943), 21.
7. "Artists in Exile Hold Stimulating Show," *Art Digest* (March 15, 1942), 9.
8. "Comment," *Art Digest* (Dec. 1, 1941), 3.
9. *The New York Times* (March 17, 1939).
10. Seckler, 13.
11. Berezov Archives.
12. Seckler, 29.
13. Fine notes on *Victory Boogie-Woogie*. Tremaine Archives.
14. Steven Naifeh and Gregory White Smith, *Jackson Pollock: An American Saga* (New York: Clarkson N. Potter, Inc., 1989), 389.
15. Jacqueline Bograd Weld, *Peggy: The Wayward Guggenheim* (New York: E. P. Dutton, 1986), 305.
16."Mondrian: An Artist's Observations and Comments on His Work," 7–8. Tremaine Archives.
17. David Sylvester, *Interviews with American Artists* (New Haven: Yale University Press, 2001), 81.
18. *Art Digest* (Jan 1, 1941), 11.
19. Dore Ashton, *The New York School: A Cultural Reckoning* (New York: The Viking Press, 1972), 118.
20. "Hans Hofmann Continues Despite the War," *Art Digest* (May 15, 1942), 29.
21. Sidney Geist, "Prelude: The 1930's," *Arts* (Sept. 1956), 53.
22. John P. O'Neill, ed., *Barnett Newman: Selected Writings and Interviews* (New York: Alfred A. Knopf, 1990), 29–30. Newman also wrote the foreword to the catalog of the exhibition of the American Modern Artists, which was mounted in protest to the Artists for Victory show.
23. Ashton, 128.
24. Berezov Archives.
25. Terenzio, 225.
26. Maurice Berezov was 40 years old when the war began and did not serve. Motivated by the deteriorating world situation and his pride at being a U.S. citizen, in 1940 he wrote and illustrated a children's book titled American Heroines featuring stories of women whose actions had affected the courses of the American Revolution and the Civil War. By dint of historical fact, Britain was one of the chief enemies in the book, which may have been the reason Berezov could not find a publisher.
27. "The Passing Shows," *ARTnews* (June-July 1943), 40.
28. Peyton Boswell, Jr. "Comments," *Art Digest* (May 15, 1944), 3.
29. "From None to Ten," *Art Digest* (May 15, 1943), 8.
30. *The Nation* (May 29, 1943). Fine papers/AAA.
31. *ARTnews* (Aug-Sept. 1943), 41.

32. Riley, "Non-Objective Museum Holds Loan Show," *Art Digest* (Nov. 1, 1943), 12.
33. "Fifty-Seventh Street in Review," *Art Digest* (Nov. 15, 1943), 18.
34. Seckler, 9.
35. Terenzio, 26.
36. Seckler 10.
37. Hitchcock, *Painting Toward Architecture* (New York: Duell, Sloan and Pearce, 1948), 82.
38. "In Staccato" was included in *Geometric Abstraction in America*, presented by the Whitney Museum of American Art, March 20-May 13, 1962.
39. Seckler, 7.
40. Solomon R. Guggenheim Archives.
41. Ibid.
42. Ibid.
43. Joan M. Lukach, *Hilla Rebay: In Search of the Spirit in Art* (New York: George Braziller, 1983), 99.
44. December 24th, 1943, Solomon R. Guggenheim Archives.
45. Solomon R. Guggenheim Archives.
46. Ashton, 110.
47. Solomon R. Guggenheim Archives.
48. Lukach, 156.
49. *Art Digest* (Nov. 1, 1945), 18.
50. Lukach, 152.
51. "The Passing Shows," *ARTnews* (March 15–31, 1944), 20. "Hans Hofmann Teacher-Artist," *Art Digest* (March 15, 1944), 13.
52. Krasner's name is written on the bottom of the printed list of participating artists, although years later she said she did not take part because she did not want to be in an all-woman exhibition. List is in Berezov Archives. See also *Woman's Art Journal* (Spring/Summer 1999), 61–62.
53. Weld, 294.
54. Russo, 133.
55. Russo, 52.
56. Henry McBride, "Women Surrealists," *New York Sun*, (Jan. 18, 1943).
57. *ARTnews* (Jan 15–31,1943), 20.
58. Jewell, "The Women Again," *The New York Times* (June 17, 1945). *ARTnews* (June, 1945).
59. Rubinstein, 268–69.
60. Terenzio, 77–78.
61. "Northwest Coast Indian Painting," catalog written by Barnett Newman, Betty Parsons Gallery, September 30–October 19, 1946.
62. Terenzio, 85.
63. Lee Krasner, New York, October 17, 1971. Quoted in Virginia Dortch, Peggy Guggenheim and Her Friends (Milan: Berenice, 1994), 110.
64. *Art Digest* (1st January 1940), 18.
65. Jewell, "Our Annual Non-Objective Field Day," *The New York Times* (March 12, 1939).
66. Munro, 110.
67. Rubinstein, 300.
68. Munro, 268.
69. Larsen, 331.
70. See Jenni L. Schlossman, "Loren MacIver: Turning the Ordinary into the Extraordinary," *Woman's Art Journal* (Spring/Summer 2000) for a full discussion.
71. *ARTnews* (Feb 5 1937), 15.

72. Seckler, 39.
73. *Museum of Modern Art Bulletin*, 4.
74. Ruthven Todd, "Hayter Paints a Picture." Berezov Archives.
75. Maude Riley, "Dynamics in Color," *Art Digest* (Jan 1, 1945).
76. Rosamund Frost, "Graphic Revolution: Studio 17," *ARTnews* (August 1–31, 1944), 11.
77. Other participants were Sue Fuller, Jacques Lipchitz, Andre Masson, Joan Miró, Nina Negri, Abraham Rattner, and Anne Ryan.
78. Terenzio, 193. Motherwell graduated from Stanford University, worked toward but did not complete his Ph.D. in philosophy at Harvard, and then studied art history at Columbia University.
79. *Art Digest* (April 1, 1944), 3.

CHAPTER III: GOING SOLO

1. Motherwell, *Modern Artists in America*, No. 1, 118.
2. A Deidre Robson, *Prestige, Profit and Pleasure: The Market for Modern Art in New York in the 1940s and 1950s* (New York: Garland, 1995), 112.
3. Maude Riley, "Perle Fine," *Art Digest* (March 1, 1945) n.p.
4. "The Passing Shows," *ARTnews* (March 1–14, 1945), 7, 25.
5. "8 by 8 and 107 by 25," *ARTnews* (March 15–31,1945), 17. Fine was also in "The Women: An Exhibition of Paintings by Contemporary American Women" at Western College, Oxford, Ohio, along with Krasner, Sage and Lamba.
6. Hilda Loveman, *Limited Edition* (December 1945), 5. Quoted in Guilbaut, endnote 52, 230. There is uncertainty as to the first use of the phrase.
7. "The Eye-Spring of Arshile Gorky," *Art Digest* (March 15, 1945). "Jackson Pollock," *Art Digest* (April 1, 1945), 59.
8. "Insufficient Evidence," *Art Digest* (June 1, 1945), 12.
9. James Johnson Sweeney, *Harper's Bazaar* (April 1944), 126.
10. Michael Leja, *Reframing Abstract Expressionism* (New Haven, Ct.: Yale University Press, 1993), 262.
11. Fortess.
12. Housley.
13. Solomon R. Guggenheim Archives, Feb 20, 1946.
14. Ibid.
15. Louise Nevelson, *Dawns & Dusks: Taped Conversations with Diana MacKown*, (New York: Alfred A. Knopf, 1990), 75.
16. *Art Digest* (Feb.1, 1944),10.
17. Ibid.
18. Berezov Archives.
19. Berezov Archives, undated note.
20. Nevelson, 94.
21."Reviews & Previews," *ARTnews* (April 1946), 57.
22. Ben Wolf, *Art Digest* (April 15, 1946), 18.
23. *The Print Collector*, n.d. except 1946, Berezov Archives. Fine's painting *Juxtaposition of Soft Black Form* was printed in *Art Digest* (Jan.1, 1946), 16, accompanying the review of the exhibition at the Museum of Non-Objective Painting.
24. Press release M. H. De Young Museum, August 8, 1947, Berezov Archives. *San Francisco Chronicle*, August 14, 1947. *Berkeley Gazette*, August 15, 1947. Fine papers/AAA.
25. Lukach, 253.
26. Guilbaut, 153.
27. Ibid.
28. Letter dated January 16, 1950, Museum of Non-Objective Painting letterhead, Fine

papers/AAA.
29. Baldwin, 20–21.
30. Jean Franklin, "Perle Fine," *The New Iconograph* (Fall, 1947), 22–25. In her writing, Fine frequently used italics for emphasis.
31. Gibson, 15.
32. In the photograph, the painting is hung horizontally, but Fine reoriented it vertically at a later date.
33. Franklin, 23.
34. Ibid., 25.
35. "Self-Designated Business Man, Frank Crowninshield Works in an Office Where the Walls are Hung with Modern Art," *ARTnews* , (Feb 3, 1934).
36. Berezov Archives.
37. Nicholas Fox Weber, *Patron Saints: Five Rebels Who Opened America to a New Art. 1928–1943* (New Haven: Yale University Press, 1992), 55–56.
38. Louchheim, "Abstraction on the Assembly Line," *ARTnews* (December 1947), 52.
39. Fine papers/AAA.
40. "Fifty-Seventh Street in Review," *Art Digest* (Jan 15, 1947), 20.
41. *The New York Times* (Jan. 14, 1947) Berezov Archives.
42. "Reviews & Previews," *ARTnews* (Jan 1947), 44.
43. Greenberg review, n.d. copy in Berezov Archives.
44. *Art Digest* (Nov. 1, 1947), 7.
45. Lukach, 249.
46. Nevelson, 100.
47. Solomon R. Guggenheim Archives. Even in his death, Nierendorf succeeded in advancing the careers of the artists he championed because the Guggenheim Foundation decided to purchase his entire estate. Among its 730 works were 121 paintings by Klee, as well as many by Chagall, Fine, Gris, Léger, Kandinsky, and Picasso. Lukach, 249.

CHAPTER IV: PROVINCETOWN INTERLUDE

1. Copy of Fine speech, August 1950, Berezov Archives.
2. Stuart Preston,"Provincetown in 1949," *The New York Times* (August 21, 1949). Among others in the exhibition were William Baziotes, Bultman, John Grillo, Weldon Kees, Motherwell, Pollock, Rothko, and Theodoros Stamos.
3. Schwartz, "Pioneer in Abstraction: Perle Fine," Women Artists News, IX/5–6 (Summer 1984) 24–25.
4. Terenzio, 226.
5. "Provincetown, Montparnesse under the Sun." n.d. Berezov Archives.
6. Ibid.
7. Ibid.
8., Berezov Archives, note.
9. "Art Schools," *Art Digest* (August 1, 1949), 30.
10. "Art School News," *Art Digest* (April 15, 1950).
11. Schwartz, 24–25.
12. Seckler, 23.
13. Schwartz, 25.
14. Berezov Archives.
15. Terenzio, 226.
16. Seckler, 12.
17. Berezov Archives.
18. Seckler, 22.
19. Newspaper clipping, August 26, 1948, Berezov Archives.

20. Fine joined the Federation in the late 1940s by which time it no longer had a political agenda. She served as corresponding secretary in 1952.
21. *Art Digest* (Nov. 15, Dec. 1 1947), 5. Daniel Catton Rich to Perle Fine, Dec. 3, 1947, Fine papers/AAA, as quoted in Gibson, *Abstract Expressionism*, 87.
22. *The New York Times*, June 5, 1949, Betty Parsons Papers/AAA.
23. "Vernissage," *ARTnews* (Sept. 1949), 13.
24. "Peyton Boswell comments: The True and the False," *Art Digest* (Sept. 15, 1949).
25. Written from Provincetown. Berezov Archives.
26. *Art Digest* (Sept.15, 1949).
27. Berezov Archives.
28. Fine's paintings in Réalités Nouvelles were *Times Square Cacophony* and *Ballet of Spring*. Berezov's paintings were *Peinture* and *Peinture H2*.
29. Included among the Europeans were Hans Hartung and Nicholas de Stael. Exhibition catalog, Berezov Archives.
30. Berezov Archives

CHAPTER V: MONDRIAN AND THE NATURE OF CLASSICISM

1. James Johnson Sweeney, *Mondrian* (New York: The Museum of Modern Art, 1953), 15.
2. Virginia Lee Rembert, *Mondrian, America and American Painting*, Ph.D. Diss., 310. Quoted in Housley, 89.
3. Housley, 74.
4. Sweeney, 16.
5. Mondrian File, Tremaine Archives.
6. Ibid.
7. Ibid.
8. Ibid. "Comments and Observations," Mondrian File, Tremaine Archives.
9. Ibid.
10. Sandler radio interview with Fine, WRFM, April 8, 1963.
11. Gudrun Inboden, and Thomas Kellein, *Ad Reinhardt* (Germany: Staatsgulerie Stuttgart, 1985), 125.
12. *ARTnews* , (Jan. 1947), 8. Letter to the editor (Feb 1947).
13. "The Passing Shows," *ARTnews* (Nov. 15–30, 1943), 21.
14. *Art Digest* (April 1, 1945).
15. Seckler interview with Busa, 13.
16. Mondrian File, Tremaine Archives.
17. *Art Digest* (Feb 1, 1949), 16.
18. John P. O'Neill, ed., *Barnett Newman: Selected Writings and Interviews* (New York: Alfred A. Knopf, 1990), 256.
19. Terenzio, 21–22.
20. Art (May 3, 1947). Copy in Berezov Archives.
21. "Vernissage," *ARTnews* (March 1946), 15.
22. Art (May 3, 1947). Copy in Berezov Archives.
23. Quoted in Matthew Spender, *From a High Place: A Life of Arshile Gorky* (New York: Alfred A. Knopf, 1999), 289.
24. Quoted in Nancy Jachec, *The Philosophy and Politics of Abstract Expressionism* (Cambridge: Cambridge University Press, 2000), 146. Leja maintains that while there was a tie to Existentialism, "there is reason to argue that the subjective identities shaped by the artists and imbricated in their paintings were already highly developed by them." Leja, 249.
25. Berezov Archives.

26. Munro, 268–269.
27. Bruno Alfieri, "A Short Talk on the Pictures of Jackson Pollock." *L'Arte Moderna* (June 8, 1950), translation in Betty Parsons Papers/AAA. Quoted in Kingsley, *Turning Point,* 199.
28. Rosenberg's essay "The American Action Painters" was published in *ARTnews* in 1952, but by then it sounded more like a swan song than a battle cry.
29. Rosenberg thought that a good portion of Pollock's western persona was an act. In a book review of *Jackson Pollock* by Bryan Robertson, he wrote: "Pollock's whackdoodle was a revival, stimulated and a bit modified by western movies. He wore the high boots, the blue jeans and the 'neckercher'; he crouched on his heels and pulled up blades of grass when he talked; he liked to go to saloons and play at bustin' up the joint." *ARTnews* (Feb. 1961), 35.
30. Mondrian File, Tremaine Archives.
31. *ARTnews* (December 1948), 24–25, 62.
32. "Editor's Letters," *ARTnews* (January 1949), 6.
33. "Editor's Letters," *ARTnews* (February, 1949), 6.
34. Motherwell, *Modern Artists in America*, No. 1 (New York: Wittenborn Schultz, 1951), 20.
35. Fine papers/AAA. Also Berezov Archives.
36. Schwartz, 25.

CHAPTER VI: THE TURBULENT DECADE

1. Prices ranged from $300 to $850. Berevoz Archives.
2. Devree, "By Herself," *The New York Times* (June 5, 1949), 6.
3. Reed, "Fifty-seventh Street in Review: Canvases Lit With Color," *Art Digest* , (July 1, 1949). For Reinhardt, see Reed, "Without Subjects," *Art Digest* (Nov. 1, 1949), 26. For Newman, see Reed, "Newman's Flat Areas," *Art Digest* (Feb 1 , 1949), 16.
4. Jon Schueler, *The Sound of Sleat: A Painter's Life* (New York: Picador, 1999), 195.
5. A. Deirdre Robson, *Prestige, Profit and Pleasure: The Market for Modern Art in New York in the 1940s and 1950s* (New York: Garland, 1995), 249.
6. Ibid., 261.
7. Thomas B Hess, *Willem de Kooning* (New York: George Braziller, Inc., 1959), 11–12.
8. "Peyton Boswell comments: Modern Manifesto Repercussions," *Art Digest* (April 15, 1950), 5, (May 1, 1950), 5.
9. The New York School of the 1950s is undergoing a much needed reassessment. See Marika Herskovic, *American Abstract Expressionism of the 1950s: An Illustrated Survey* (Franklin Lakes, New Jersey: New York School Press, 2003).
10. Ashton, 3.
11. Quoted in Rubinstein, 269.
12. Robert Hughes, *American Visions: The Epic History of Art in America* (New York: Alfred A. Knopf, 1997), 492.
13. Housley.
14. Parsons Papers, Fine file/AAA. Paintings were sold by Fine to Smith College and the Provincetown Art Association, among others, during this period.
15. Weld, 306.
16. Lee Hall, *Betty Parsons: Artist, Dealer, Collector* (New York: Harry N. Abrams, Inc., 1991),100.
17. Doris Brian, *Art Digest* (Oct. 1, 1950), 11.
18. Paul Cummings, interview, AAA, Nov. 24, 1971.
19. Robson, 322, endnote 64.
20. Schwartz, 25.

21. Gibson, 85.
22. Seckler, 35.
23. Ibid., 36.
24. Ibid., 14.
25. Ibid.,15.
26. Ibid.
27. Ibid.
28. Ibid., 16.
29. Ibid. 17.
30. Ibid. 16.
31. Ibid., 17.
32. Quoted in Naifeh and Smith, 750.
33. Seckler, 14.
34. Munro, 216.
35. Seckler, 14.
36. Housley.
37. Seckler, 30.
38. Alcopley, "The Club, Its First Three Years," typed memoir, owned by Ibram Lassaw.
39. B. H. Friedman, *Jackson Pollock: Energy Made Visible* (New York: McGraw-Hill Book Company, 1972), 113.
40. Berezov Archives.
41. Paul Bird, "Big Met Show Finds Americans Now Speak Universal Language," *Art Digest* (Dec. 1, 1950), 7. "Jackson Pollock: Is He the Greatest Living Painter in the United States?" *Life* Vol. 27 (August 28, 1949), 42–43, 45. The photo of the Irascibles was published in January 15, 1951.
42. Deborah Solomon, *Jackson Pollock: A Biography* (Cooper Square Press ed. 2001), 218.
43. Friedman, xiv.
44. Freed/Schapiro.
45. Berenice D'Vorzon interview with Housley, August 2004.
46. Friedman, xviii.
47. Schueler, 248.
48. Housley.
49. Seckler, 11.
50. Devree, *The New York Times* (February 25, 1951), n.p.
51. Parsons Papers, AAA.
52. Robert Goodnough, "Reviews and Previews: Parsons to March 10," *ARTnews* (March 1951), 46.
53. Frank O'Hara, *Jackson Pollock* (George Braziller, Inc., 1959), 29.
54. Parsons papers, AAA.
55. Hall, 102.
56. Ibid.,103.
57. Robert Skinner, interview with Housley, April 2002. While Skinner had met Fine earlier, he did not get to know her personally until the 1960s when he taught art history, often taking his students to visit her in her studio.
58. Fine Papers/AAA.
59. Rae Ferren interview with Housley, August 2004. Thomas B. Hess, "Reviews and Previews, Ninth Street to June 10," *ARTnews* (Summer 1951), 47. Other women who took part in all the shows were Elaine de Kooning, Hartigan and Mitchell. Frankenthaler, only 23 at the time of her inclusion in the first show, had work in five of the six, Krasner in four of the six.
60. Berezov Archives.

61. Thomas B. Hess, "The New York Salon," *ARTnews* (February 1954), 25. For a full discussion of the New York Annuals, see Marika Herskovic, ed., *New York School, Abstract Expressionists: Artists Choice by Artists* (Franklin Lakes, NJ: New York School Press, 2000).
62. Brian O'Doherty, "Death of a Gallery" (n.d.), Fine papers/AAA.
63. Thomas McCormick, "Second to None: Six Artists of the New York School," exhibition catalog (Chicago: Thomas McCormick Gallery, 2001), 10.
64. Larry Campbell, "Reviews and Previews," *ARTnews* (Dec. 1952), 43. Fine quote in Berezov Archives.
65. Fairfield Porter, Parsons Papers/AAA.
66. Berezov Archives.
67. Seckler.
68. Terenzio, 167.
69. Freed/Schapiro.
70. Parsons Papers/AAA.

CHAPTER VII: THE SPRINGS

1. Sherrill Foster, "Profile: An Interview with Perle Fine Working Around the Clock," *The Hamptons Scene* (October 11, 1980), n.p.
2. Fine's actual address was Amagansett, The Springs (East Hampton) being on the other side of the road. Housley.
3. Seckler,17.
4. Other artists in East Hampton included: Brach, Brooks, Cherry, Dine, Ernst, Ferren, Gottlieb, Greene, Hartigan, Johnson, King, Marca-Relli, Mitchell, Morris, Motherwell, Nivola, Ossorio, Rivers, Rothko, Schapiro, and Sterne.
5. Tony Kornheiser, "East End's Winter of Content," *Newsday* (Sunday March 16, 1975), 1–6.
6. Undated questionnaire in Berezov Archives, asking "How did the community affect your work?"
7. Ibid.
8. Tony Vevers, "Abstract Expressionism in Provincetown," *New York-Provincetown: A 50s Connection*, (Provincetown: Provincetown Art Association and Museum, 1994), 6.
9. Questionnaire, Berezov Archives.
10. Housley interview Ferren.
11. Kornheiser, 1.
12. Ibid.
13. Berezov Archives, March 4, 1959.
14. Foster, n.p.
15. Sandler, April 8, 1963, Casper Citron Program, Station WRFM.
16. Seckler, 20.
17. Foster, n.p.
18. Housley interview.
19. Beginning in 1957, Krasner rented an apartment in New York City and spent summers in The Springs.
20. In 1954, the AAA presented a joint exhibition with the Japan Abstract Art Club, which opened in New York and traveled to Tokyo. A symposium "Abstract Art and the World Today" was held at the Museum of Modern Art, with Franz Kline and Alfred Barr among the panelists. In 1956, the "Painters Eleven" of Canada participated in a joint exhibition.
21. John Ferren, "Stable State of Mind," *ARTnews* (May 1955), 22.
22. Fairfield Porter, "Reviews and Previews, Third Annual," *ARTnews* (Jan 1955), 47.

23. Ibid.
24. Philip Pearlstein, "The Private Myth," *ARTnews* (Sept. 1961), 42. Statements were also published by Pat Adams, Bourgeois, Enrico Donati, Fine, Sally Hazalet, John Hultberg, Lester Johnson, Lassaw, Lewitan, Nevelson, George Spaventa, and Richard Stankiewicz.
25. "Wittenborn to June 30," *Art Digest* (June 1955), 27. James R. Mellow, Arts (Dec. 1955), 21. Two prints were featured in "14 Painter-Printmakers," in the December 1955 issue of *Arts*.
26. Ad Reinhardt, "Letters to the Editor," *ARTnews* (Jan. 1959), 6.
27. Berezov Archives.
28. Seckler, 25.
29. Ibid.
30. Undated note, Berezov Archives.
31. Housley interview.
32. John Ashbery, "Reviews and Previews," *ARTnews* (March 1958), 14.
33. Berezov Archives.
34. Baur solicited comments from the artists which he incorporated into the exhibition catalog. Fine wrote: "When I first moved my studio to the country, and the wonder and grandeur of the world of nature captivated me completely, I felt I must find new means to express these things." See John I. H. Baur, *Nature in Abstraction: The Relation of Abstract Painting and Sculpture to Nature in Twentieth Century American Art,* (New York: The Whitney Museum of American Art, 1958), 8.
35. "Statement," It Is (No. 2, Autumn 195), 14. See also Herskovic, *New York School*, 138.
36. Helen De Mott, "In the Galleries," ARTnew (April 1960), 60.
37. Edith Burckhardt, "Reviews and Previews," *ARTnews* (April 1959), 56.
38. Martica Sawin, "In the Galleries," Arts (April 1957), n.p.
39. See Thomas B. Hess, "Art of Assemblage," *ARTnews* (Nov., 1961).
40. Scrap, April 19, 1961. Berezov Archives.
41. Seckler, 18–19.
42. Ibid.
43. Ibid.

CHAPTER VIII: PAINTING IN THE SHADOW OF THE GRID

1. Rosenberg wrote the catalog text for Fine's solo exhibition at the Tanager Gallery. Berezov Archives.
2. Quoted in German publication *Das Kunstwerk*, n.d.. Copy of statement is in Berezov Archives.
3. Michael Fried quoted in Hal Foster, *Discussions in Contemporary Culture*, Seattle: Bay Press, 1987. 73. See also Meyer, 231.
4. Quoted in "The New Art," exhibition catalog, Wesleyan University 1964 (Middletown, Conn.: Wesleyan University, 1964), 3.
5. Seckler, 21, 28.
6. O Hara, 29.
7. Schueler, 195.
8. "Reviews and Previews," *ARTnews* (Jan. 1960), 13.
9. Henry Geldzehler, *Making it New: Essays, Interviews, and Talks*, (New York: Turtle Point Press, 1994), 348.
10. Rosen, *Making Their Mark*, 14.
11. Russo, 52.
12. Lawrence Campbell, "Reviews and Previews," *ARTnews* (April 1963), 54.

13. Sandler, 66.
14. Virtually the same statement appears in "Artists of East Hampton," exhibition catalog, Phoenix Gallery Nov. 15-Dec. 12, 1980 (Frederick MD: University Publications of America, Inc.) Copy of catalog is in Guild Hall Archives. Berezov Archives.
15. Interview April 8, 1963, Casper Citron Program, Station WRFM. Transcription in Berezov Archives.
16. Campbell, 54.
17. Seckler, 26.
18. Undated note, Berezov Archives.
19. O'Hara, 11.
20. Berezov Archives.
21. Fortess interview, July 18, 1976.
22. Dated March 24, 1975, Berezov Archives.
23. The letter was written by John Hopkins to W. P. McEwen, Dean of Faculties, Hofstra, Dec. 13, 1965. It was a recommendation for tenure.
24. Russo, 51.
25. Ibid., 48.
26. Rubinstein, 301.
27. Russo, 48.
28. Berezov Archives.
29. Taped interview, interviewer unidentified, n.d. Berezov Archives.
30. Fortess, July 18, 1976.
31. Joan Wheeler, "New Honors for Artist," n.d., Malden is listed as newspaper location. Berezov Archives.
32. Russo, 50.
33. Seckler, 39.
34. David Deitcher, *Perle Fine: Major Works 1954–1978*, exhibition catalog, Guild Hall, East Hampton, Sept. 23-Oct. 29, 1978.
35. Charlotte Willard, "Paintings and Wood Collages," *New York Post*, (Feb.11, 1967), 14.
36. Seckler, 37.
37. Berezov Archives.
38. Ibid.
39. Ibid.
40. Ibid.
41. Ibid.
42. Wheeler, "New Honors for Artist," n.d., Berezov Archives.
43. Others in the exhibition were: Baziotes, de Kooning, Gorky, Hofmann, Motherwell, Newman, Pollock, Pousette-Dart, Reinhardt, Rothko, Stamos, Still, and Tomlin. Perle Fine to The Whitney Museum of American Art, Sept. 22, 1976, and October 5, 1976, Artist File, Whitney Museum of American Art, New York. Quoted in Joan Marter, "Women and Abstract Expressionism: Painting and Sculpture, 1945–1959," Sidney Mishkin Gallery, (New York: Baruch College CUNY, 1997), 6.
44. Seckler, 25.
45. Russo, 53.
46. Ibid., 47.
47. Berezov Archives.
48. Edgar Buonagurio, "Perle Fine," *Arts Magazine* (February 1973), 29.
49. Irene Rousseau, "Perle Fine," *Arts Magazine* (June 1982), 6.
50. Sandler, *American Art*, 74.
51. Abbott interview with Housley, August 2004. Seckler, 36.
52. Peter Frank, exhibition catalog. Copy in Berezov Archives.

53. Marjorie Welish, "Perle Fine at Andre Zarre," *Art in America* (March/April 1978), 135–136.
54. Berezov Archives.

EPILOGUE

1. Housley.
2. Berezov Archives.
3. Ferren, D'Vorzon, Housley interviews.
4. Ibid. No date.
5. *Scrap* (April 19, 1961) Fine papers/AAA.

SELECTED BIBLIOGRAPHY

BOOKS

Ashton, Dore. *The New York School: A Cultural Reckoning.* New York: The Viking Press, 1972.

Auping, Michael. *Abstract Expressionism: The Critical Developments.* New York: Harry N. Abrams, Inc. in association with the Albright-Knox Art Gallery, 1987.

Denby, Edwin. *Willem De Kooning.* New York: Hanuman Books, 1988.

Dortch, Virginia. *Peggy Guggenheim and Her Friends.* Milan: Berenice, 1994.

Foster, Hal. *Discussions in Contemporary Culture.* Seattle: Bay Press, 1987.

Friedman, B. H. Jackson. *Pollock: Energy Made Visible.* New York: McGraw-Hill Book Company, 1972.

Geldzahler, Henry. *Making It New: Essays, Interviews, and Talks.* New York: Turtle Point Press, 1994.

——— *New York Paintings and Sculpture: 1940–1970.* New York: E. P. Dutton & Co., Inc. 1969.

Gibson, Ann Eden. *Abstract Expressionism: Other Politics.* New Haven: Yale University Press, 1997.

——— *Issues in Abstract Expressionism: The Artist-Run Periodicals.* Ann Arbor/London: UMI Research Press, 1990.

Guilbaut, Serge. *How New York Stole the Idea of Modern Art: Abstract Expressionism, Freedom and the Cold War.* Translated by Arthur Goldhammer. Chicago: The University of Chicago Press, 1983.

Hall, Lee. *Betty Parsons: Artist, Dealer, Collector.* New York: Harry N. Abrams, Inc., 1991.

——— *Elaine & Bill: Portrait of a Marriage, The Lives of Willem and Elaine de Kooning.* New York: Cooper Square Press, 1993.

Harris, Mary Emma. *The Arts at Black Mountain College.* Cambridge: The MIT Press, 1987.

Herskovic, Marika, ed. *American Abstract Expressionism of the 1950s: An Illustrated Survey.* New Jersey: New York School Press, 2003.

——— *New York School, Abstract Expressionists: Artists Choice by Artists.* New Jersey: New York School Press, 2000.

Haskell, Barbara. *Agnes Martin.* New York: Whitney Museum of American Art, 1992.

Hess, Thomas B. and Elizabeth C. Baker, ed. *Art and Sexual Politics: Why Have There Been No Great Women Artists?* New York: Collier Books, 1971.

——— Hess, Thomas B. *Willem de Kooning.* New York: George Braziller, Inc., 1959.

Hitchcock, Henry-Russell. *Painting Toward Architecture.* New York: Duell, Sloan and Pearce, 1948.

Hobbs, Robert Carleton and Gail Levin. *Abstract Expressionism: The Formative Years.* Ithaca and London: Cornell University Press, 1978.

Hobbs, Robert. *Lee Krasner.* New York: Harry N. Abrams, Inc., 1999.

Housley, Kathleen *L. Emily Hall Tremaine: Collector on the Cusp.* Meriden, Ct.: Tremaine Foundation, University Press of New England, 2001.

Hughes, Robert. *American Visions: The Epic History of Art in America.* New York: Alfred A. Knopf, 1997.

Inboden, Gudrun and Thomas Kellein. *Ad Reinhardt.* Germany: Staatsgulerie Stuttgart, 1985.

Jachec, Nancy. *The Philosophy and Politics of Abstract Expressionism.* Cambridge: Cambridge University Press, 2000.

Janis, Sidney. *Abstract & Surrealist Art in America.* New York: Reynal & Hitchcock, 1944.

Jones, Caroline A. *Machine in the Studio: Constructing the Postwar American Artist.* Chicago and London: The University of Chicago Press, 1996.

Kingsley, April. *The Turning Point: The Abstract Expressionists and the Transformation of American Art.* New York: Simon & Schuster, 1992.

Krauss, Rosalind. *Bachelors.* Cambridge: The MIT Press, 1999.

Leja, Michael. *Reframing Abstract Expressionism.* New Haven, Ct.: Yale University Press, 1993.

Lipsey, Roger. *An Art of Our Own: The Spiritual in Twentieth Century Art.* Boston: Shambhala, 1997.

Lukach, Joan M. *Hilla Rebay: In Search of the Spirit in Art.* New York: George Braziller, 1983.

Lynes, Russell. *Good Old Modern.* New York: Atheneum, 1973.

Meech, Julia. *Frank Lloyd Wright and the Art of Japan: The Architect's Other Passion.* New York: Japan Society and Harry N. Abrams, Inc., 2001.

Meyer, James. *Minimalism: Art and Polemics in the Sixties.* New Haven: Yale University Press, 2001.

Motherwell, Robert, ed. *Modern Artists in America, No. 1.* New York: Wittenborn Schultz,1951.

Munro, Eleanor. *Originals: American Women Artists.* New York: Touchstone Book, Simon and Schuster, 1979.

Naifeh, Steven W. *Culture Making: Money, Success, and the New York Art World.* Princeton, NJ: Princeton University, 1976.

Naifeh, Steven and Gregory White Smith. *Jackson Pollock: An American Saga.* New York: Clarkson N. Potter, Inc., 1989.

Nevelson, Louise. *Dawns & Dusks: Taped Conversations with Diana MacKown.* New York: Charles Scribner's Sons, 1976.

O'Hara, Frank. *Jackson Pollock.* New York: George Braziller, Inc., 1959.

O'Neill, John P., ed. *Barnett Newman: Selected Writings and Interviews.* New York: Alfred A. Knopf, 1990.

Ratcliff, Carter. *The Fate of a Gesture: Jackson Pollock and Postwar American Art.* New York: Farrar, Straus, Giroux, 1996.

Rembert, Virginia Pitts. *Piet Mondrian in the USA: The Artist's Life and Work.* USA: Parkstone Press, LTD, 2001.

Robson, A. Deirdre. *Prestige, Profit and Pleasure: the Market for Modern Art in New York in the 1940s and 1950s.* New York: Garland Publishing, Inc. 1995.

Rose, Barbara. *Autocritique: Essays on Art and Anti-Art, 1963–1987.* New York: Weidenfield & Nicolson, 1988.

Rosen, Randy and Catherine C. Brawer. *Making Their Mark: Women Artists Move Into the Mainstream, 1970–85.* New York: Abbeville Press, 1989.

Rosenberg, Harold. *Art & Other Serious Matters.* Chicago: The University of Chicago Press, 1985.

Rubinstein, Charlotte Streifer. *American Women Artists from Early Indian Times to the Present.* Boston: G. K. Hall, 1982.

Russo, Alexander. *Profiles of Women Artists.* Frederick, MD: University Publications of America, Inc., 1985.

Sandler, Irving. *American Art of the 1960s.* New York: Harper & Row, 1988.

——— *Art of the Post Modern Era: From the Late 1960s to the Early 1990s.* New York: IconEditions, Harper Collins, 1996.

——— *The New York School: The Painters and Sculptors of the Fifties.* New York: Harper & Row, 1978.

Schapiro, Miriam. *Art: A Woman's Sensibility*. Valencia: California Institute of the Arts, 1975.

Schwabacher, Ethel. *Hungry for Light*. Bloomington: Indiana University Press, 1993.

Scott, William B. and Peter M. Rutkoff. *New York Modern: The Arts and the City*. Baltimore: The Johns Hopkins University Press, 1999.

Seitz, William C. *Arshile Gorky, Paintings, Drawings, Studies*. Garden City, New York: Doubleday & Co. and the Museum of Modern Art, 1962. Exhibition catalog, The Museum of Modern Art in collaboration with The Washington Gallery of Modern Art.

Seuphor, Michel. *Dictionary of Abstract Painting*. New York: Tudor Publishing Company, 1958.

Slobodkina, *American Abstract Artists: Its Publications, Catalogs, and Membership*. Great Neck, New York: Urquhart-Slobodkina, 1979.

Solomon, Deborah. *Jackson Pollock: A Biography*. New York: Cooper Square Press edition 2001.

Spender, Matthew. *From a High Place: A Life of Arshile Gorky*. New York: Alfred A. Knopf, 1999.

Steiner, Raymond J. *The Art Students League of New York: A History*. Saugerties, NY: CSS Publications, Inc., 1994.

Sweeney, James Johnson. *Mondrian*. New York: The Museum of Modern Art, 1953.

Sylvester, David. *Interviews with American Artists*. New Haven: Yale University Press, 2001.

Terenzio, Stephanie, ed., *The Collected Writings of Robert Motherwell*. New York: Oxford University Press, 1992.

Weber, Nicholas Fox. *Patron Saints: Five Rebels Who Opened America to a New Art, 1928–1943*. New Haven: Yale University Press, 1992.

Weld, Jacqueline Bograd. *Peggy: The Wayward Guggenheim*. New York: E. P. Dutton, 1986.

MAJOR ARTICLES, UNPUBLISHED PAPERS AND DISSERTATIONS

Baldwin, Benjamin. "Perle Fine." *Arts & Architecture*, May 1947, 20–21.

Fine, Perle. "Mondrian: An Artist's Observation and Comments on His Work." Tremaine Archives, Emily Hall Tremaine Foundation, Meriden, Ct.

Franklin, Jean. "Perle Fine." *The New Iconograph,* Fall 1947, 22–25.

Housley, Kathleen L. "The Tranquil Power of Perle Fine's Art." *Woman's Art Journal*, Vol. 24, No. 1, Spring/Summer 2003, 3–10.

Larsen, Susan Carol. The American Abstract Artists Group: A History and Evaluation of Its Impact Upon American Art. Ph.D. Diss., Northwestern University, 1975. Ann Arbor: Xerox University Microfilms, 1975.

Rembert, Virginia Lee. "Mondrian, America and American Painting." Ph.D. Diss., Columbia University, 1970. Ann Arbor: University Microfilms, 1971.

Schwartz, Therese. "Pioneer in Abstraction: Perle Fine." *Women Artists News* IX/5–6, Summer 1984, 24–25.

EXHIBITION CATALOGS

Ad Reinhardt. New York: The Museum of Modern Art, The Museum of Contemporary Art, Los Angeles, Rizzoli International Publications, Inc., 1991.

American Abstract Artists: Pioneers of Abstract Art. New York: Sidney Mishkin Gallery, Baruch College/CUNY, 1996.

American Art, 1934–1956, Selections from the Whitney Museum of American Art. Montgomery: Montgomery Museum of Fine Arts, 1978.

Nature in Abstraction: The Relation of Abstract Painting and Sculpture to Nature in Twentieth Century American Art. New York: The Whitney Museum of American Art, 1958.

New York—Provincetown: a 50s Connection. Provincetown, MA: Provincetown Art Museum, 1994. From the collections of Drs. Thomas and Marika Herskovic and the Provincetown Art Association and Museum.

Perle Fine: Major Works: 1954–1978. East Hampton, NY: Guild Hall,1978.

Reclaiming Artists of the New York School: Toward a More Inclusive View of the 1950s. New York: Sidney Mishkin Gallery, Baruch College/CUNY, 1994.

Women and Abstract Expressionism: Painting and Sculpture, 1945–1959. New York: Sidney Mishkin Gallery, Baruch College/CUNY, 1997.

FINE INTERVIEWS

Fortess, Karl. Audiotape, July 1976, Berezov Archives.

Freed, Hermine and Miriam Schapiro. Video and audio tape, n.d., Pollock-Krasner Center, East Hampton, NY.

Herskovic, Marika and Thomas Herskovic. American Abstract Expressionists: Artists of the 9th Street Show-Perle Fine. Videotape, 1991. Pollock-Krasner Center, East Hampton, NY, Berezov Archives.

Sandler, Irving. Transcript. April 8, 1963 Casper Citron Program, Station WRFM. Berezov Archives.

"Teaching Art." Audiotape, n.d., no interviewer, Berezov Archives.

ARCHIVES OF AMERICAN ART, SMITHSONIAN INSTITUTE, INTERVIEWS AND PAPERS

James Brooks, interview conducted by Dorothy Seckler, June 10, 1965.

Peter Busa, interview conducted by Dorothy Seckler, Sept. 5, 1965.

Nicolas Carone, interview conducted by Paul Cummings, May 11, 1968.

Perle Fine, interview conducted by Dorothy Seckler, January 19, 1968.

Perle Fine papers, microfilm, AAA-SI N/735.

Grace Hartigan, interview conducted by Julie Haifley, May 10, 1979.

Robert Motherwell, interview conducted by Paul Cummings, November 24, 1971.

Betty Parson Papers, Perle Fine file, AAA-N68-64.

INTERVIEWS CONDUCTED BY HOUSLEY

Mary Abbott, August 2004

David Berezov, March 2002

Madelyn Berezov, March 2002

Arlene Bujese, August 2004

Berenice D'Vorzon, August 2004

Rae Ferren, August 2004

Charlotte Fine, January 2003

Dorothy Fine, January 2003

Eleanor Fine, January 2003

Marika Herskovic, November 2002

Margaret Kerr, March 2003

Ernestine Lassaw, March 2003

Robert Richenburg, March 2003

Robert Skinner, April 2002

EXHIBITIONS

SOLO EXHIBITIONS

1945: Marian Willard Gallery, NYC
1946: Nierendorf Gallery, NYC
1947: Nierendorf Gallery, NYC
1947: M. H. De Young Memorial Museum, San Francisco, CA
1949: Betty Parsons Gallery, NYC
1951: Betty Parsons Gallery, NYC
1952–53: (Dec.-Jan.) Betty Parsons Gallery, NYC
1955: Tanager Gallery, NYC
1957: Tanager Gallery, NYC
1958: Tanager Gallery, NYC
1960: Tanager Gallery, NYC
1961: Franklin Gallery, Cornell University, Ithaca, NY
1961: Robert Keene Gallery, Southhampton, NY
1961: Graham Gallery, NYC
1963: Graham Gallery, NYC
1964: Graham Gallery, NYC
1967: Graham Gallery, NYC
1972: Joan Washburn Gallery, NYC
1973: Andre Zarre Gallery, NYC
1974: Hofstra University, Hempstead, NY
1976: Andre Zarre Gallery, NYC
1977: Andre Zarre Gallery, NYC
1978: "Major Works, 1954–1978," Retrospective, Guild Hall Museum, East Hampton, NY
1982: Ingber Gallery, NYC
1984: Ingber Gallery, NYC
1997: Perle Fine Works on Paper, Hirschl & Adler Galleries, NYC.

GROUP EXHIBITIONS: MULTI-YEAR

American Abstract Artists (AAA), 1945 through 1970s
Federation of Modern Painters and Sculptors, beginning in 1950s
Guild Hall Museum, East Hampton, annuals for artist members beginning in 1955
The Museum of Non-Objective Painting (Solomon R. Guggenheim Museum), 1943, '44,'45, '46, '47
9th St. Show, and New York Annuals, Stable Gallery, 1951, 1953–57
Pittsburgh International Exhibition of Contemporary Painting and Sculpture (Carnegie Internationals) 1958, 1961
Salon des Réalités Nouvelles, Paris, France, 1947, 1950
Silvermine Annual Exhibitions, New Canaan, Ct., 1960s
Tanager Gallery Group Shows, 1955–62
Virginia Museum Biennials, (Purchase prize 1948)
Whitney Museum of American Art Annuals and Biennials, 1946, 47, 51, 52, 54, 55, 58, 61, 72

GROUP EXHIBITIONS: SINGLE YEAR

1943: Spring Salon for Young Artists, Art of this Century, NYC.
1944: Second Spring Salon for Young Artists, Art of this Century, NYC.
Group Exhibition, Puma Gallery, NY.
Print and Etching Exhibition, Wittenborn Gallery, NY.
1945: The Women: An Exhibition of Paintings by Contemporary Women, Alumnae Hall Gallery, Western College, Oxford, Ohio.
The Women, Art of This Century, NYC.
1946: Thirty-First Annual Exhibition, Society of American Etchers.
Print Exhibition (organized by Hayter), Paris, France.
1947: Works on Paper, Stanhope Gallery, Boston, MA.
Spring Annual, Watkins Gallery, The American University, Washington, D.C.
Painting Toward Architecture, Tremaine Collection, circ., Wadsworth Atheneum, Hartford, CT.
1948: Abstract and Surrealist American Art, Chicago Art Institute, Chicago, IL.
1949: New England Painting and Sculpture, Institute of Contemporary Art, Boston, MA.
Traveling exhibition, European museums, Solomon R. Guggenheim Museum.
Group Exhibition, Gallery 200, Provincetown, MA.
Ten Women Who Paint, Tryon Gallery, Smith College, Northhampton, MA.
1950: Post-Abstract Painting 1950: France, America, Hawthorn Memorial Gallery and the Provincetown Art Association, Provincetown, MA.
American Painting Today–1950, The Metropolitan Museum of Art, NYC.
Contemporary American Women Painters and Sculptors, location unknown.
1952: Lithographs, Wittenborn One-Wall Gallery, NYC.
1953: Nine Women Artists, Bennington College Gallery, Bennington, VT.
Painting and Sculpture Exhibition, New School for Social Research, NYC.
1955: Eleven New Artists of the Region, Guild Hall Museum, East Hampton, NY.
Ninth Annual Print Exhibition, Brooklyn Museum, Purchase Award.
The American Federation of Art–Contemporary Trends, circ. 14 colleges and museums.
1956: Exhibition, New York City Center Gallery, NYC.
1957: 14 Painter-Printmakers, Kraushaar Galleries, Brooklyn Museum, NY.
A Review of the Season, Signa Gallery, East Hampton, NY.
1958: Nature in Abstraction: The Relation of Abstract Painting and Sculpture to Nature in Twentieth-Century American Art, circ., Whitney Museum of American Art, NYC.
"Collage in America," Zabriskie Gallery, NYC, in cooperation with the American Federation of Art.
Exhibition, New York City Center Gallery, NYC.
1959: Painters, Sculptors, Architects of the Region, Guild Hall, East Hampton, NY.
10th Street, The Contemporary Arts Association of Houston, Houston, TX.
Modern Drawing, European and American, Bertha Schaefer Gallery, NYC.
A Review of the Season, Signa Gallery, East Hampton, NY.
1960: McNay Art Institute, San Antonio, TX.
Second Annual Art Exhibit, Brookhaven National Laboratory.
Mexican Biennial, Palacio de Bellas Artes, Mexico City, Mexico.
Art Today, Brooks Memorial Gallery, Memphis, TN.
1961: International Watercolor Biennial, Brooklyn Museum, NY.
Geometric Abstraction in America, Whitney Museum of American Art, NYC.
The Art of Assemblage, circ., Museum of Modern Art, NYC.
1962: Art in America, location unknown.

Provincetown: A Painter's Place, American Federation of Art.
Lyricism in Abstract Art, American Federation of Art, location unknown.
Women Artists in America Today, Mt. Holyoke College, South Hadley, MA.
1963: Hans Hofmann and his Students, circ., Museum of Modern Art, NYC.
1965: Women Artists in America, 1707–1964, The Newark Museum, Newark, NJ.
Exhibition, Long Island University, Southhampton, NY.
1967: Selection 1967: Recent Acquisitions in Modern Art, University Art Museum, University of California, Berkeley, CA.
Amerikanische Druckgrapik eine neue Formensprache, location unknown.
1972: Museum of Non-Objective Painting Exhibition, Washburn Gallery, NYC.
1973: 8 Contemporary American Artists, State University of New York at Binghamton, NY.
1977: Perspective, Freedman Art Gallery, Albright College, Reading, PA.
1978: Exhibition, Women at the Laundry, East Hampton, NY.
Artists of Suffolk County, Heckscher Museum, Huntington, NY.
1979: Women Artists of Eastern Long Island, Guild Hall Museum, East Hampton, NY.
The Springs Artists Exhibition, Ashawagh Hall, East Hampton, NY.
Around Jackson Pollock, East Hampton, 1946–56,
15 Abstract Expressionists, Cultural Center, Paris, France.
Artists of East Hampton, Phoenix I Gallery (Arlene Bujese), Maryland.
1980: Geometric Tradition in American Painting: 1920–1980, Marilyn Pearl Gallery, NYC.
1981: American Artists, The Early Years, Summit Art Center, Summit, NJ.
Drawings, Phoenix II Gallery (Arlene Bujese), Washington D.C.
1982: Modern Masters, Women of the First Generation, Mabel Smith Douglas Library, Rutgers University, New Brunswick, NJ.
1984: The Return of Abstraction, Ingber Gallery, NYC.
Some Major Artists of the Hamptons Then and Now: 1960s-1980s,
Elaine Benson Gallery, Bridgehampton, NY.
1986: A Colorful Retrospective, Works on Paper, Ingber Gallery, NYC.
1990: East Hampton Avant-Garde: A Salute to the Signa Gallery, Guild Hall Museum, East Hampton, NY.
1994: Reclaiming Artists of the New York School: Toward a More Inclusive View of the 1950s, Baruch College Gallery, City University of NY.
Women and Abstract Expressionism: Painting and Sculpture, 1945–1959, Baruch College, City University, NY.
New York–Provincetown: A '50s Connection, Provincetown Art Association and Museum, MA.
2001: Abstract Expressionism: Second to None, Thomas McCormick Gallery, Chicago, IL.
2004: Abstract Expressionism: Second to None, Revised and Expanded, Thomas McCormick Gallery, Chicago, IL.

ACKNOWLEDGMENTS

Perle Fine was not a letter-writer, a journal-keeper, or a string-saver. Her focus on art was so total, I am certain she would have preferred for me to use her paintings as the sole documentation of her life. There are few letters between her and Maurice Berezov, her husband, during their years of maintaining two residences: an apartment in New York City, and a house and studio in East Hampton, Long Island. The papers in Fine's archives are chiefly catalogues, copies of reviews, and drafts of statements about the meaning of art. Fortunately, what does exist has been carefully maintained by David and Madelyn Berezov, Nashville, Tenn. Before I visited them in March 2002, I feared I would find papers shoved in shoe boxes, and canvases leaning against damp cellar walls — a nightmare of disorganization and decay. Instead, I found that Madelyn had put everything in chronological order in three-ring binders, and the paintings were stored carefully in a climate-controlled room. Furthermore, David and Madelyn welcomed me into their home, gave me space to work, and went to great lengths to facilitate my research.

So also, my trip to Malden, Mass., to interview Fine's remaining relatives, her sisters-in-law Charlotte and Dorothy and her niece Eleanor, resulted in the formation of new friends. Graciously, they shared their memories with me of a woman they adored, showing me with great pride the paintings they own.

Drs. Marika and Thomas Herskovic possess probably the best collection of Fine's work in the world. Marika is deeply knowledgeable about the New York School and is dedicated to bringing about a full reassessment, having edited and published two books on the subject. Twice she let me wander freely around her art-filled home, even getting down on her hands and knees with me to study a painting up close. If it meant rearranging a closet in order to reach a painting in storage, she did so without complaint, in fact, with a sense of high adventure.

The Archives of American Art (AAA), Smithsonian Institute, has a single microfilm file of Fine's papers, mostly newspaper clippings, a few letters, and photographs of paintings. There is also a file among the papers of Betty Parsons covering the years 1948 to 1953 when Fine was associated with Parsons's gallery. Of particular worth are the interviews conducted by Dorothy Seckler for the AAA, and by Alexander Russo for his book *Profiles of Women Artists.* The Solomon R. Guggenheim Museum has letters from the 1940s between Fine and Baronness Hilla Rebay. My thanks to Ann Butler, archivist, for making copies available to me.

I would like to thank Barbara Jenkins, a friend and artist, who helped me select the paintings and who read the draft of my manuscript. Early in my research, she accompanied me to Guild Hall in East Hampton to see Fine's "A Woven Warmth." Her immediate response was: "How beautiful! It took great intelligence and enormous experience to paint that." Without realizing it, she had echoed and confirmed Harold Rosenberg's assessment of Fine's art. My thanks also go to Joan McCarthy who read an early draft of the book and helped me put all the black and white photographs onto computer files. And finally, thanks to my husband Timothy J. Housley for his unwavering support and encouragement.

I never knew Perle Fine. My interest in her was sparked by my research for the book *Emily Hall Tremaine: Collector on the Cusp*, published in 2001 by The Tremaine Foundation and distributed by University Press of New England. Tremaine was a legendary collector of modern art. The architect Philip Johnson described her as having "eyes like gimlets" because of her uncanny ability to spot talent. Tremaine thought highly of Fine's art, and I trusted her judgment, even when the difficulty of finding material and locating paintings made me question whether a full biography could be written. In retrospect, I'm glad I did.

ABOUT THE AUTHOR

Kathleen L. Housley is an independent writer and researcher with a strong interdisciplinary background spanning American history and women's studies. Housley's second book, *Emily Hall Tremaine, Collector on the Cusp* was a 2002 finalist for the Library of Congress/ Connecticut Center of the Book Award. In the biography, praised for its balance and its contextual range, Housley assesses the convoluted role of the art collector in relation to artists, dealers, and art institutions during the second half of the twentieth century.

Housley has written on both Tremaine and Fine for *Woman's Art Journal,* and has published articles, poetry and book reviews in numerous publications, including *The Christian Century, Image,* and *New England Quarterly.*

Housley's first book, *The Letter Kills But the Spirit Gives Life: The Smiths, Abolitionists, Suffragists, Bible Translators* (1993) won the Award of Merit from the Connecticut League of Historical Societies in 1994 and has been used as a text in women's studies courses.

Housley has a Masters Degree in Liberal Studies from Wesleyan University, (Middletown, Connecticut), and is an Affiliated Scholar at Trinity College (Hartford), an honorary position granted by the Board of Trustees in recognition of her scholarly work.

INDEX

CREDITS

Photo Credits:
Fine and Sisters, Malden, Mass. Courtesy of the Fine family.
Fine at Wadsworth Atheneum, Dec 1947: Wadsworth Atheneum Museum of Art, Hartford, CT. Courtesy of the Wadsworth Atheneum and Edward Saxe.
All other photos were taken by Maurice Berezov ©A.E. Artworks.

Cover Design: Michael Storrings

Cover Photograph: Perle Fine in her Provincetown Studio, early 1950s.
Maurice Berezov/A.E. Artworks

Typographic Design: Kari Grimsby

Pl. 1. Perle Fine. *In Staccato* (1941), oil on canvas, 30 x 30". Location unknown.

Pl. 2. Perle Fine. *Midnight* (1942), gouache on cardboard, 11 x 9 3/4". Private collection.

Pl. 3. Perle Fine. *Spring Feeling* (1945),
watercolor on canvas, 12 x 16".
Location unknown.

Pl. 4. Perle Fine. *Untitled* (1945), oil on canvas, 38 x 63". Collection of Drs. Tom and Marika Herskovic.

Pl. 5. Perle Fine. *Forms Fugitive* (1945), oil on canvas, 60 x 34". Private collection. Courtesy of Hirschl & Adler Galleries, New York.

Pl. 6. Perle Fine. *Three Clowns* (1946), gouache on paper, 26 x 21".
Collection of Dr. Melodie Mayberry-Stewart.

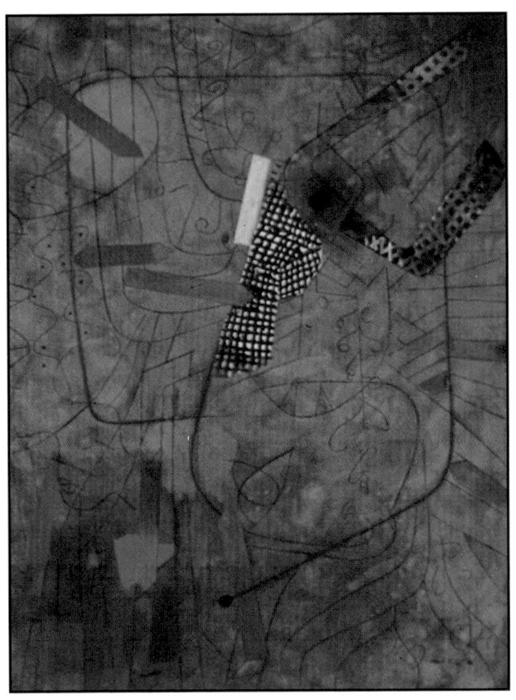

Pl. 7. Perle Fine. *Tyranny of Space* (1946), gouache on paper, 26 x 21". Location unknown.

Pl. 8. Perle Fine. *Pink Harlequin* (1948), oil on canvas, 44 x 38".
Private collection. Maurice Berezov Photograph © A. E. Artworks.

Pl. 9. Perle Fine. *Bicycle Forms* (1949), gouache on paper. Collection of Jack Berezov. Maurice Berezov Photograph © A. E. Artworks.

Pl. 10. Perle Fine. *Painting No. 10* (1950), oil and sand on canvas, 48 x72". Private collection. Courtesy of Thomas McCormick Gallery, Chicago.

Pl. 11. Perle Fine. *Thor* (1951), enamel, gouache, aluminum foil on paper, 21 x 27". Private collection. Maurice Berezov Photograph © A. E. Artworks.

Pl. 12. Perle Fine. *Wide To the Wind* (1952), collage and mixed media on paper, 10 x 25". Collection of Tom and Darleen Furst, Rockford, Illinois. Courtesy of Thomas McCormick Gallery, Chicago.

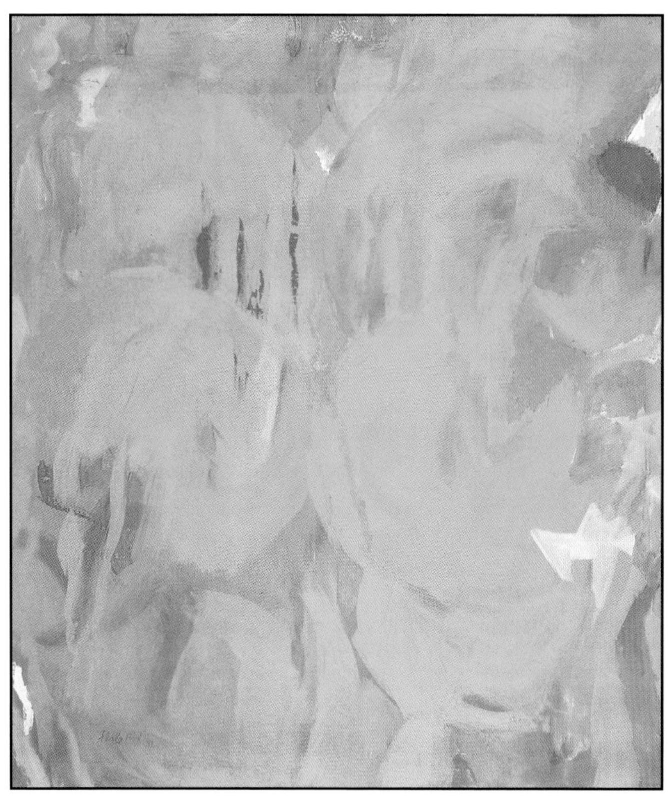

Pl. 13. Perle Fine. *Untitled, Prescience Series* (1952), oil on canvas, 43 ½ x 37 ½". Private collection. Courtesy of Thomas McCormick Gallery, Chicago.

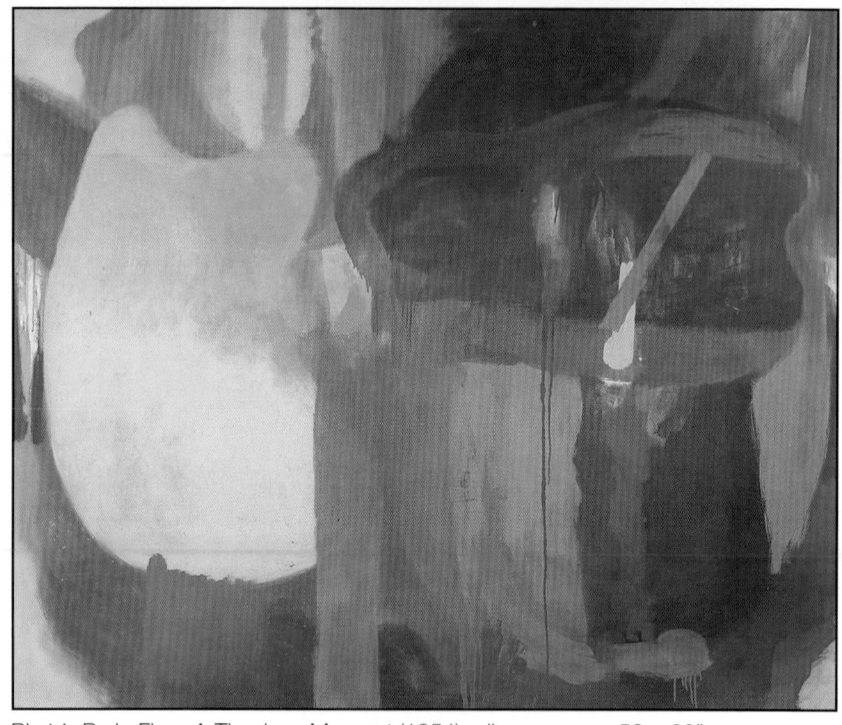

Pl. 14. Perle Fine. *A Timeless Moment* (1954), oil on canvas, 50 x 60". Collection of Drs. Tom and Marika Herskovic.

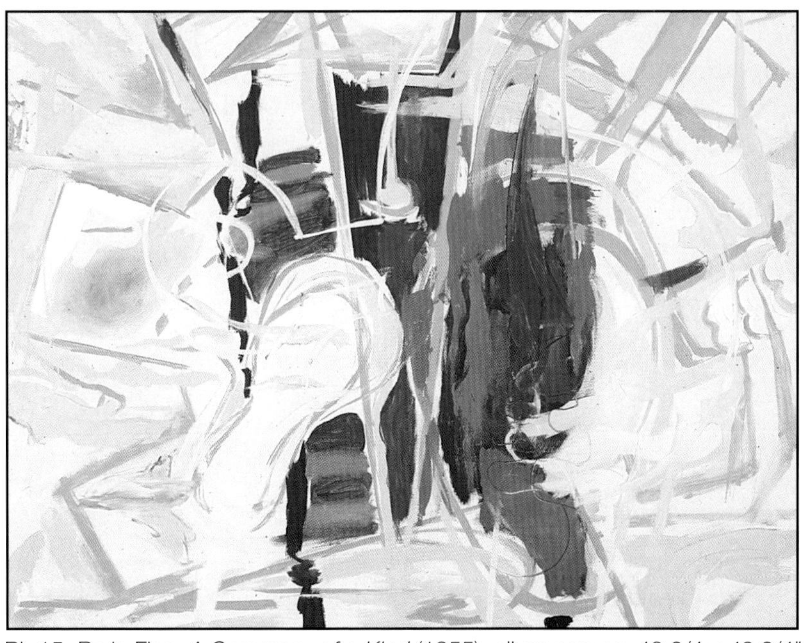

Pl. 15. Perle Fine. *A Ceremony of a Kind* (1955), oil on canvas, 43 3/4 x 49 3/4". Collection of Drs. Tom and Marika Herskovic.

Pl. 16. Perle Fine. *Astraea* (1956), oil and collage on canvas, 58 x 68". Private collection. Courtesy of Thomas McCormick Gallery, Chicago.

Pl.17. Perle Fine. *The Wind and the Sea* (1956), oil and collage on canvas, 57 x 70". Collection of Norman and Lois Muse. Courtesy of Thomas McCormick Gallery.

Pl. 18. Perle Fine. *Black Waterfall* (1957), oil on canvas, 68 x 66". Private collection. Courtesy of Thomas McCormick Gallery.

Pl. 19. Perle Fine. *The Early Morning Garden* (1957), oil and collage on canvas, 44 x 36". Collection of Art Enterprises, Ltd. Courtesy of Thomas McCormick Gallery.

Pl. 20. Perle Fine. *Untitled* (1957), oil and collage on canvas, 14 x 12". Private collection. Courtesy of Thomas McCormick Gallery, Chicago.

Pl. 21. Perle Fine. *The Roaring Wind* (1958), oil on canvas, 42 x 52 3/16".
Collection of Drs. Tom and Marika Herskovic.

Pl. 22. Perle Fine. *Tournament* (1959), oil on canvas, diptych, 57 x 66" each panel. Private collection. Maurice Berezov Photograph © A. E. Artworks.

Pl. 23. Perle Fine. *Encounter a.k.a. Brouhaha, Foldover Series* (1959), gouache and collage on paper, 22 x 30". Private collection. Courtesy of Thomas McCormick Gallery.

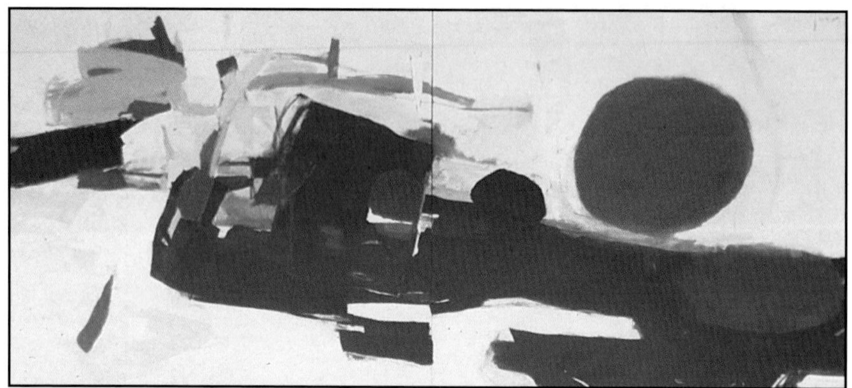

Pl. 24. Perle Fine. *Flood Cloud* (1960), oil on canvas, 86 x 156". Courtesy of A. E. Artworks. Maurice Berezov Photograph © A. E. Artworks.

Pl. 25. Perle Fine. *Breakthrough* (1961) oil on canvas, 56 x 86". Private collection. Courtesy of Thomas McCormick Gallery.

Pl. 26. Perle Fine. *Vibrant Beat, #13* (1961), 79 x 38". Collection of A. E. Artworks. Maurice Berezov Photograph © A. E. Artworks.

Pl. 27. Perle Fine. *Study for Cool Blue* (1961), 10 ½ x 13 3/4". Private collection. Maurice Berezov Photograph © A. E. Artworks.

Pl. 28. Perle Fine. *A Vigorous Now* (1966), wood and oil collage, 14 x 18". Private collection. Maurice Berezov Photograph © A. E. Artworks.

Pl. 29. Perle Fine. *Cross Currents* (1966), wood and oil collage, 30 x 30". University of California, Berkeley Art Museum. Gift of the artist.

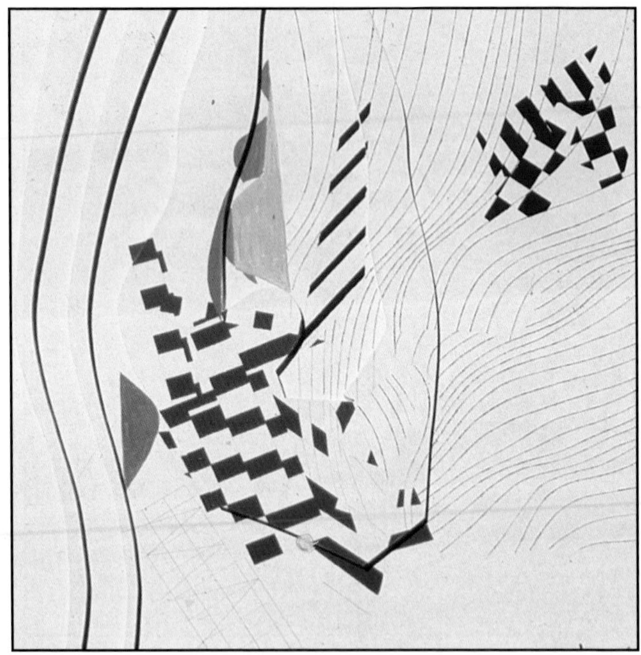

Pl. 30. Perle Fine. *Silences Still* (1966), wood collage and acrylic, 30 x 30". Private collection.